T0304103

Globalism and Regional Economy

The book covers the results of trial and error of regional economies in Japan, Korea, Austria, New Zealand, and the UK over the past two decades. Since the end of the Cold War, regional economies have been struggling to meet the demands of global change, and are trying to find a new approach based on "inter-regional cooperation" to survive and develop further.

This book focuses on the circumstances of regional economies worldwide as well as three important issues of concern: commercial and policy issues, international trade, and promoting a regional approach in international tourism. The book presents case studies of five countries and examines the possibility of application to other regions. Although every region has suffered from the decline of traditional industries in the face of international competition, academic analysis of successful cases is particularly useful and relevant to the reforms of regional economies and their development. This book also discusses the current problems of FTAs, tourism, medical management, and regional management and suggests possible short-term development strategies. Regional economies have begun a number of initiatives in these fields in the globalized world. The book demonstrates the current results of such initiatives.

The book also explores new patterns of collaboration between regions of different countries following their recent initiatives.

Susumu Egashira is a Professor of History of Economic Thought at Otaru University of Commerce, Japan. He received his PhD in Economics from Kyoto University. He was a visiting scholar to Cambridge University in 2000 and 2001. His research interests are in the fields of economic thought and environmental economics, and he has become interested in inter-regionalism as a way for regional economies to survive in a globalized world.

Routledge Studies in the Modern World Economy

Globalism and Regional Economy

Edited by Susumu Egashira

Routledge
Taylor & Francis Group

LONDON AND NEW YORK

First published
2014 by Routledge
2 Park Square, Milton Park, Abingdon, Oxon, OX14 4RN

and by Routledge
711 Third Avenue, New York, NY 10017

Routledge is an imprint of the Taylor & Francis Group, an informa business

British Library Cataloguing in Publication Data
A catalogue record for this book is available from the British Library

Library of Congress Cataloging-in-Publication Data
Globalism and regional economy/edited by Susumu Egashira.
pages cm. – (Routledge studies in the modern world economy; 118)
Includes bibliographical references and index.
1. Regional economics. 2. Globalization. I. Egashira, Susumu.
HT388.G577 2013
330.9–dc23   2013000958

ISBN: 978-0-415-81719-6 (hbk)
ISBN: 978-0-203-75110-7 (ebk)

Typeset in Times New Roman
by Sunrise Setting Ltd, Paignton, UK

Printed and bound in Great Britain by
TJ International Ltd, Padstow, Cornwall

Contents

Figures

Tables

Contributors

Makoto Anazawa is a Professor of International Trade at Otaru University of Commerce. He is the author of numerous articles and books on industrialization policies, foreign direct investment, and multinational corporations in Southeast Asia, especially Malaysia.

Luisa Andreu is an Associate Professor of Marketing at the Department of Marketing, University of Valencia. She holds Bachelor and Doctoral degrees in Economics and Business Administration from the University of Valencia, and a Master of Science in Tourism Management and Marketing from the International Centre for Tourism at Bournemouth University. She has been Co-Chair of the congress "Advances in Tourism Marketing Conference" in 2005, 2007, and 2011. Her research interests include the analysis of consumer behavior, tourism marketing, corporate social responsibility, and online marketing.

Ryoya Asaoka is an undergraduate student of the Department of Health Sciences at Hokkaido University. He studies health policy making using the geographical information system supervised by Professor Katsuhiko Ogasawara.

Rafael Currás-Pérez is currently an Associate Professor in the Department of Marketing at the University of Valencia, Spain. He is a graduate of the Polytechnic University of Valencia and obtained his PhD from the University of Valencia in 2007. His research interests include corporate social responsibility, online consumer behavior, corporate communication, tourism marketing, and non-lucrative marketing. His research has been published in the *Journal of Business Ethics*, *European Journal of Marketing*, *Tourism Management*, *Journal of Product and Brand Management*, *Journal of Marketing Communications*, *Marketing Intelligence and Planning*, *Universia Business Review*, *Corporate Reputation Review*, *International Review on Public and Nonprofit Marketing*, and the best Spanish refereed journals.

Susumu Egashira is a Professor of History of Economic Thought at Otaru University of Commerce. He has published on the history of economic thought, evolutionary economics, and agent-based computer simulation models, and is the author of *Studies of Friedrich Hayek* (1990). He is the Editor of *Evolutionary and Institutional Economic Review*.

Masahiro Endoh is a Professor of International Economics at Keio University. He has published papers on both theoretical and empirical analysis of international trade and regional trade agreements. He is a former associate professor of International Economics at Otaru University of Commerce. His forthcoming book in Japanese is about the Hokkaido economy.

Kenji Fujimori is an Associate Professor of the Community-hospital-instructor Supporting Center at Hokkaido University Hospital. He is co-editor of the books *Introduction to Diagnosis Procedure Combination Data Analysis* (2007) and *Practical Use of Diagnosis Procedure Combination Data for Acute Disease in Regional Medicine* (2011).

Juergen Gnoth is interested in consumer behavior, tourism services marketing, place branding, and marketing ethics. He is a leading member of the Tourism Research and Place Branding Group and an international and cross-cultural researcher. The main focus of his research lies with the constructs of experiences networks, intentions, expectations, image, and satisfaction, but also with understanding and measuring the influence of emotions on consumption behavior. He deals closely with Tourism New Zealand, and members of the tourism industry, such as hotels, airlines, operators, and consultants to keep his teaching up-to-date and relevant. Juergen is a member of a number of editorial boards including the *Journal of Travel Research* and *Annals of Tourism Research*, for which he also served as the Associate Editor for the Research Notes sector for more than 12 years.

Shoji Haruna is a Professor of Applied Microeconomics at Okayama University, Japan. He has published many articles on industrial organization and international economics and is the author of *Market Economies and Labor-Managed Firms* (in Japanese).

Tomonori Hasegawa is a Professor of Social Medicine at Toho University School of Medicine. He graduated from Tokyo University School of Medicine in 1985. His academic activities cover health policies and performance measurement of health systems. He was engaged in health sector reform in Japan as an advisory member of the Cabinet Office. He is a board member of the Japan Council for Quality Health Care, the Japanese Society of Transplantation (where he is the Chairperson of the Ethical Committee), the Japanese Society of Hospital Administration, and the Japanese Society of Healthcare Management (Editor in Chief).

Chan-Guk Huh is a Professor of International Economics at the National Chungnam University, Korea. He has published on macroeconomics and international economics in Korea as well as in the US. He served as an economist and for the Federal Reserve System of the US, and was also the Director of Economic Research at the Korea Economic Research Institute before holding his current position. He is currently working on issues related to Northeast Asian economic integration.

Tomoki Ishikawa is a Masters course student of the Graduate School of Health Sciences at Hokkaido University. He studies health policy making using the geographical information system supervised by Professor Katsuhiko Ogasawara.

Naoto Jinji is an Associate Professor at Kyoto University, Japan. He has published numerous articles on international trade in journals such as the *Canadian Journal of Economics* and *Review of International Economics*.

Sachiko Kazekami is an Associate Professor of Economics at Chukyo University. Her research interests include the effect of globalization on labor demands, labor market adjustments, mobility of the labor market, and different effects of a labor demand shock on local labor markets. She is also involved in some projects of job creation.

Nozomi Kichiji is a Professor of Economics at Asahikawa University. He has published on network theory including circulation flow of community currency and traffic line of tourists. He is co-editor of the book *Topological Aspects of Critical Systems and Networks* (2007).

Ralf T. Kreutzer is a Professor of Marketing at Berlin School of Economics and Law. He is the author of numerous articles and books on marketing topics, including principles of marketing, dialogue marketing, online marketing, and corporate reputation management. He also works as a marketing and management consultant in different industries in Germany and other countries.

Gunther Maier is a Professor at the Institute for the Environment and Regional Development, Department of Socioeconomics at WU Vienna University of Economics and Business. He is the Director of the Institute and also directs the Research Institute of Spatial and Real Estate Economics at this university. He is actively involved in the European Regional Science Association and the Regional Science Association International. He has published/edited seven books and numerous articles in international journals on issues in regional economics, quantitative methods, and related topics. His research ranges from spatial microeconomics, regional development processes, and cluster policy to real estate markets, the role of universities, and the quality of scholarly journals.

Katsuhiko Ogasawara is a Professor of the Graduate School of Health Sciences at Hokkaido University. He has published many articles on health informatics and health policy making. He is the co-author of "Filmless versus film-based systems in radiographic examination costs: an activity-based costing method" (2011) and "Willingness to pay for municipality hospital services in rural Japan: a contingent valuation study" (2011).

Yuji Sase is a Masters course student of the Graduate School of Health Sciences at Hokkaido University. He studies health policy making using the geographical information system supervised by Professor Katsuhiko Ogasawara.

Yu Hong Sun is an Associate Professor of Economics at Dongbei University of Finance and Economics. She is the author of numerous articles and two books on international economic integration, including *The Networks of Global*

FTAs and the Integration Strategy of Developing Countries (2007), and *Cross-Regional Bilateral FTA: Analysis of Political and Economic Motivation* (2008). She has undertaken research at national or provincial levels, including "The evolutionary trend of non-trade clauses in North–South FTAs and China's countermeasures."

Kenichi Tamai is a Professor of Management at the Graduate School of Business at Otaru University of Commerce. He is the author of *Strategy Formation and Organizational Culture* (1982).

Akiko Tanaka graduated from Meiji Gakuin University in Tokyo with a Bachelor degree in English Literature from the Faculty of Literal Arts. During her working career she gained a variety of work experience in fields such as guest relations, event management, public relations, and marketing in tourism. She has also worked as the Project Manager for Tourism and Economic Development in the Vienna Representative Office in Tokyo. She studied Tourism Management at the MODUL University Vienna and completed a MBA degree in 2011.

Alfred Taudes is a Professor at WU Vienna University of Economics and Business. He has published several books and more than 120 articles on information systems and operations management. He is the editor of the book *Adaptive Information Systems and Modelling in Economics and Management Science* (2005).

Tomochika Toguchi is a Lecturer at the College of Economics and Environmental Policy, Okinawa International University. His research interests include agricultural and environmental economics and landscape research in agriculture.

Michaela Trippl is an Associate Professor at the Department of Human Geography at Lund University, Sweden. She is an active member of the European Regional Science Association and the Regional Studies Association. Michaela Trippl has published three books and numerous articles in journals such as *Research Policy*, *Regional Studies*, *Economic Geography*, and *Environment and Planning A*. Her main research interests include cluster development and policy, regional innovation systems, long-term regional structural change, as well as labor mobility and regional development.

Xingyuan Zhang is a Professor of Applied Microeconomics at Okayama University, Japan. His recent research has focused on innovation and technology spillovers with many articles in these fields.

Preface

Introduction

Although the fusion of global economic institutions that began after the end of the Cold War has become an inevitable tide, this process contains a number of problems. The movement that originally objected to globalization vigorously from the viewpoint of the protection of traditional society and cultures has gradually changed, and all countries have now begun to consider strategies for both resistance and coexistence.

While most scholars believe that a universal economic system will be dominant sooner or later, the global situation has changed once again following Lehman's collapse. On the one hand, because the existing governmental system cannot respond to a borderless economy represented by international capitals, global cooperation is required. On the other hand, the relative decline in the significance of central governments has made the self-help development of regional economies more important.

In particular, even regional economies, cultures, and societies are being encouraged to internationalize. For example, regional firms often cooperate in order to expand overseas. Moreover, international regional cooperation can occur without the support of a central government, or large companies, whose head offices are located in capital cities. Whereas interregional cooperation once meant cooperation in one country, cooperation across national borders will become even more important in the future.

The chapters in this book focus on the current revival of regional economies in Japan, China, Korea, Austria, New Zealand, and the UK, and use the examples of other countries to suggest solutions to these present difficulties. At the 100th anniversary symposium of the Otaru University of Commerce in 2011, where the original papers were presented, economists and management scientists from the six countries above, together with the US, were invited to discuss interregional cooperation under the theme "Globalization and Regional Economy." The topics for debate included why regional economies that had merely been the recipients of globalization in the past are now looking for a way to revitalize on the wave of globalization, and why and how some of them have been successful.

Moreover, the decline in national economies after Lehman's collapse suggests that local areas have to formulate economic strategies that take advantage of their regional characteristics in order to survive. For example, the economic indexes of Hokkaido (where the Otaru University of Commerce is located) have indicated different macroeconomic trends from those of Japan. Therefore, if we just expect the effects of central government policy, the regional divide may widen.

The 13 papers in this book describe the current situations and efforts for survival of regional economies in several countries. They are a result of interregional cooperation among academics and the lessons drawn from other countries.

Japanese and Asian economies after the end of the Cold War

The end of the Cold War was not only a turning point in the history of the world; it was also important for Japan in two senses. First, the economic bubble in Japan began to burst in 1991. Second, the political reason for the US to protect its Western allies (economically) from socialism had disappeared. Capitalism thus became the global standard economic system after the collapse of socialist countries, and globalization, namely the international unification of markets, progressed. The Japanese economy critically missed out on this wave because of economic depression.

Although Asian countries have increased industrial production based on foreign capital and low labor costs, Japanese firms have moved production bases to foreign countries. As a consequence, domestic production, which formerly caused the semiconductor industry in Silicon Valley to grind to a halt, has begun to lose traction.

Whilst regional economies in Japan suffered from the depression in the early 1990s, they remained relatively optimistic because the Japanese economy recovered from 1994 to 1996. The appreciation of the yen, around 1995, and rapid influx of foreign capital from the offshore market critically influenced Japan's manufacturing industry. Before that time, there were a number of cases of large companies moving production bases to developing countries but fewer similar cases involving SMEs (small to medium-sized enterprises). However, changing trade conditions and stiff competition with emerging countries meant that even SMEs were forced to move their production bases to lower-wage regions.

In 2010, 99.7 percent of Japanese firms were SMEs and 80 percent of paid workers were employed by these companies. These figures were much higher than those in the US, Korea, and other countries, implying that the role of SMEs is relatively much more important in Japan. In particular, important technologies in Japan, such as the complex, high-precision dies used to produce components for many industries, are supported by SMEs. The movement of SME production bases thus seriously influenced local economies and forced a switch in the industrial structures of regions.

Farming areas in Japan had supplied cheaper labor in high economic growth periods during the 1960s and early 1970s, but they lost their wage advantage in the 1980s because of international competition. The only solution was for local economies to break into niche businesses or attract branches of large companies. However, they were unable to do so in the face of growing globalization in the 1990s. Monetary and human capital was lost from local areas to large cities such as Tokyo, and most local economies are nowadays supported by the local distribution of central government taxes. The Japanese government's plan to overcome the monetary crisis of 1997 has completely failed and has left a huge budget deficit.

Further, the role of Japan in the global economy has been diminished by developing countries in Asia in the 20 years since the end of the Cold War. A long depression and low birth rates and longevity have also widened the gap between urban and rural areas, and the significance of local economies for globalization has become increasingly blurred during this period.

Free trade agreements (FTAs) as the main approach to international trade

The 1997 Asian currency crisis was a turning point for Japan and for the whole of Asia. It seriously affected the economies of developing countries in Asia and forced them to change their business models. They suffered from the rapid depreciation of their currencies and even public unrest; however, some saw the crisis as a chance to break away from developmental dictatorship after the intervention of the IMF. In particular, the Korean economy, which traditionally had a dual structure, largely reformed its economic system and this encouraged the development of internationally successful multinationals such as Samsung.

Moreover, China welcomed foreign capital and new technologies and it truly began to become the "factory of the world." The Chinese government kept a more favorable rate of exchange and retained control over the supply of labor and resources. Although China has maintained its one-party regime, it has lower corporate taxes than Japan and the US and encourages free competition. The government has further distinguished between rural and urban areas in order to control wages, while foreign firms advancing into China have been obliged to facilitate technological transfers. China was thus well prepared to lead international competition in manufacturing industries before 2000.

In addition, the conclusion of bilateral FTAs increased trade among participating countries but caused a deterioration of trade conditions for non-member nations. In this sense, FTAs have a strong character of administrated trade. However, non-strategic industries, such as agriculture in Japan and Korea, react sharply, and it often takes a longer period of time to coordinate interested domestic parties compared to the actual negotiation of the FTAs themselves. In part one of this book, the meaning of FTAs for Asian countries is discussed. In Chapter 2, Kazekami and Endoh discuss how the trade of intermediate and final goods influences the demand for labor in manufacturing industries in Japan, where, as in other countries, industrial bases tend to relocate to local areas where wages and property prices are relatively low. However, the overseas transfer of large corporations and subsidiaries negatively affects employment. This empirical study is thus important for considering whether FTAs will prevent the loss of firms and improve employment conditions in local areas.

In Chapter 3, Sun discusses China's FTA strategy by empirically investigating the present situation and the perspectives of FTAs in China and in ASEAN (Association of South East Asian Nations) countries. This study shows that China's bilateral FTA networks may disturb the formation of an East Asian-wide FTA, a viewpoint that is important because this tendency to create an economic bloc – not only by China, but also by others – suggests a fundamental problem of FTAs. These originally appeared as an alternative to WTO (World Trade Organization) negotiations, which had made little progress. It remains to be seen whether the unification of a number of FTAs will mean the birth of a worldwide free trade area, or whether economic blocs led by influential countries will determine future global economic and political relations.

The Chinese government has imposed a duty of technological transfer on foreign firms that relocate their production bases to China, aiming to encourage product and process innovation in developing countries. However, the technological advantages of advanced countries have disappeared, thanks to a combination of technology transfers and foreign capital flows, and industries in advanced countries have rapidly lost their market shares by exporting to low-wage developing countries. It is thus important to assess how FTAs, which have the opportunity to change international relationships, may influence such technological transfers. In Chapter 4, Jinji *et al.* empirically investigate how regional integration affects technology spillovers among trade partners. The main finding from estimating a gravity model is that technology spillovers between trade partners are higher if these countries enjoy regional integration.

Regional integration will be completed only by the introduction of a single currency such as the euro. It can be said that if there is only a limited currency system, which is not completely independent from participating countries, a dominant currency or strong cooperative monetary policy could establish economic integration. In Chapter 5, Huh discusses the issue of currency cooperation in East Asia from the viewpoint of recent global as well as regional development. He presents several options for East Asian countries, such as segmented groupings and currency cooperation.

Soon after the Asian currency crisis, Kiichi Miyazawa, who was the Minister of Finance in Japan at that time, proposed the concept of an Asian Monetary Fund, but the proposals were eventually discarded because of objections by non-Asian countries. Since that time, even though they have continued to fear the disturbance of domestic economies by huge international capital inflows, developing countries in Asia have adopted the strategy of accepting long-term capital flows in order to enable economic development.

Strategy for survival: tourism promotion

Owing to globalization, some regional economies in advanced countries have been forced to shift from primary and secondary industries to tertiary industries. In particular, a number of local economies have tried to make tourism their main industry, based on the belief that this is a relatively easy option if they have historical or natural resources. It is thought that if they are creative, then tourism will be a high performance industry, requiring little capital investment. However, international competition in attracting tourists, as well as competition among domestic regions, has increased markedly in recent times.

For example, Hokkaido in Japan promotes ecotourism and food tourism, but it is difficult to differentiate many of its designated sightseeing areas. Moreover, most tourists come from Asian countries such as China, Taipei, and Korea, and their needs are not necessarily met by the tourist resources in Hokkaido. In particular, the main objective of Chinese visitors is to enjoy not only natural environments but also shopping opportunities. Hokkaido's tourist industry also lacks the marketing ability to attract more tourists. In addition, cheaper travel packages have led to low-quality service, and Hokkaido's reputation among domestic tourists is declining as a result.

This implies that tourism needs careful marketing and intensive investment in order to succeed. In Chapter 6, Gnoth *et al.* describe the tourism promotion strategy adopted by New Zealand, which has utilized special events such as the America's Cup. The chapter explores how events may become catalysts for the goals set by tourist destinations. It also examines how well businesses cooperate and it analyzes the role industrial organizations play in achieving tourism goals. The roles of industry and direct marketing organizations are also discussed.

However, in most of the regions trying to change their economic structures, the existing industry has usually declined and been underfunded. If such regions plan to draw tourists from other countries (under such budget constraints), they must utilize e-commerce as a main strategy. In Chapter 7, Taudes and Tanaka present a comparative study in e-marketing strategies between Austria and Hokkaido and point out the problems with Hokkaido's e-commerce approach. Their study shows that Austria has a dynamic e-tourism management system, whereas that of Hokkaido is rather static. They also find many opportunities to improve the quality of websites, particularly in terms of improving market effectiveness.

Moreover, efforts are necessary to both exploit new tourist resources and utilize existing ones. In Chapter 8, Kichiji uses a network analysis to analyze tourist attractions and to propose new tourist strategies for both the regional government and for firms. The findings of this chapter may help managers and local government officers in the tourism sector to understand tourist traffic lines.

Green tourism mostly receives research attention in advanced countries where such natural resources are scarce. However, the protection of rural landscapes has led to the regulation of land use, making it difficult for the local government to prioritize different ventures such as ecotourism or residential development.

The Niseko area in Hokkaido, on which Toguchi's study in Chapter 9 focuses, is a traditional ski resort that has well-known hot springs, although the main industry in this area has been agriculture.

However, numbers of Japanese ski tourists have decreased since the late 1990s, though Australian tourists have visited the region, and some have even built holiday homes there. But following the collapse of Lehman Brothers, numbers of Australian inhabitants rapidly decreased. On the other hand, the Chinese began to purchase properties. As a result, houses which are liked by Australian and Chinese tourists have been built in the traditional farming landscape. The dilemma for the local government is whether to protect the landscape as a resource for green tourism or promote the real estate sector, which is also an important source of income for local inhabitants. How a local government balances the interests of inhabitants and regulates development in this situation is a difficult political economic problem. In Chapter 9, Toguchi assesses the landscape at a micro-perspective level in order to understand local objectives and determine how targets are derived from the perception of a rural landscape.

In an advanced country, tourism alone does not have the potential to be a main industry or to stimulate a nation's economy as it does in a developing country. However, we should not ignore tourists' capacity to establish a local brand. Local brands are crucial for both attracting investment from abroad and for exporting local goods, and thus the promotion of tourism is vital from the viewpoint of local integrated policy.

Local healthcare in a changing society

Over the past decade, Asian countries have increased exports to the US; this has overcome the bursting of the IT bubble and continued to develop. The Japanese economy also recovered from 2004 to 2006, but its structure was largely different from that seen previously. For example, the benefits of the economic recovery were concentrated in urban areas, and, as a result, economic indexes of local areas such as Hokkaido show different behaviors from that of Japan as a whole. Indeed, many local governments have a large fiscal deficit, and this is is accelerated by the increasing movement of younger workers to cities, which unbalances the population structure in local areas. Moreover, the proportion of people above 65 years old in Japan is more than 25 percent in 2012. This problem of an aging society will also begin to affect Korea and China in 2040. In particular, China, which has a one-child policy, is predicted to become the most significantly aging society of all time.

An aging population increases the nation's social security burden, particularly the cost of medical care. Indeed, every healthcare system in the world suffers from fiscal problems in some form. Moreover, it is impossible to offer fair treatment to all people because medical treatment is advanced and thus it becomes more expensive every day. In this sense, it is difficult to both maintain the public healthcare system and to improve its level of service. In Chapter 10, Hasegawa investigates healthcare quality with particular focus on the influence of rapid aging in Japan. This empirical study provides important information for policymakers in South Korea and Chinese Taiwan, which are also suffering from rapid aging and which share a common cultural background with Japan.

In Chapter 11, Ogasawara *et al.* consider a similar problem from the viewpoint of the number and distribution of doctors. This chapter discusses the appropriate distribution of medical resources in large and underpopulated areas such as Hokkaido, which faces a serious aging society problem. According to this empirical study, Hokkaido may face a serious shortage of medical staff within 20 years and it needs to formulate comprehensive measures to solve this problem.

Because Japan has maintained a high-quality social security system, including universal health insurance coverage, it can act as a model case study for other aging countries in terms of rapid changes in the family unit (and in social institutions) due to rapid economic growth. Over the next ten years, the experience of Japan will yield important lessons for other countries.

Marketing strategies to survive globalization

Globalized competition suggests that not only large business but also SMEs in all industries will have to become multinationals. This also means that not only companies located in urban areas, with abundant human resources, but also local domestic-oriented companies will have to internationalize. Although the subsidiaries of large manufacturing firms are expanding overseas with the expectation of a distribution route, a company that has to explore the market by itself needs elaborate marketing in advance. However, marketing in a domestic market is fundamentally different to that in a foreign market.

By contrast, in Chapter 12, Kreutzer presents a case study to investigate how Heidelberg Druckmaschinen AG achieved its dominant market position, survived the financial crisis, and managed its turnaround. The future challenges that Heidelberg must overcome in order to keep this position are also analyzed.

In the final chapter, Tamai examines the competitiveness of manufacturing firms in Japan. Although it is frequently pointed out that the advantage of the Japanese economy is based on a high level of technology supported by SMEs, the actual level of technology is rarely measured. Tamai thus empirically examines the competiveness of SMEs in the manufacturing industry in order to clarify its foundations.

In many cases, local SMEs have insufficient funds and poor market research capacities to advance overseas. Moreover, the services and food industries need more efforts and funds to survive intense international competition compared with the manufacturing industry, which has considerable technical advantages. To compensate for this disadvantage, companies from different industries in a region can work together to internationalize – in some cases, with the assistance of the local government. If this kind of regional project were to become popular, the reconstruction and integration of regional industries in Japan may occur in the near future, since many companies within a region can be influenced. Moreover, the niche strategy of avoiding urban markets, in which large businesses compete intensively, and penetrating local smaller markets overseas (often incurring lower initial costs) will prevail. A matching strategy between firm size and market size will ultimately decide the direction of cross-border interregionalism.

How regional economies can survive in the future

The economic tide of circulating international capital, which strongly influences a nation's economy, was temporarily dampened after Lehman's collapse. Even the rapid development of the Chinese economy has slowed as a result. The Chinese government is switching from an export-oriented policy to one that aims to increase domestic consumption. The policy for demand creation plans to activate not only large cities such as Beijing and Shanghai, but also local markets. This means that China will shift from being "the factory of the world" to "the market of the world" and competition in the Chinese market will move from large cities to local areas.

Japan has finally found a globalization strategy that will allow regional economies to recover. Previously, regional economies usually had relationships with foreign countries only through the central government or large companies that had head offices in Tokyo. However, the central government has stuttered since Lehman's collapse and local economies have continued to stagnate. Moreover, accumulated government deficit, which is more than one quadrillion yen, highlights the limits of government and demonstrates a lack of initiative in the reconstruction plan and in Japan's reaction to the serious nuclear accident following the Great East Japan Earthquake in 2011. Furthermore, the establishment of administration by the Democratic Party means that recent political momentum in Japan has moved from local-oriented to urban-oriented politics.

However, local inhabitants may begin to acknowledge their situations and revitalize their economies themselves. Some papers in this book are empirical studies of recovering in a regional economy. Actions such as a local company beginning to explore foreign markets without an agency in Tokyo, and a local city planning to establish its brand in the international market, would have been unthinkable a quarter of a century ago. In this sense, globalization is allowing local cities to realize such plans. The international economic rules of trade are being upgraded and international competition is reducing the cost of transactions. It is also now far easier for local companies to perform in foreign markets than ever before.

Regional policy by the central government is also changing in this regard. In the opening article of this book, Maier criticizes the use of neoclassical economics in regional policymaking and proposes new ideas from the agglomeration viewpoint. He also discusses the understanding of regional economies as developing "clusters" and shows the theoretical possibility of policies that could have a continuous effect.

However, there remain many barriers to overcome when local economies aim to advance overseas. In particular, a shortage of funds is a serious problem. It seems as though this will be the main focus for how we attract international funds to local companies and industries. Asia must continue to be the most active economic region in the world, as the success of local economies in Japan is largely dependent on whether it can obtain active and capable people that use their skills before they grow too old.

Makoto Anazawa and Susumu Egashira

1 Regional policy in a globalized economy

Gunther Maier and Michaela Trippl

Introduction

Economic policy intervention in general and regional economic policy intervention in particular can be justified by two sets of arguments: an efficiency argument and an equity argument (Richardson 1978; Fürst *et al.* 1976; Armstrong and Taylor 1993). The efficiency argument is usually rooted in the notion of market failure and the need for policy to correct for it. In the case of substantial externalities, transaction costs or other major barriers to free trade and free resource allocation, it is the aim of policy to remove these barriers to allow market forces to allocate resources more efficiently. Rooted in the belief that market forces (when they can operate uninhibitedly) lead to an efficient allocation of resources, such a policy is expected to lead to higher efficiency of resource allocation and, consequently, higher welfare, since formerly underutilized resources are now used in an optimal way.

The equity argument, on the other hand, views it as morally unacceptable and politically risky when certain groups of society, or certain regions or sectors, do not get their adequate share of economic welfare. Excessive disparities in income, for example, may be seen as a threat to the existence of a state or an economic and political union like the European Union, and should therefore be counteracted by respective policy measures. The cohesion-oriented part of EU regional policy is solidly rooted in this set of arguments. Combatting regional disparities through various policy instruments like provision of information, public investment, public support for private investment, and provision of infrastructure are traditional tasks of regional policy makers.

In either case, the policy maker intervenes in the economic system with the aim of moving it away from one undesirable, or less desirable, state to another more desirable one. In the case of the efficiency argument, the policy will allow the economic system to better utilize the available resources, thus generating growth and a higher level of welfare. In the case of the equity argument, the policy will redistribute resources between regions and thus lead to a new distribution of economic activities, which policy makers suspect is politically more desirable for the population. In either case, policy intends to make a lasting impression on the economic system rather than just generating short-term effects. In this sense, a successful form of regional economic policy is one that steers the economic system toward a new, more desirable development path, which the economic system will then follow automatically without continuous policy intervention.

These arguments show that the policy maker needs an excellent understanding of how the economic system works. In order to design policies in such a way that they lead to the desired outcome, the regional policy maker needs to know which way the economic system will react to his/her policy incentives. This knowledge may come from theoretical knowledge, past experience, or the experience of comparable regions. This issue is of particular relevance to regional policy makers in a globalized economy, where the regional economic system is not only integrated into the national one, but, through numerous linkages, also connected to the economic systems of other countries and their regions.

In the recent two decades, our understanding of how the economic system works has changed considerably. At the micro level, substantial doubt has been raised about the validity of the basic assumptions of the standard neoclassical model used to analyze the behavior of economic actors (Tversky and Kahneman 1974, 1981; Smith 2000; Camerer and Loewenstein 2003). Contributions at the macro level have led to new perspectives on the role of trade (Krugman 1979, 1984, 1986; Ethier 1982; Eaton and Grossman 1986), on growth processes (Grossman and Helpman 1991; Aghion and Howitt 1998), and on the significance and relevance of spatial agglomerations of economic activities (Krugman 1991; Fujita and Thisse 2002; Fujita *et al.* 1999). Many of these arguments have led to policy suggestions and have been picked up by policy makers and policy consultants. In a regional context, cluster policies (e.g. Porter 1998), which attempt to form and support spatial agglomerations of related economic activities, have received widespread attention and have been developed and implemented by many regional authorities around the world.

Although such new views of how the economic system works are obviously adopted willingly by regional policy makers, it seems to us that this adoption is selective and quite incomplete. Policy makers tend to accept certain arguments and conclusions from new theoretical developments, while ignoring or pushing aside others. This may lead to inconsistent policies, the effectiveness of which can be seriously questioned.

In this chapter we will investigate various views of how the economic system works and what their consequences are for regional policy. As far as the views of the operation of the economic system are concerned, we take on a rather abstract perspective and distinguish between the "neoclassical view" on the one hand and the "agglomeration view" on the other. The second section of the chapter is devoted to a comparative discussion of these two views. We argue that these are actually the only two comprehensive views of the operation of the economic system currently available, and that all the above mentioned theoretical advances can be subsumed under the "agglomeration view."

While the "neoclassical view" provides only few arguments for regional policy, the "agglomeration view" actually requires (regional) policy intervention, as we will discuss in the third section of the chapter. However, the same characteristics ascribed to the economic system by the "agglomeration view" that call for regional policy, also challenge the adequate implementation of regional policy. The non-linear relations between key elements of the economic system that the "agglomeration view" postulates imply that the reaction of the economic system to a policy intervention crucially depends on when, where, and in what intensity the policy measure is implemented. The chapter closes with a concluding section.

The theoretical background of regional economic policy

When we want to analyze the opportunities that regional policy has for influencing the long-term economic prosperity of a region, we need some understanding of how a regional economy works. As we have already mentioned in the introduction, at a general level we can distinguish between two main views:

1 the "neoclassical view," and
2 the "agglomeration view."

Both views that we will discuss in more detail below take a comprehensive look at the economy and its various elements and interactions. In a general equilibrium perspective, they take into account commodity, labor, capital, and various other markets as well as the transfers between these markets and between the spatial units considered.

The two views differ by their treatment of agglomeration forces and transportation costs. The neoclassical view excludes both agglomeration economies[1] and transportation costs by assumption. This simplifies the formal structure of the model and allows us to derive some very clear and specific results. The agglomeration view, on the other hand, allows for positive agglomeration forces that are counteracted by transportation costs. Depending on the relationship between these forces, the models of the agglomeration view lead to different results. Since the other assumptions of the neoclassical view usually remain unchanged in agglomeration view models, one can view the neoclassical view as a special case of the agglomeration view. The former results from the latter when we assume that neither agglomeration economies nor transport costs exist in the economy.

Neoclassical view

In regional economics the neoclassical view results from the application of the principles and assumptions of neoclassical economics to a regional economy. The neoclassical view has been formalized by Arrow and Debreu (1954) and is taught to students today as mainstream economics. Neoclassical economics is based on a set of assumptions and its theoretical conclusions are deduced therefrom. The most important tool of neoclassical economists is mathematics, in particular calculus. The application of these assumptions, and of the economic toolbox, has led to a consistent set of arguments and to principles that are widely shared by economists. In the context of our chapter, a brief discussion of the neoclassical view is justified by the influence it still tends to have on policy considerations. Most of the market principles that guide the design and implementation of some of our policies are derived from the – fairly limited – perspective of the neoclassical view.

The most important assumptions of the neoclassical view are utility/profit maximization, perfect information, perfect mobility, and perfect competition. The neoclassical assumptions guarantee that economic actors always pursue their self-interest and in doing so are not restricted by limited information, transaction, and mobility costs or power of rival actors. Market prices always reflect the scarcity in the respective market and signal opportunities to increase their utility or profit. Because of the assumptions, actors will always pursue these opportunities. In the context of our chapter, the assumption of "perfect competition" and the assumption of "perfect mobility" are of particular relevance.

The assumption of "perfect competition" implies that production takes place according to a linear homogeneous production function. This implies that changing all the inputs to a production process by a certain factor changes the output by the same factor. So, irrespective of the scale of production, the costs per unit remain the same, larger or smaller units do not have an economic advantage over others, and agglomeration economies are excluded by assumption. In summarizing, it can be said that in the neoclassical view there is no economic incentive toward the concentration of production. If such an incentive existed in one sector, for example, it would work toward the concentration of all the global production in this sector in one location. Because of the assumption of perfect mobility, there is no force counteracting this concentration tendency. This would generate one monopolist in this sector, contradicting the requirements of perfect competition.

The assumption of perfect mobility eliminates one of the most important elements of spatial economics: transport costs. The assumption implies that all goods, services, and individuals can be transferred across space without any costs in terms of money, time, and effort. This assumption guarantees that there is "one" market with many suppliers and customers, instead of various spatial markets, which conflict with perfect competition because of their limited numbers of actors.

Because of the assumption of perfect mobility it is difficult for neoclassical economics to deal with regions and space. When we relax this assumption and allow for physical distance and transportation costs, we either conflict with other neoclassical assumptions, like perfect competition, or end up in the perverse structure of "backyard capitalism" (Mills 1972; Starrett 1978). With transportation costs, it is profitable for producers to break up production facilities and to locate them as closely as possible to the location of the customers. Because of the assumption of perfect competition, which implies the absence of agglomeration economies, this can be pursued until all products are produced in the backyard of their respective customer. In this "backyard capitalism" there are only subsistence industrialists and no large-scale production facilities that require external labor. No products are shipped from one location to another, no workers commute from home to work. Although transportation costs are the ultimate reason for this structure, in equilibrium, no resources are used for transport.

This line of reasoning shows clearly how the assumption of perfect competition and the assumption of perfect mobility are related. If we want to avoid outcomes of complete concentration and of "backyard capitalism," then whenever we relax one of the assumptions, we also have to adjust the other. They relate to counteracting forces in a spatial economy. Agglomeration economies pull production together while transportation costs push them apart.

An immediate consequence of its assumptions is that the neoclassical model is a linear model. This has a number of important implications for its policy recommendations:

- *Marginal changes lead to marginal reactions*: In all markets, a small increase in demand yields a small increase in the respective price, which in turn stimulates a small increase in supply, which brings supply and demand back to equilibrium. There are no threshold levels that need to be crossed before markets react. Consequently, there are no beaten paths that the economy will follow, nor can it be locked into a specific equilibrium by the structure it generates.
- *There exists only one equilibrium outcome*: This equilibrium is Pareto-efficient and socially optimal. The assumptions ensure continuously increasing supply and continuously decreasing demand curves, which intersect at one point and thereby define the market equilibrium. Since actors will trade or produce only when they can increase their utility or profit, everyone reaches the highest level of the objective function that can be achieved under the existing constraints. The resulting equilibrium is therefore optimal for every individual actor as well as for society as a whole.
- *Disturbances are washed away over time*: They lead to deviations from equilibrium, which triggers market forces that bring the economy back toward equilibrium. Therefore, disturbances can only have a temporary effect that disappears over time. The long run outcome of the economy cannot be changed by external disturbances.

These implications lead to the famous policy recommendation of neoclassical economics, that when all the assumptions hold, policy should adopt a "hands off" approach and not intervene in the economy. Policy is only needed to correct for deviations ("market failure") from the neoclassical set of assumptions. This task corresponds to the "efficiency argument" mentioned in the introduction. When the assumptions hold, the market mechanism generates the optimal outcome through its "invisible hand" and does not need any help from policy makers. Policy interventions may actually just generate disturbances that temporarily prevent the system from reaching the equilibrium. Moreover, according to the neoclassical view, policy interventions only have temporary effects and cannot alter the outcome in the long run. At best they are useless, but, at worst, they are probably even damaging and a waste of resources.

It is quite obvious that policies aiming to concentrate production in one region do not fit into the framework of the neoclassical view of the economy. In a neoclassical economy, any such attempt to concentrate production in one region will immediately generate counteracting forces that will disperse production again. The concentration of production generated by, say, a cluster policy, will drive up wages and drive down capital rents in the respective region relative to others (Borts and Stein 1964), which will stimulate workers to move toward this region and capital to move away from it. Through this effect, the perfect mobility of resources will again dissolve the production agglomeration. Consequently, such a concentration policy will not work in a neoclassical economy and the funds allocated to this policy will simply be wasted.

Agglomeration view

In the late 1980s, the neoclassical view was more and more criticized. The main source of criticism was its inability to explain long-run economic growth. In the neoclassical model, because of diminishing marginal returns to capital, growth in the long run depends on the rate of innovation. Moreover, the rate of innovation cannot be explained within the model, because innovation appears as a public good and will therefore not be produced by profit maximizing entrepreneurs.

Attempts to resolve this problem led to models that relaxed the assumption of perfect competition and allowed for agglomeration economies. Work by Romer (1986, 1987, 1990), Rebelo (1991), Barro and Sala-i-Martin (1991), and others popularized "endogenous growth models," which turned out to be major elements in the development of the agglomeration view. Another important contribution was the idea of "monopolistic competition," developed by Dixit and Stiglitz (1977). Their model combined product specific monopolies with competition between the products and became a cornerstone in many formal agglomeration-view models.

Krugman (1991) and others extended these ideas to two identical regions and investigated the economic relations between them. This approach became known as "new economic geography" (NEG). In order to avoid uninteresting corner solutions, they introduced transportation costs as a force counteracting the concentrating tendencies of agglomeration economies. The relation between the centripedal force of agglomeration economies and the centrifugal force of transport costs turns out to be a key parameter for the performance of the NEG models.

The new economic geography version of the agglomeration view has developed out of the neoclassical view and therefore shares many of its basic assumptions. As has been mentioned above, the agglomeration view can be seen as a generalization of the neoclassical view, as it introduces agglomeration forces and transportation costs into its basic structures. The implications of this seemingly minor adjustment are quite dramatic. Because of these changes, the agglomeration view models become non-linear and specific results depend, to a large extent, on specific functional forms of equations and on parameter values. The vast majority of the respective literature discusses model specifications, assumptions, and their implications for the properties of the model. The literature dealing with policy consequences is much more limited. An important exception is the book by Baldwin *et al.* (2003), which deals with the relation between economic geography and public policy. Although it lays out the properties of economic geography models from a policy perspective, it does not take the step that our chapter does, i.e. to examine conceptually the implications these properties have for a specific form of policy.

The most important properties of the agglomeration-view model can be explained easily by using Krugman's famous "tomahawk bifurcation" (Figure 1.1). This graph shows the relationship between transportation costs on the horizontal axis and the share of production of region 1 in a two-region model. The model that produces this graph is a general equilibrium model that allows capital and labor in the industry sector to move freely between the regions. To keep production from concentrating completely in one of the two regions, the NEG models typically assume that, in addition to the industry sector, there is another sector (e.g. agriculture), which is not mobile between the regions.

When transportation costs are high, the firms try to stay close to the consumers of the immobile sector. Since agglomeration forces are weak relative to transport costs, it does not pay for them to cluster production in one of the two regions. Since production distributes equally between the regions according to the workers/customers in the immobile sector, industrial workers also split equally between the two regions. The result is a stable equilibrium with 50 percent of production, workers, and customers being located in region 1.

When transport costs are low relative to agglomeration economies, the latter dominate the distribution of production. It pays for producers in the industry sector

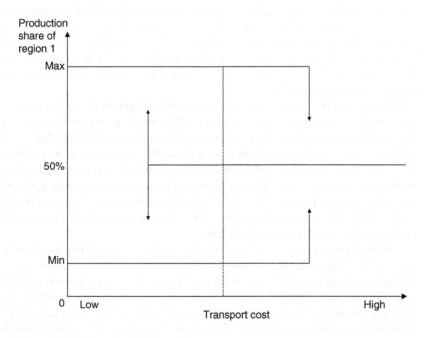

Figure 1.1 The tomahawk bifurcation.

to concentrate all their production in one of the two regions and to serve both regions from there. The benefits of concentrated production outweigh the costs of transporting the products to the customers in the other region. Since industrial jobs are concentrated in one region, industrial workers will also migrate to this region, thus strengthening the concentration of demand, as well as that of labor. This stabilizes the concentrated production equilibrium, where all industrial production will be located in just one region. Only the immobile sector is left in the other region.

Since the two regions are assumed to be identical, the model cannot predict in which one of the two regions industrial production will concentrate. When transport costs are low enough, a small random disturbance may decide between the two options. It is important to note that both are stable equilibria; once reached, none of the economic actors can gain by deviating from the respective equilibrium.

Contrary to the neoclassical model, the NEG-model yields multiple equilibria. This is the first important property to note. In the range of medium transport costs, there are three of them. As indicated by the dashed vertical line in Figure 1.1, production may be concentrated in region 1 (intersection with the top line), or in region 2 (intersection with the bottom line), or it may be split evenly between the two regions (intersection with the middle line). In the latter case, industry finds enough demand in each of the regions to keep production located there. Concentrating it in one of the regions would be uneconomical because of the costs of transporting the products to the other region.

The second property of the tomahawk bifurcation is "path dependence." Which of the three equilibria in a medium transport costs case is realized depends on the path the economy has taken before. When the economy has reached this situation through declining transport costs, it will reach this area with production equally split between the regions (the only stable equilibrium at high transport costs). Since equal distribution is also a stable equilibrium at medium transport costs, this distribution will remain.

When the medium transport costs case is reached through increasing transport costs, production will already be concentrated in one of the regions. Since this is also a stable equilibrium in the medium transport costs case, this distribution will persist as well. Contrary to the neoclassical model, where the effects of disturbances fade away over time and the model always returns to one equilibrium, in the agglomeration view model, the long-term result may depend crucially upon previous development patterns. Because of this dependence of the long-run outcome on the development path, policy interventions may lead the regional economy to one long-term outcome vis-à-vis another.

A third important property is "catastrophic changes" (indicated by the arrows in Figure 1.1). Suppose that the medium transport costs equilibrium has been reached through declining transport costs. Because of the arguments made above, production will remain equally split between the regions. However, when transport costs decline even further, this equal distribution equilibrium becomes unstable. At this point all the production and all the industrial workers will be attracted to one of the two regions. Since this change is not gradual, as is typical for neoclassical models, it is called "catastrophic." At this point, usually called a "bifurcation point," the economy can "choose" between – in this case – two future development paths. One implies the concentration of industrial production and of industrial workers in region 1; the other implies their concentration in region 2.

When viewed over time, these mechanisms imply a development path like the one sketched in Figure 1.2. This is known as the "pitchfork bifurcation." On the vertical axis, the graph again shows the share of production in region 1 in a system of two identical regions. Instead of a parameter value, as in Figure 1.1, we now show time on the horizontal axis. So, the economy always moves from left to right through this graph.

The bifurcation point is located at time t_0. At this point in time, the equal distribution equilibrium that characterized the system up to this point cannot be sustained any longer and the system will either move to the upper branch (all industry concentrated in region 1) or to the lower branch (all industry concentrated in region 2) of the pitchfork. This pitchfork bifurcation diagram will play a central role in the next section of the chapter.

When the economy (in its development over time) approaches such a bifurcation point, the existing equilibrium loses stability and the system can switch to another development path. From an a-priori point of view, various possible paths of development exist for the region. At the bifurcation points, the economy may move onto one or the other. Once the path is chosen, path dependence sets in and stabilizes the development path until – maybe – another bifurcation point is

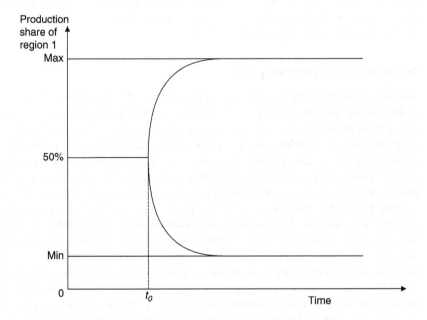

Figure 1.2 The pitchfork bifurcation.

reached. When the economy is approaching a bifurcation point, relatively small random events or policy interventions may suffice to guide it toward one of the available development paths. At stable periods (away from any bifurcation points) even after substantial policy interventions, the economy may return to the stable equilibrium path just like in a neoclassical economy.

Through agglomeration forces, the entry of a new producer into a regional economy has positive implications for all the firms already existing in the region. Consequently, these agglomeration forces imply an externality. Because of this externality, the neoclassical result, that the equilibrium is Pareto-efficient and socially optimal, does not hold any longer in the case of the agglomeration view. The equilibrium that is reached through the market mechanism may be both economically inefficient and socially undesirable. Under the assumptions of the agglomeration view, a Pareto-efficient and socially optimal equilibrium is actually a rather unlikely coincidence.

In the neoclassical view, the standard treatment for externalities that threaten the optimality of the market equilibrium is to internalize them. In order to be able to identify the correct amount of treatment required, the externality under investigation should be the only one in the economy so that the rest of the economy works according to neoclassical assumptions. In the agglomeration view, however, the externalities (i.e. the agglomeration forces) are not just an isolated nuisance; they are an essential part of the economy. They are abundant and spread out throughout the economy. Removing them through internalization would, on the one hand, be extremely difficult because of their widespread effect, and would, on the other hand, lead to the above mentioned structure of "backyard capitalism" and the reintroduction of all the conceptual problems that have eventually led to the development of the agglomeration view.

Implications for regional policy

The two views about the way the economic system works that we have discussed in the previous section imply very different lessons for regional policy and regional policy makers. While – with the exception of the correction of market failures – regional policy is considered useless, or even harmful, from the viewpoint of the neoclassical theory, the agglomeration view implies an explicit need for active regional policy intervention. Since the outcome generated by the market mechanism is distorted by the externalities that characterize the agglomeration view, it is unlikely that the outcome generated by the market is optimal and that policy is required to steer the regional economy toward a more desirable development path. Because of the different development paths that the economy may take in the agglomeration view, policy can also be quite effective. If policy manages to move the regional economy from an undesirable to a desirable development path, it will have a decisive long-term impact, because the regional economy will stay on the desirable development path without further policy intervention. In this respect, the agglomeration view is much more encouraging than the neoclassical view for regional policy makers.

But while the fundamental properties of the agglomeration view imply a need for regional policy, the same fundamental properties make the design of an appropriate regional policy extremely difficult. Because of the non-linearities introduced by externalities and agglomeration economies, the response of the economic system to policy intervention depends on the specific context. Let us illustrate this point by using Figure 1.2 again. At time t_0 the system reaches a bifurcation point. The former stable 50 percent equilibrium loses stability the closer in time we get to the bifurcation point. Small random disturbances will lead to stronger fluctuations of the region's production share than in previous periods. At time t_0 these disturbances will eventually push the system to the upper or lower branch of the pitchfork. There, the stabilizing mechanisms of the new development path will set in, the region will either win production share at the expense of the other region (upper branch) or lose production share to the other region (lower branch).

The implication for the policy maker is that the economic system reacts differently to his/her policy interventions, depending on the time of the intervention. When the policy maker attempts to keep a fair (i.e. 50 percent) share of production for the region, his/her experience from the past is that of a neoclassical view economic system: Since equal distribution of production was a stable equilibrium in previous periods (way to the left of t_0), small deviations from this distribution always disappeared over time and the system returned to the desired production share. Depending on his/her beliefs, the policy maker may attribute this fact either to the intrinsic stability of the economic system at the desired production share, or to the clever policy fine-tuning he/she may have applied in the past. In any case, when the same economic system approaches t_0, it starts to react strangely from the policy maker's point of view. The fluctuations of the production share increase, and production facilities and workers move in and out of the region in larger numbers. Based on his/her knowledge and experience from the past, the policy maker will either see this as an unusually large deviation from the stable equilibrium, and expect the system to return to its previous behavior over time, or try to scale up budget and policy instruments in order to match the larger-scale problems. But, what the policy maker will most likely not recognize is that the problem is changing insofar as the process that has worked in his/her favor in the past – path dependence – keeping the production share at the 50 percent level, begins to work in his/her disfavor and pushes the region away from the desired level. A policy that is scaled up and proportional to the magnitude of the problem, but based on previous experience with the response of the economic system, will turn out to be insufficient to overcome the inertia of the path dependent process.

By the time the increased budget and new policy instruments are available, the system has probably already passed the bifurcation point. The region has started to move along the new development path and path dependence has set in. If the region has previously been fortunate and has taken off on the upper branch of the pitchfork diagram, it will be perceived as a role model for successful regional development. Its regional policy will be investigated for the secrets of its success and referenced as a "best practice" policy model. If the region has been unfortunate in the past, it has entered the lower branch of the pitchfork diagram.

Path dependence has set in and has locked it into a de-industrialization process. Based on experience from the past, policy will be upgraded further, to address the problems of the region. But, since resource allocation will be based on the experience of the past, most likely, the amount of money invested will not be sufficient to overcome the increasing level of path dependence.

These arguments show that neither economic theory, nor past experience, nor the experience of other regions can be of much guidance for the policy maker: although agglomeration-view models typically allow for bifurcation points in development paths, predicting their position would require precise knowledge of the internal structure of the economic system and of all its relevant parameters. Today's agglomeration view models are highly stylized sketches of economies, and are in no way able to characterize real (regional) economic systems; one can even doubt that they ever will be able to do this. In this way, they can alert us to possible future development scenarios, but they do not allow for precise predictions. However, without accurate knowledge of the location of bifurcation points on the region's development path, the regional policy maker cannot adapt policy instruments accordingly. The policy that is adequate at a certain point on the development path may be inadequate at another point in time. This also implies that past experience is of little value in those periods of change. Since circumstances change with time, and also with the application of regional policy instruments, measures that were successful in the past may not work at a later stage, in part because the success of the policy in the past has changed the circumstances.

Similarly, the success stories of other regions cannot easily be transferred. On the one hand, the specific circumstances of the best practice region at the time of its success are probably different from the ones in the target region. On the other hand, the success of the regional policy in the best practice region itself changes the circumstances so much that a transfer of the best practice policy becomes problematic. The success of Silicon Valley inspired many regions to try to imitate its policy and strategy. All of them, however, were in a disadvantaged position as they had to compete against Silicon Valley's well-established computer industry.

In real world settings, the problems that the regional policy maker faces are much larger than we have described above. In reality, of course, there are not just two regions competing for production activities, as most agglomeration view models assume, but many. Regional economies are not homogeneous but composed of various sectors with different organizational structures, legal frameworks, technological capabilities, and linkages to the rest of the economy. All these elements may reach bifurcation points at different periods in time and therefore respond differently to policy incentives at different times. So, the regional policy maker faces at least three problems when designing a regional policy:

1 *When* (at what point in time) to apply a policy intervention,
2 *Where* (to what sector, location, group of companies) to apply a policy intervention, and
3 *How much* (with what intensity) to apply the policy intervention.

As we have seen before, the response of the economic system to a policy intervention will depend upon its position relative to a bifurcation point. The same policy that is highly successful when applied at the right time (at the bifurcation point) will be unsuccessful when applied too early or too late. As far as the target of regional policy intervention is concerned, sectors that are in their nascent state of development, or near a bifurcation point in their development path, would be the obvious targets. However, as the discussion above has shown, they are difficult to identify. The fact that policy has been applied successfully to a sector in another region does not really help, because of the impact this success has on the circumstances for future regional policy. Even when the policy maker picks the right timing and the right target for his/her policy intervention, he/she is still left with the problem of choosing the optimal dose of intervention: When the regional economic system is at the bifurcation point, a very small intervention may be enough to tip the scale and push the system toward the desirable development path. When path dependence is at work, on the other hand, a substantial amount of money may temporarily have positive effects, but may not be enough to overcome path dependence and to keep the regional economic system from returning to the undesirable development path.

In a globalized economy, what we called "circumstances" in the discussion above are generated to a large extent by the economic activities and policies of many other countries, their regions, and sectors. The stronger linkages of globalization lead to increased interdependence between the countries, regions, and sectors. They challenge regional policy makers even further. Through globalization, the circumstances of regional policy making become more complex as well as more dynamic. The externalities and agglomeration economies of the agglomeration view imply that shocks entering through these linkages will not necessarily disappear over time, but may accumulate through the regional economic system and spread further to other regions. Since, in a globalized economy, it is quite difficult to keep regional problems contained in the respective region, regional policy has gained in importance and responsibility. Unfortunately, regional policy makers have to face this challenge with less guidance coming from regional economic theory.

Conclusions

In this chapter, we have discussed the challenges of regional policy in a globalized economy from the viewpoint of recent developments in economic theory. In recent years, many of the theoretical developments in economics highlight externalities and positive agglomeration effects. We aggregate these developments under the term "agglomeration view" and contrast this with the traditional "neoclassical view" of the economic system. While the neoclassical view leads to a single stable equilibrium and smooth development paths, the agglomeration view allows for multiple equilibria, bifurcation points, catastrophic changes, and path dependence.

These characteristics of the agglomeration-view economic system have two important implications for regional policy and regional policy makers: On the one hand, they imply an active role for regional policy and show that regional policy is generally needed in order to reach a socially desirable result. On the other hand, the externalities and agglomeration economies that characterize the agglomeration view imply highly complex system dynamics that make it difficult for economic theory to provide guidance to regional economic policy. Since the reaction of the regional economic system to policy interventions depends upon the specific circumstances of the system, our agglomeration view models in their current crude form cannot provide reliable guidance. Neither can previous experience nor the experience of other regions offer much help. The continuous evolution of circumstances in a globalized economy on the one hand, and the effects of the successful application of a policy in the past or in another region on the other, lead to fundamentally incomparable circumstances that question the value of that experience. In particular, we see at least three areas that challenge the regional policy maker: (1) when to apply a regional policy intervention, (2) where to apply it, and (3) how much of it to apply.

Note

1 We use the term "agglomeration economies" here in a broad sense. They include all effects of concentration of production irrespective of them being within a plant, firm, or sector (economies of scale) or between those units ("external economies," "localization economies," "urbanization economies").

References

Aghion, P. and Howitt, P. (1998) *Endogenous Growth Theory*, Cambridge, MA.: MIT Press.

Armstrong, H. and Taylor, J. (1993) *Regional Economics and Policy*, New York, London: Harvester Wheatsheaf.

Arrow, K.J. and Debreu, G. (1954) "Existence of an Equilibrium for a Competitive Economy," *Econometrica* 22: 265–290.

Baldwin, R.E., Forslid, R., and Martin, P. (2003) *Economic Geography and Public Policy*, Princeton, NJ: Princeton University Press.

Barro, R.J. and Sala-i-Martin, X. (1991) "Convergence across States and Regions," Discussion Paper Nr. 629, Economic Growth Center, Yale University, New Haven, CN.

Borts, G.H. and Stein, J.L. (1964) *Economic Growth in a Free Market*, New York: Columbia University Press.

Camerer, C.F. and Loewenstein, G. (2003) "Behavioral Economics: Past, Present, Future," in Camerer C.F., Loewenstein G., and Rabin, M. (eds), *Advances in Behavioral Economics*, Princeton, NJ: Princeton University Press.

Dixit, A.K. and Stiglitz, J.E. (1977) "Monopolistic Competition and Optimum Product Diversity," *American Economic Review* 67: 297–308.

Eaton, J. and Grossman, G. (1986) "Optimal Trade and Industrial Policy under Oligopoly," *Quarterly Journal of Economics* 101: 383–406.

Ethier, W. (1982) "National and International Returns to Scale in the Modern Theory of International Trade," *American Economic Review* 72: 389–405.

Fujita, M. and Thisse, F.-J. (2002) *Economics of Agglomeration; Cities, Industrial Location and Regional Growth*, Cambridge: Cambridge University Press.

Fujita, M., Krugman, P.R., and Venables, A.J. (1999) *The Spatial Economy*, Cambridge, MA: MIT Press.

Fürst, D., Klemmer P., and Zimmermann, K. (1976) *Regionale Wirtschaftspolitik*, Tübingen: J.C.B. Mohr.

Grossman, G. and Helpman, E. (1991) *Innovation and Growth in the Global Economy*, Cambridge, MA: MIT Press.

Krugman, P.R. (1979) "Increasing Returns, Monopolistic Competition, and International Trade," *Journal of International Economics* 9: 469–479.

Krugman, P.R. (1984) "Import Protection as Export Protection," in Kierkowski, H. (ed.), *Monopolistic Competition and International Trade*, Oxford: Oxford University Press.

Krugman, P.R. (1986) *Strategic Trade Policy and the New International Economics*, Cambridge, MA: MIT Press.

Krugman, P.R. (1991) "Increasing Returns and Economic Geography," *Journal of Political Economy* 99: 483–499.

Mills, E.S. (1972) "An Aggregative Model of Resource Allocation in a Metropolitan Area," in Edel, M. and Rothenburg, J. (eds), *Readings in Urban Economics*, New York: Macmillan.

Porter, M.E. (1998) "Clusters and the New Economics of Competition," *Harvard Business Review* 76: 77–90.

Rebelo, S. (1991) "Long Run Policy Analysis and Long Run Growth," *Journal of Political Economy* 99: 500–521.

Richardson, H.W. (1978) *Regional and Urban Economics*, New York: Penguin Books.

Romer, P.M. (1986) "Increasing Returns and Long Run Growth," *Journal of Political Economy* 94: 1002–1037.

Romer, P.M. (1987) "Growth Based on Increasing Returns Due to Specialization," *American Economic Review* 77(2): 56–62.

Romer, P.M. (1990) "Endogenous Technological Change," *Journal of Political Economy* 98: 71–102.

Smith, V.L. (2000) *Bargaining and Market Behavior: Essays in Experimental Economics*, Cambridge: Cambridge University Press.

Starrett, D. (1978) "Market Allocations of Location Choice in a Model with Free Mobility," *Journal of Economic Theory* 17: 21–37.

Tversky, A. and Kahneman, D. (1974) "Judgment Under Uncertainty: Heuristics and Biases," *Science* 185: 1124–1131.

Tversky, A. and Kahneman, D. (1981) "The Framing of Decisions and the Psychology of Choice," *Science* 211: 453–458.

Part I

Free trade areas in Asia

2 The effect of intermediate and final goods trade on labor demand in Japanese firms*

Sachiko Kazekami and Masahiro Endoh

Introduction

How trade affects wages and jobs is well established as a research topic, and this theme continues to attract the attention of researchers with respect to various economic activities. In 2010 in Japan, at monetary policy meetings and in various speeches and town meetings, members of the policy board of the Bank of Japan repeatedly cited strengthening "globalization" and growing "competition" with foreign countries as reasons why the real wages of Japanese workers had not increased despite the (then) economic upturn. More recently, the sharp appreciation of the nominal Japanese yen has sparked the argument that such sudden yen appreciation encourages Japanese firms to outsource their activities, partly or completely, to developing countries, thereby decreasing the number of domestic jobs. As Japanese firms have increased their economic transactions with Asian countries in the past decade or two, concern about the negative effect this may have on fair wages and stable employment in Japan has emerged.

This chapter uses firm-level data on Japan's manufacturing and service industries in order to evaluate how firms' trade activities affect their labor demands according to type of employment, gender, and education. We consider this chapter to have three distinguishing characteristics that set it apart from previously published papers on the topic. First, it classifies workers according to type of employment, gender, and academic background. Second, it divides trade effects into trade-induced factor-biased technology changes and trading volume changes. Finally, it divides trade activities into intermediate goods imports and final goods exports and distinguishes between different trading partners.

*The authors appreciate the financial support provided by the Ministry of Education, Culture, Sports, Science, and Technology in Japan, Chukyo University, and Keio University. The authors are also grateful to the Ministry of Health, Labor, and Welfare, the Ministry of Economy, Trade, and Industry, and the Ministry of Internal Affairs and Communications Statistics Bureau for providing us with the Basic Survey on Wage Structure, the Basic Survey of Japanese Business Structure and Activities, and the Establishment and Enterprise Census. We constructed the employer–employee data set ourselves using these data.

The first characteristic of our study is that it considers factors such as type of employment and gender when estimating how trade affects wages. Much previous research examines how imports affect workers by skill level (Feenstra and Hanson 1999; Ekholm and Hakkala 2006; Ahn *et al.* 2008). These studies report that imports of intermediate goods from low-income countries affect labor composition by shifting labor requirements to highly-skilled workers. Other studies note that offshoring increases the ratio of non-regular workers to all workers (Machikita and Sato 2011; Tomiura *et al.* 2011). Recent research using employer-employee data has resulted in ample information on both companies and workers. These studies mainly explore the impact of exports and whether the high wages of exporters are caused by changing worker pool composition, an increasing return on highly skilled workers, or growing productivity (Frias *et al.* 2012; Krishna *et al.* 2011).

Little is known, however, about how trade affects workers by type of employment or by gender. Many previous empirical studies examine the impact of exports and imports on workers only according to their education levels or the division between production and non-production workers, while many theoretical studies model labor by skill level. However, the variety of types of employment arrangements has greatly expanded in recent years. Specifically, the number of workers working a non-traditional number of hours and/or non-traditional contract periods has greatly increased in many developed countries, while, at the same time, disparities in treatment and pay among these workers are being recognized. In addition, it is natural to assume that the female labor market is segregated from that of male workers in East Asian countries, given that the average wage of female workers is relatively much lower, even after controlling for factors such as education, age, and occupation. In this chapter, we assume that trade affects wages differently according to type of employment, gender, and academic background.

The second characteristic of our research is that it estimates two types of trade effects separately: the internationalization of firm activities and the increase in international transactions. The term "trade" in this context has two meanings. The first is that the enterprise begins to conduct international activities, which changes its production process and thus its factor components. The second is that the growth in trade increases demand for complementary workers with trade goods, while decreasing that for substitute workers. Thus, the firm's factor components change. We expect that the increase in a firm's volume of trade from zero to one million dollars (termed the "start-up effect") has a different effect from that of the increase in trade from one to two million dollars ("volume effect"), even though both effects are caused by an increase in trade volume of one million dollars. This study thus captures and clarifies how trade affects groups of individual workers based on trade-induced factor-biased technology changes (from the start-up effect) and trading volume changes (from the volume effect).[1]

The third characteristic of our study is that it takes account of both intermediate goods imports and final goods exports by firms simultaneously and differentiates between trade partners geographically. Most previous papers, including those mentioned above, examine only the effects of either exports or imports on firms' labor demands. In addition, some studies overlook differences in the origin and destination of trade even though it is natural to assume that international transactions with developed countries influence Japanese labor demand differently to those with developing countries. By contrast, the present chapter examines these aspects inclusively. We consider the intermediate goods imports of Japanese firms as an indicator of how much they outsource their activities to foreign countries.

The remainder of this chapter is organized as follows. In the second section, we describe the empirical approach and data set. The third section proposes the empirical results. The final section presents our conclusion.

Empirical approach

Empirical model

We begin by assuming that capital, input goods, and output goods can be treated as fixed factors over one year or more, whereas labor should be treated as a variable. Assuming that the variable cost function in firm i has a translog form, we can write this as:

$$
\begin{aligned}
\ln C_i = \alpha_i &+ \sum_j \beta_j \ln w_{ij} + \frac{1}{2} \sum_j \sum_k \gamma_{jk} \ln w_{ij} \ln w_{ik} + \sum_l \delta_l \ln x_{il} \\
&+ \sum_j \sum_l \zeta_{jl} \ln w_{ij} \ln x_{il} + \frac{1}{2} \sum_l \sum_m \eta_{lm} \ln x_{il} \ln x_{im} + \sum_n \kappa_n z_{in} \\
&+ \sum_j \sum_n \lambda_{jn} z_{in} \ln w_{ij} + \sum_l \sum_n \mu_{ln} z_{in} \ln x_{il} + \frac{1}{2} \sum_n \sum_o \nu_{no} z_{in} z_{io},
\end{aligned}
$$
(2.1)

where C_i represents total variable costs for firm i, w_{ij} is the wages of the optimally chosen workers in labor category j in firm i, x_{il} is the fixed inputs or outputs l in firm i, and z_{in} is the structural variable n in firm i, including industry dummies, that shifts variable costs.

Differentiating the translog cost function (2.1) with respect to wages w_{ij} yields the payments made to workers in labor category j in firm i relative to variable costs, which we denote by the cost shares S_{ij}:

$$
S_{ij} = \beta_j + \sum_k \gamma_{jk} \ln w_{ik} + \sum_l \zeta_{jl} \ln x_{il} + \sum_n \lambda_{jn} z_{in},
$$
(2.2)

where $S_{ij} = w_{ij} L_{ij} / \sum_k w_{ik} L_{ik}$ and L_{ij} is demand for labor in labor category j, which depends on gender, education level, and type of employment. As for the fixed input and output factor x_{il}, we use three variables: tangible fixed assets, total outputs, and total inputs. The structural variable z_{in} includes the factors that represent a firm's international economic transactions, such as an overseas affiliates dummy, exports and imports dummies, the ratio of final goods exports to three regions (Asia, North America and Europe, and "others") to total sales, the ratio of intermediate goods imports from these three regions to its total purchase of intermediates, and 75 industry dummies.

We also calculate the elasticities of factor demand using the estimation results. The elasticities of labor demand in labor category j with respect to wages for labor categories j and k are:

$$\varepsilon_{jj} = \frac{\partial \ln L_{ij}}{\partial \ln w_{ij}} = \frac{\gamma_{jj} + S_{ij}^2}{S_{ij}} - 1, \tag{2.3}$$

$$\varepsilon_{jk} = \frac{\partial \ln L_{ij}}{\partial \ln w_{ik}} = \frac{\gamma_{jk} + S_{ik}S_{ij}}{S_{ij}}, \tag{2.4}$$

where L_{ij} denotes demand for labor in labor category j, expressed in man-hours. To ensure that the translog cost function is homogeneous of degree one in wages, we impose $\sum_k \gamma_{jk} = \sum_l \zeta_{jl} = \sum_n \lambda_{jn} = 0$. Without loss of generality, we impose the symmetry requirement that $\gamma_{ij} = \gamma_{ji}$. These characteristics also satisfy the condition of $\sum_k \varepsilon_{jk} = 0$. We estimate share equations using the iterative seemingly unrelated regression model. Since the sum of labor cost shares equals one, one equation needs to be dropped, and this model can thus be applied independent of the deleted equation.

The semi-elasticity of labor demand in category j with respect to the structural variable n is demonstrated by:

$$\varepsilon_{jn} = \frac{\partial \ln L_{ij}}{\partial z_{il}} = \frac{\lambda_{jn}}{S_{ij}}. \tag{2.5}$$

We use the cost share S_{ij} of the sample means to calculate the above elasticities.[2]

Data

Detailed information on both workers and companies, such as type of employment, trade, and sales, does not exist in one survey in Japan. Therefore, we construct an employer–employee data set using the Basic Survey on Wage Structure and the Basic Survey of Japanese Business Structure and Activities from 2008. The Basic Survey on Wage Structure is conducted by the Ministry of Health, Labor, and Welfare on private establishments that have five or more regular employees and public establishments that have ten or more regular employees. Further, it includes workers selected using the uniform sampling method from among these establishments in order to obtain a clear picture of the wage structure across Japan and to provide detailed information about the breakdown of Japanese workers' education levels, ages, genders, employee types, and workplaces. The Basic Survey of Japanese Business Structure and Activities is conducted by the

Ministry of Economy, Trade, and Industry, and it covers enterprises that have 50 or more employees and excess capital or investment funds valued at over 30 million yen. Covered industries include mining, manufacturing, wholesale and retail trade, and the food and drink industry.

Because the unit of workers data used by the Basic Survey on Wage Structure is work establishment, whereas the unit of company data from the Basic Survey of Japanese Business Structure and Activities is enterprises, we use the Establishment and Enterprise Census to link both data sets. This census is conducted on all establishments in Japan in order to compile a complete directory that serves as the master sampling framework for various statistical surveys, including the Basic Survey on Wage Structure by the Statistics Bureau. This census is conducted by the Ministry of Internal Affairs and Communications.[3]

The number of enterprises covered by both the Basic Survey of Japanese Business Structure and Activities and the Establishment and Enterprise Census was 25,513 in 2008. Meanwhile, the number of enterprises and employees covered by both the Basic Survey on Wage Structure and the Establishment and Enterprise Census in 2008 was 26,156 and 863,135, respectively. Therefore, by connecting the Basic Survey of Japanese Business Structure and Activities and the Basic Survey on Wage Structure and by deleting enterprises that have missing data, we compile a data set of 5,050 enterprises.

We employ two definitions to refer to labor categories depending on type of employment. The first definition (Definition A) is used to classify workers into the following ten categories by gender, education level, and period of employment (hired for a definite or an indefinite period): (A1) male graduates of secondary education schools, hired for a definite period, (A2) male graduates of secondary education schools, hired for an indefinite period, (A3) male graduates of higher education schools and universities, hired for a definite period, (A4) male graduates of higher education schools and universities, hired for an indefinite period, (A5) male temporary employees, (A6) female graduates of secondary education schools, hired for a definite period, (A7) female graduates of secondary education schools, hired for an indefinite period, (A8) female graduates of higher education schools and universities, hired for a definite period, (A9) female graduates of higher education schools and universities, hired for an indefinite period, and (A10) female temporary employees.

The second definition (Definition B) is used to classify workers into the following ten categories by gender, education level, and position of employment (non-regular or regular staff): (B1) male graduates of secondary education schools, non-regular staff, (B2) male graduates of secondary education schools, regular staff, (B3) male graduates of higher education schools and universities, non-regular staff, (B4) male graduates of higher education schools and universities, regular staff, (B5) male temporary employees, (B6) female graduates of secondary education schools, non-regular staff, (B7) female graduates of secondary education schools, regular staff, (B8) female graduates of higher education schools and universities, non-regular staff, (B9) female graduates of higher education schools and universities, regular staff, and (B10) female temporary employees.

We do not expect the estimation results based on Definitions A and B to differ much from each other, since "employment for a definite period" and "employment for an indefinite period" in Definition A roughly correspond to "non-regular worker" and "regular worker" in Definition B for each gender and at each education level. This is because most employment for a definite period is for non-regular workers, while most employment for an indefinite period is for regular workers in Japan. Table 2.1 shows the percentage of each labor classification by gender and by labor definition in 2008. For example, 51.41 percent of male employees graduated from junior and senior high schools after completing their educations. Among them, 4.38 percent are working under fixed-term contracts and 5.11 percent are working as non-regular workers; thus, the two figures are similar. Likewise, 47.03 percent are working for an indefinite period and 46.30 percent are working as regular workers. In Japan, the employment status of male and

Table 2.1 Categories of workers

Male workers		
Definition A	*Employment for a definite period*	*Employment for an indefinite period*
Graduates of secondary education schools	4.38%	47.03%
Graduates of higher education schools and universities	1.62%	37.75%
Short-time worker	9.22%	
Definition B	*Non-regular worker*	*Regular worker*
Graduates of secondary education schools	5.11%	46.30%
Graduates of higher education schools and universities	1.66%	37.71%
Short-time worker	9.22%	
Female workers		
Definition A	*Employment for a definite period*	*Employment for an indefinite period*
Graduates of secondary education schools	8.34%	21.78%
Graduates of higher education schools and universities	3.43%	14.86%
Short-time worker	51.59%	
Definition B	*Non-regular worker*	*Regular worker*
Graduates of secondary education schools	10.97%	19.15%
Graduates of higher education schools and universities	3.75%	14.54%
Short-time worker	51.59%	

female workers is different, however. More than 80 percent of male employees are indefinite-period workers or regular workers, whereas more than 50 percent of female employees are short-time workers.

The hourly wage in labor category j in firm i, w_{ij}, is calculated by dividing the sum of the contractual cash earnings of employees in labor category j in firm i by the sum of the actual number of their scheduled hours and overtime worked. As for the fixed inputs or outputs l in firm i, x_{ij}, we consider the following three factors: x_{i1} is the value of tangible fixed capital, x_{i2} is the total sales of final goods, and x_{i3} is the total purchases of intermediate goods. In addition, we consider nine factors as the structural variable n in firm i, z_{in}. Here, z_{i1} is a dummy variable that proxies for whether firm i has a foreign subsidiary ($z_{i1} = 1$) or not ($z_{i1} = 0$); z_{i2} is a dummy variable that proxies for whether firm i exports its products on its own ($z_{i2} = 1$) or not ($z_{i2} = 0$); z_{i3} is a dummy variable that proxies for whether firm i imports its intermediates (except from the Middle East) on its own ($z_{i3} = 1$) or not ($z_{i3} = 0$); z_{i4} is a ratio of the final goods firm i exports to Asia to its total sales; z_{i5} is a ratio of the final goods firm i exports to North America and Europe to its total sales; z_{i6} is a ratio of the final goods firm i exports to other countries to its total sales; z_{i7} is a ratio of the intermediate goods firm i imports from Asia (except the Middle East) to its total purchase of intermediates; z_{i8} is a ratio of the intermediate goods firm i imports from North America and Europe to its total purchase of intermediates; z_{i9} is a ratio of the total intermediate goods firm i imports from other countries (except the Middle East) to its total purchase of intermediates. We report detailed descriptive statistics in Table 2.2.

Main results

Semi-elasticities of labor demand with trade

Table 2.3 presents the semi-elasticities of labor demand with the foreign subsidiary dummy, exports and imports dummies, and exporting and outsourcing ratios. The coefficients estimated by equation (2.2) are shown in Appendixes 1 and 2. The figures presented in Table 2.3 are calculated from equation (2.5) by using the estimated results of λ_{jn} in Appendixes 1 and 2 as well as the cost shares S_{ij} in Appendix 3. The italic font means that the estimated result λ_{jn} to obtain the figure is statistically significant at the 10 percent level. Since the two definitions of labor categories produce similar results, we focus on the results of Definition A. The following explanations thus concern the figures represented in the italic font.

The overseas affiliate dummy (z_{i1}) positively affects demand for male and female graduates of higher education schools and universities, hired for an indefinite period (L_{iA4} and L_{iA9}), but negatively affects demand for male graduates of secondary education schools, hired for a definite period (L_{iA1}), and that for female temporary employees (L_{i10}). It can be inferred that multinational companies prefer to recruit workers that have a high level of education both to operate overseas affiliates and to work in the headquarters in Japan for an indefinite period as regular staff. By contrast, since both male workers that have low and intermediate

Table 2.2 Descriptive statistics

Variables		Mean	Std. Dev.	Min	Max
ln w_{iA1}	log of firm i's hourly wage: male graduates of secondary education schools, hired for a definite period	1.03	1.27	0.00	4.17
lnw_{iA2}	log of firm i's hourly wage: male graduates of secondary education schools, hired for an indefinite period	2.67	0.86	0.00	4.12
ln w_{iA3}	log of firm i's hourly wage: male graduates of higher education schools and universities, hired for a definite period	0.62	1.16	0.00	4.61
ln w_{iA4}	log of firm i's hourly wage: male graduates of higher education schools and universities, hired for an indefinite period	2.73	0.86	0.00	4.41
ln w_{iB1}	log of firm i's hourly wage: male graduates of secondary education schools, non-regular staff	1.16	1.27	0.00	3.99
ln w_{iB2}	log of firm i's hourly wage: male graduates of secondary education schools, regular staff	2.69	0.85	0.00	4.17
ln w_{iB3}	log of firm i's hourly wage: male graduates of higher education schools and universities, non-regular staff	0.66	1.16	0.00	4.50
ln w_{iB4}	log of firm i's hourly wage: male graduates of higher education schools and universities, regular staff	2.74	0.85	0.00	4.41
ln w_{i5}	log of firm i's hourly wage: male temporary employees	0.72	1.09	0.00	4.90
ln w_{iA6}	log of firm i's hourly wage: female graduates of secondary education schools, hired for a definite period	0.77	1.09	0.00	3.41
ln w_{iA7}	log of firm i's hourly wage: female graduates of secondary education schools, hired for an indefinite period	1.95	1.13	0.00	3.84
ln w_{iA8}	log of firm i's hourly wage: female graduates of higher education schools and universities, hired for a definite period	0.47	0.96	0.00	4.23
ln w_{iA9}	log of firm i's hourly wage: female graduates of higher education schools and universities, hired for an indefinite period	1.77	1.26	0.00	3.84
ln w_{iB6}	log of firm i's hourly wage: female graduates of secondary education schools, non-regular staff	0.95	1.13	0.00	3.47
ln w_{iB7}	log of firm i's hourly wage: female graduates of secondary education schools, regular staff	1.94	1.15	0.00	3.84

Table 2.2 Continued

Variables		Mean	Std. Dev.	Min	Max
$\ln w_{iB8}$	log of firm i's hourly wage: female graduates of higher education schools and universities, non-regular staff	0.53	1.00	0.00	3.56
$\ln w_{iB9}$	log of firm i's hourly wage: female graduates of higher education schools and universities, regular staff	1.76	1.27	0.00	3.84
$\ln w_{i10}$	log of firm i's hourly wage: female temporary employees	1.12	1.12	0.00	4.91
$\ln x_{i1}$	log of firm i's tangible fixed capital	7.66	1.94	0.00	16.06
$\ln x_{i2}$	log of firm i's total sales of final goods	9.34	1.62	5.52	16.23
$\ln x_{i3}$	log of firm i's total purchases of intermediate goods	8.45	2.11	0.00	16.20
z_{i1}	a dummy variable that proxies for whether firm i has a foreign subsidiary (1) or not (0)	0.24	0.42	0.00	1.00
z_{i2}	a dummy variable that proxies for whether firm i exports its products on its own (1) or not (0)	0.24	0.42	0.00	1.00
z_{i3}	a dummy variable that proxies for whether firm i imports its intermediates (except from the Middle East) on its own (1) or not (0)	0.23	0.42	0.00	1.00
z_{i4}	a ratio of the final goods firm i's exports to Asia to its total sales	0.02	0.06	0.00	0.80
z_{i5}	a ratio of the final goods firm i's exports to North America and Europe to its total sales	0.01	0.06	0.00	0.86
z_{i6}	a ratio of the final goods firm i's exports to other countries to its total sales	0.00	0.03	0.00	0.72
z_{i7}	a ratio of the intermediate goods firm i's imports from Asia (except the Middle East) to its total purchase of intermediates	0.03	0.11	0.00	1.00
z_{i8}	a ratio of the intermediate goods firm i's imports from North America and Europe to its total purchase of intermediates	0.01	0.06	0.00	1.00
z_{i9}	a ratio of the total intermediate goods firm i's imports from other countries (except the Middle East) to its total purchase of intermediates	0.00	0.02	0.00	0.74

Note: Number of observations, 5050.

Table 2.3 Semi-elasticities of labor demand on structural variables

	L_{iA1}	L_{iA2}	L_{iA3}	L_{iA4}	L_{i5}	L_{iA6}	L_{iA7}	L_{iA8}	L_{iA9}	L_{i10}
z_{i1}	-0.167	-0.034	-0.104	0.075	-0.081	-0.014	0.010	-0.070	0.138	-0.152
z_{i2}	-0.075	-0.016	0.222	0.056	-0.092	-0.156	-0.077	-0.159	0.111	-0.057
z_{i3}	0.053	-0.036	-0.033	0.031	-0.056	0.273	-0.003	0.169	-0.102	0.006
z_{i4}	-0.218	-0.058	-0.447	0.137	0.353	0.621	0.017	0.818	-0.813	0.001
z_{i5}	0.175	-0.130	-0.675	0.246	-0.123	0.166	0.188	-0.266	-0.427	-0.264
z_{i6}	-1.608	0.206	-1.336	-0.043	-0.242	-0.041	0.071	0.150	-0.144	0.122
z_{i7}	0.634	-0.103	0.377	0.018	0.027	-1.052	0.154	-0.543	0.206	0.209
z_{i8}	-0.432	-0.123	-1.222	0.260	0.481	-0.641	0.070	-1.063	0.674	-0.523
z_{i9}	1.072	0.098	1.038	-0.343	0.502	0.376	0.254	0.908	-0.312	-0.047

	L_{iB1}	L_{iB2}	L_{iB3}	L_{iB4}	L_{i5}	L_{iB6}	L_{iB7}	L_{iB8}	L_{iB9}	L_{i10}
z_{i1}	-0.097	-0.039	-0.127	0.078	-0.067	0.047	-0.033	-0.059	0.138	-0.144
z_{i2}	-0.011	-0.022	0.371	0.051	-0.093	-0.225	-0.022	0.002	0.071	-0.059
z_{i3}	-0.058	-0.023	0.002	0.026	-0.065	0.208	0.005	0.061	-0.090	-0.002
z_{i4}	-0.330	-0.059	-0.417	0.135	0.286	0.634	0.030	0.471	-0.728	-0.031
z_{i5}	0.198	-0.113	-0.858	0.234	-0.131	-0.123	0.261	-0.348	-0.362	-0.270
z_{i6}	-0.879	0.139	-0.663	-0.055	-0.204	0.180	-0.017	0.137	-0.114	0.130
z_{i7}	0.486	-0.109	0.323	0.038	0.002	-0.486	0.003	-0.138	0.170	0.200
z_{i8}	-0.317	-0.134	-1.096	0.243	0.402	-0.200	0.031	-0.777	0.695	-0.556
z_{i9}	1.606	0.168	1.000	-0.395	0.393	-0.414	0.459	0.167	-0.335	-0.142

Note: The italic font means that the estimated result λ_{jn} to obtain the figure is statistically significant at the 10% level.

levels of education hired for a definite period and female temporary employees are not required for the management of overseas affiliates, their positions and working hours are reduced in order to leave financial space to increase the positions and working hours of highly educated employees.

The exports dummy (z_{i2}) positively affects demand for male graduates of higher education schools and universities (L_{iA3} and L_{iA4}) and that for female graduates of higher education schools and universities, hired for an indefinite period (L_{iA9}). We can see that companies selling their products on the international market need workers that have a high level of education, which is the factor-biased technology change induced by their exporting activities. By contrast, the imports dummy (z_{i3}) has a mixed effect on female workers. The factor-biased technology change induced by companies' importing activities increases labor demand for female workers that have junior or senior high school diplomas hired for a definite period (L_{iA6}), but decreases that for female workers that have higher professional school, junior college, university, or graduate school diplomas, hired for an indefinite period (L_{iA9}). These two categories are thus symmetrical in the sense of workers' educational levels and contract periods, but it is difficult to interpret what these symmetrical effects stem from.

As for the structural variables concerning the ratios of final goods exports and intermediate goods imports (z_{i4} to z_{i9}), the Heckscher–Ohlin model makes the following predictions. Japan is relatively abundant in workers that have a high level of education compared with other Asian countries and developing countries, but its relative abundance of factors is scarcely different from that of the developed countries in North America and Europe. Japan thus exports goods that are intensive in workers that have a high level of education to Asian countries and other developing countries, whereas it imports goods that are intensive in workers that have low and intermediate levels of education from these countries. Therefore, it is expected that an increase in the ratio of exports to and imports from Asian countries and other developing countries (z_{i4}, z_{i6}, z_{i7}, and z_{i8}) shifts an average Japanese firm's labor demand towards workers that have a high level of education (L_{iA3}, L_{iA4}, L_{iA8}, and L_{iA9}), whereas it shifts it away from workers that have low and intermediate levels of education (L_{iA1}, L_{iA2}, L_{iA6}, and L_{iA7}). By contrast, the ratio of exports to, and imports from, North American and European countries (z_{i5} and z_{i8}) does not shift a firm's labor demand in a particular direction to a significant degree.

These estimation results, however, support only two predictions regarding Japanese trade with Asian countries and other developing countries: the negative effect of z_{i6} on L_{iA1} and the negative effect of z_{i7} on L_{iA6}. For trade with Asian countries, z_{i4} negatively affects L_{iA9}, whereas z_{i7} positively affects L_{iA1}. Both, therefore, represent the opposite of the prediction by the Heckscher–Ohlin model. In addition, it is difficult to explain why z_{i7} has the opposite effect on L_{iA1} and L_{iA6}, in the same categories except gender.

Regarding Japanese trade with North American and European countries, some variables show statistically significant positive or negative figures. For example, z_{i5} shifts labor demand towards male graduates of higher education schools and universities, hired for an indefinite period (L_{iA4}), while z_{i8} shifts labor demand towards male and female workers that have a high level of education, hired for an indefinite period (L_{iA4} and L_{iA9}). The variable z_{i8} also shifts labor demand away from male workers that have a high level of education, hired for a definite period (L_{iA3}), and from female temporary employees (L_{iA10}). These results may reflect the fact that international transactions require highly-educated employees regardless of trading partners and that as trade volume increases, companies increase their labor demands for them. Moreover, the Heckscher–Ohlin model has little power of prediction.

Elasticities of labor demand with wages

Table 2.4 presents the elasticities of labor demand with wages. The figures presented in Table 2.4 are calculated from equations (2.3) and (2.4) by using the estimated results of γ_{jj} and γ_{jk} in Appendixes 1 and 2 as well as the cost shares S_{ij} and S_{ik} in Appendix 3. The italic font means that the estimated results γ_{jj} and γ_{jk} to obtain the figure are statistically significant at the 10 percent level. Similar to the discussion in the previous subsection, we focus on the results of Definition A.

First, we examine the values of ε_{jj} (the diagonal in Table 2.4). It is interesting to note that the impact of increasing wages in one labor category on labor demand in the same category differs with respect to workers' employment periods. For instance, demand for labor provided by workers hired for a definite period (L_{iA1}, L_{iA3}, L_{iA6}, and L_{iA8}) increases as their own wages (w_{iA1}, w_{iA3}, w_{iA6}, and w_{iA8}) increase. This result might stem from supply-side factors, namely definite-period workers increase their working hours when they receive a rise in their hourly wages. As for the other labor categories, the elasticities of labor demand with wages are negative. This either reflects companies' expected responses to a rise in wages or comes from supply-side factors, in that workers hired for an indefinite period, and temporary employees, decrease their working hours as their wages increase, because this increases their demand for leisure.

Second, as for the value of ε_{jk}, a rise in hourly wages in one labor category increases demand for labor of the opposite gender that has the same educational attainment and same type of employment and that, for labor, has the same type of employment and of the same gender, but different educational levels. For example, in Table 2.4, if w_{iA1} (hourly wage of male graduates of secondary education schools, hired for a definite period) increases, it would correspondingly increase labor demand for L_{iA6} (labor of the same educational attainment and the same type of employment as L_{iA1}, but where the gender is female) and L_{iA3} (labor of the same gender and same educational attainment as L_{iA1}, but where educational attainment is higher). We can see this pattern in all ten hourly wages in the upper table of Table 2.4. These findings imply that the workers of one category hired for a definite period are complementary to those of the opposite gender or of different educational attainment hired for a definite period. They also suggest that the workers of one category hired for an indefinite period are substitutes for those of the opposite gender or of different educational attainment hired for an

Table 2.4 Elasticities of labor demand on wages

	L_{iA1}	L_{iA2}	L_{iA3}	L_{iA4}	L_{i5}	L_{iA6}	L_{iA7}	L_{iA8}	L_{iA9}	L_{i10}
w_{iA1}	0.025	0.009	0.171	−0.010	0.047	0.139	−0.039	−0.144	−0.051	0.001
w_{iA2}	0.113	−0.383	−0.198	0.258	0.095	0.021	0.436	−0.292	0.073	0.152
w_{iA3}	0.069	−0.006	0.612	−0.004	−0.055	−0.028	−0.027	0.044	−0.005	−0.018
w_{iA4}	−0.111	0.231	−0.098	−0.380	0.163	−0.111	0.086	−0.090	0.418	0.159
w_{i5}	0.039	0.006	−0.111	0.012	−0.190	−0.079	−0.030	−0.191	−0.034	0.091
w_{iA6}	0.129	0.002	−0.065	−0.009	−0.090	0.141	−0.007	0.217	−0.049	−0.012
w_{iA7}	−0.118	0.105	−0.203	0.023	−0.109	−0.023	−0.474	−0.254	0.045	0.060
w_{iA8}	−0.047	−0.008	0.036	−0.003	−0.077	0.076	−0.028	0.809	0.001	−0.013
w_{iA9}	−0.101	0.012	−0.026	0.074	−0.082	−0.102	0.030	0.003	−0.424	0.019
w_{i10}	0.002	0.033	−0.118	0.038	0.298	−0.033	0.054	−0.102	0.026	−0.440

	L_{iB1}	L_{iB2}	L_{iB3}	L_{iB4}	L_{i5}	L_{iB6}	L_{iB7}	L_{iB8}	L_{iB9}	L_{i10}
w_{iB1}	−0.129	0.019	0.127	−0.001	0.030	0.129	−0.035	−0.100	−0.064	−0.019
w_{iB2}	0.196	−0.393	−0.052	0.250	0.080	0.147	0.399	−0.226	0.086	0.160
w_{iB3}	0.043	−0.002	0.493	−0.001	−0.059	−0.025	−0.023	−0.002	−0.005	−0.024
w_{iB4}	−0.007	0.226	−0.022	−0.383	0.159	−0.098	0.085	−0.078	0.421	0.173
w_{i5}	0.021	0.005	−0.122	0.012	−0.185	−0.073	−0.024	−0.156	−0.032	0.094
w_{iB6}	0.139	0.015	−0.079	−0.011	−0.110	−0.065	0.015	0.198	−0.047	−0.014
w_{iB7}	−0.082	0.088	−0.156	0.021	−0.079	0.032	−0.476	−0.174	0.032	0.059
w_{iB8}	−0.030	−0.006	−0.002	−0.002	−0.067	0.056	−0.023	0.630	0.004	−0.015
w_{iB9}	−0.108	0.014	−0.023	0.074	−0.076	−0.074	0.023	0.025	−0.424	0.021
w_{i10}	−0.044	0.035	−0.164	0.042	0.307	−0.030	0.059	−0.115	0.030	−0.435

Note: The italic font means that the estimated results γ_{1j} and γ_{jk} to obtain the figure are statistically significant at the 10% level.

indefinite period. The clarification of the reason for this relationship between labor categories remains a topic for future research.

Conclusion

This chapter used firm-level data on Japan's manufacturing and service industries in 2008 in order to estimate how firms' trade activities affect their labor demands. Labor demands were categorized by type of employment, gender, and education. The effects of firms' export and import activities on their labor demands were divided into the start-up effect and the volume effect, and the latter was then subdivided according to trading partners. By using this method, we estimated how increasing trading volume between Japan and Asian countries affected Japanese firms' labor demands.

Our main findings are threefold. First, the start-up effect of exports increases companies' labor demands for both male and female graduates that have high levels of education hired for an indefinite period. Second, the start-up effect of imports increases labor demand for female workers that have low and intermediate levels of education hired for a definite period, but decreases labor demand for female workers that have a high level of education hired for an indefinite period. Third, regarding trade activities with Asian countries, the ratio of final goods exports to Asian countries negatively affects labor demand for female graduates that have a high level of education hired for an indefinite period, whereas the ratio of intermediate goods imports from Asian countries positively affects labor demand for male and female graduates that have low and intermediate levels of education hired for a definite period.

Although this chapter showed how trade with Asian countries affects Japanese labor demand, it failed to provide any theoretical foundation or reasons for why these rather patchy results were observed in Japan. These points remain objectives for future research.

Appendix 2.1 Estimation results 1: workers categorized by period of employment

	S_{iA1}		S_{iA2}		S_{iA3}		S_{iA4}		S_{i5}	
	Coeff.	Std. Dev.	Coeff.	Std. Dev.	Coeff.	Std. Dev.	Coeff.	Std. Dev.	Coeff.	Std. Dev.
$\ln w_{iA1}$	0.0288***	0.0006	−0.0071***	0.0008	0.0017***	0.0003	−0.0125***	0.0008	0.0004	0.0004
$\ln w_{iA2}$	−0.0071***	0.0008	0.0926***	0.0027	−0.0065***	0.0005	−0.0321***	0.0021	−0.0062***	0.0007
$\ln w_{iA3}$	0.0017***	0.0003	−0.0065***	0.0005	0.0187***	0.0004	−0.0049***	0.0005	−0.0016***	0.0003
$\ln w_{iA4}$	−0.0125***	0.0008	−0.0321***	0.0021	−0.0049***	0.0005	0.0959***	0.0025	−0.0037***	0.0007
$\ln w_{i5}$	0.0004	0.0004	−0.0062***	0.0007	−0.0016***	0.0003	−0.0037***	0.0007	0.0186***	0.0007
$\ln w_{iA6}$	0.0030***	0.0005	−0.0091***	0.0008	−0.0011***	0.0004	−0.0116***	0.0008	−0.0028***	0.0005
$\ln w_{iA7}$	−0.0059***	0.0006	0.0067***	0.0013	−0.0034***	0.0004	−0.0203***	0.0012	−0.0046***	0.0005
$\ln w_{iA8}$	−0.0016***	0.0003	−0.0062***	0.0005	0.0003	0.0003	−0.0039***	0.0005	−0.0020***	0.0004
$\ln w_{iA9}$	−0.0045***	0.0005	−0.0161***	0.0009	−0.0010***	0.0003	0.0056***	0.0009	−0.0033***	0.0005
$\ln w_{iJ10}$	−0.0022***	0.0006	−0.0159***	0.0013	−0.0023***	0.0004	−0.0124***	0.0012	0.0052***	0.0006
$\ln x_{i1}$	−0.0004	0.0006	0.0059***	0.0021	−0.0003	0.0004	0.0007	0.0020	−0.0017***	0.0006
$\ln x_{i2}$	0.0014	0.0013	−0.0155***	0.0041	0.0005	0.0007	0.0190***	0.0038	0.0038***	0.0011
$\ln x_{i3}$	−0.0018**	0.0008	0.0039	0.0027	−0.0011**	0.0005	0.0002	0.0026	−0.0001	0.0007
z_{i1}	−0.0048**	0.0024	−0.0120	0.0077	−0.0012	0.0014	0.0241***	0.0073	−0.0019	0.0021
z_{i2}	−0.0022	0.0027	−0.0056	0.0087	0.0026*	0.0016	0.0179**	0.0082	−0.0022	0.0024
z_{i3}	0.0015	0.0025	−0.0130	0.0082	−0.0004	0.0015	0.0098	0.0077	−0.0013	0.0023
z_{i4}	−0.0063	0.0144	−0.0207	0.0469	−0.0052	0.0084	0.0439	0.0442	0.0083	0.0128
z_{i5}	0.0051	0.0145	−0.0467	0.0472	−0.0079	0.0084	0.0787*	0.0446	−0.0029	0.0130
z_{i6}	−0.0465*	0.0262	0.0739	0.0852	−0.0156	0.0152	−0.0138	0.0803	−0.0057	0.0234
z_{i7}	0.0183**	0.0079	−0.0369	0.0256	0.0044	0.0046	0.0058	0.0242	0.0006	0.0070
z_{i8}	−0.0125	0.0125	−0.0442	0.0406	−0.0143**	0.0073	0.0832**	0.0383	0.0113	0.0111
z_{i9}	0.0310	0.0385	0.0353	0.1253	0.0121	0.0224	−0.1098	0.1181	0.0119	0.0344
Constant term	0.0784***	0.0063	0.3403***	0.0199	0.0477***	0.0037	0.0632***	0.0187	0.0213***	0.0056

Continued

Appendix 2.1 Continued

	S_{iA6}		S_{iA7}		S_{iA8}		S_{iA9}		S_{i10}	
	Coeff.	Std. Dev.	Coeff.	Std. Dev.	Coeff.	Std. Dev.	Coeff.	Std. Dev.	Coeff.	Std. Dev.
$\ln w_{iA1}$	0.0030***	0.0005	−0.0059***	0.0006	−0.0016***	0.0003	−0.0045***	0.0005	−0.0022***	0.0006
$\ln w_{iA2}$	−0.0091***	0.0008	0.0067***	0.0013	−0.0062***	0.0005	−0.0161***	0.0009	−0.0159***	0.0013
$\ln w_{iA3}$	−0.0011***	0.0004	−0.0034***	0.0004	0.0003	0.0003	−0.0010***	0.0003	−0.0023***	0.0004
$\ln w_{iA4}$	−0.0116***	0.0008	−0.0203***	0.0012	−0.0039***	0.0005	0.0056***	0.0009	−0.0124***	0.0012
$\ln w_{i5}$	−0.0028***	0.0005	−0.0046***	0.0005	−0.0020***	0.0004	−0.0033***	0.0005	0.0052***	0.0006
$\ln w_{iA6}$	0.0300***	0.0007	−0.0030***	0.0006	0.0018***	0.0004	−0.0043***	0.0005	−0.0030***	0.0006
$\ln w_{iA7}$	−0.0030***	0.0006	0.0381***	0.0012	0.0171***	0.0004	−0.0023***	0.0006	−0.0020**	0.0009
$\ln w_{iA8}$	0.0018***	0.0004	−0.0032***	0.0004	−0.0005	0.0004	−0.0005	0.0003	−0.0017***	0.0004
$\ln w_{iA9}$	−0.0043***	0.0005	−0.0023***	0.0006	−0.0017***	0.0003	0.0294***	0.0007	−0.0029***	0.0007
$\ln w_{i10}$	−0.0030***	0.0006	−0.0020**	0.0009	−0.0007**	0.0004	−0.0029***	0.0007	0.0373***	0.0012
$\ln x_{i1}$	−0.0014*	0.0007	0.0013	0.0011	−0.0007**	0.0004	−0.0021***	0.0008	−0.0013	0.0012
$\ln x_{i2}$	−0.0012	0.0013	−0.0124***	0.0022	0.0008	0.0007	0.0000	0.0015	0.0036	0.0023
$\ln x_{i3}$	0.0000	0.0009	−0.0022	0.0015	0.0000	0.0005	−0.0011	0.0010	0.0022	0.0015
z_{i1}	−0.0004	0.0025	0.0009	0.0041	−0.0007	0.0013	0.0078***	0.0028	−0.0118***	0.0043
z_{i2}	−0.0042	0.0029	−0.0067	0.0047	−0.0015	0.0015	0.0063**	0.0031	−0.0044	0.0048
z_{i3}	0.0074***	0.0027	−0.0002	0.0044	0.0016	0.0014	−0.0058**	0.0029	0.0005	0.0045
z_{i4}	0.0167	0.0155	0.0015	0.0251	0.0078	0.0079	−0.0460***	0.0168	0.0001	0.0260
z_{i5}	0.0045	0.0156	0.0164	0.0253	−0.0025	0.0080	−0.0241	0.0170	−0.0204	0.0262
z_{i6}	−0.0011	0.0281	0.0062	0.0457	0.0014	0.0144	−0.0082	0.0306	0.0095	0.0472
z_{i7}	−0.0284***	0.0085	0.0133	0.0137	−0.0052	0.0043	0.0117	0.0092	0.0162	0.0142
z_{i8}	−0.0173	0.0134	0.0061	0.0217	−0.0101	0.0069	0.0382***	0.0146	−0.0404*	0.0225
z_{i9}	0.0101	0.0413	0.0220	0.0672	0.0086	0.0212	−0.0176	0.0450	−0.0037	0.0694
Constant term	0.0914***	0.0067	0.2038***	0.0107	0.0388***	0.0035	0.0655***	0.0073	0.0497***	0.0111

Notes: A full set of industry dummies is included. *, **, and *** signify statistical significance at the 10%, 5%, and 1% levels, respectively.

Appendix 2.2 Estimation results 2: workers categorized by position of employment

	S_{iB1}		S_{iB2}		S_{iB3}		S_{iB4}		S_{i5}	
	Coeff.	Std. Dev.	Coeff.	Std. Dev.	Coeff.	Std. Dev.	Coeff.	Std. Dev.	Coeff.	Std. Dev.
$\ln w_{iB1}$	0.0279***	0.0006	−0.0053***	0.0008	0.0011***	0.0003	−0.0109***	0.0008	−0.0001	0.0004
$\ln w_{iB2}$	−0.0053***	0.0008	0.0896***	0.0027	−0.0046***	0.0004	−0.0334***	0.0021	−0.0065***	0.0007
$\ln w_{iB3}$	0.0011***	0.0003	−0.0046***	0.0004	0.0168***	0.0003	−0.0039***	0.0004	−0.0017***	0.0003
$\ln w_{iB4}$	−0.0109***	0.0008	−0.0334***	0.0021	−0.0039***	0.0004	0.0952***	0.0025	−0.0038***	0.0007
$\ln w_{i5}$	−0.0001	0.0004	−0.0065***	0.0007	−0.0017***	0.0003	−0.0038***	0.0007	0.0187***	0.0007
$\ln w_{iB6}$	0.0034***	0.0005	−0.0074***	0.0009	−0.0013***	0.0003	−0.0150***	0.0009	−0.0035***	0.0005
$\ln w_{iB7}$	−0.0053***	0.0006	0.0035***	0.0012	−0.0027***	0.0003	−0.0183***	0.0011	−0.0037***	0.0005
$\ln w_{iB8}$	−0.0014***	0.0003	−0.0059***	0.0005	−0.0001	0.0003	−0.0040***	0.0005	−0.0018***	0.0003
$\ln w_{iB9}$	−0.0055***	0.0005	−0.0150***	0.0009	−0.0009***	0.0003	0.0056***	0.0009	−0.0031***	0.0005
$\ln w_{i10}$	−0.0040***	0.0006	−0.0150***	0.0013	−0.0027***	0.0003	−0.0114***	0.0012	0.0054***	0.0006
$\ln x_{i1}$	0.0000	0.0006	0.0059***	0.0021	−0.0013***	0.0003	0.0011	0.0020	−0.0018***	0.0006
$\ln x_{i2}$	0.0006	0.0013	−0.0152***	0.0040	0.0012*	0.0006	0.0182***	0.0038	0.0038***	0.0011
$\ln x_{i3}$	−0.0013	0.0008	0.0034	0.0027	−0.0008*	0.0004	0.0006	0.0026	−0.0001	0.0007
z_{i1}	−0.0032	0.0024	−0.0137*	0.0076	−0.0014	0.0012	0.0248***	0.0072	−0.0016	0.0021
z_{i2}	−0.0004	0.0027	−0.0077	0.0086	0.0042***	0.0014	0.0164**	0.0082	−0.0022	0.0024
z_{i3}	−0.0019	0.0025	−0.0082	0.0081	0.0000	0.0013	0.0084	0.0077	−0.0015	0.0022
z_{i4}	−0.0110	0.0145	−0.0209	0.0464	−0.0047	0.0073	0.0432	0.0441	0.0068	0.0128
z_{i5}	0.0066	0.0146	−0.0400	0.0467	−0.0098	0.0073	0.0750*	0.0444	−0.0031	0.0129
z_{i6}	−0.0293	0.0263	0.0491	0.0843	−0.0075	0.0132	−0.0176	0.0802	−0.0048	0.0233
z_{i7}	0.0162**	0.0079	−0.0385	0.0254	0.0037	0.0040	0.0121	0.0241	0.0000	0.0070
z_{i8}	−0.0106	0.0125	−0.0475	0.0401	−0.0125**	0.0063	0.0778**	0.0382	0.0095	0.0111
z_{i9}	0.0536	0.0387	0.0597	0.1240	0.0114	0.0194	−0.1267	0.1179	0.0093	0.0342
Constant term	0.0740***	0.0063	0.3484***	0.0197	0.0383***	0.0032	0.0682***	0.0186	0.0216***	0.0056

Continued

Appendix 2.2 Continued

	S_{iB6}		S_{iB7}		S_{iB8}		S_{iB9}		S_{i10}	
	Coeff.	Std. Dev.	Coeff.	Std. Dev.	Coeff.	Std. Dev.	Coeff.	Std. Dev.	Coeff.	Std. Dev.
$\ln w_{iB1}$	0.0034***	0.0005	−0.0053***	0.0006	−0.0014***	0.0003	−0.0055***	0.0005	−0.0040***	0.0006
$\ln w_{iB2}$	−0.0074***	0.0009	0.0035***	0.0012	−0.0059***	0.0005	−0.0150***	0.0009	−0.0150***	0.0013
$\ln w_{iB3}$	−0.0013***	0.0003	−0.0027***	0.0003	−0.0001	0.0003	−0.0009***	0.0003	−0.0027***	0.0003
$\ln w_{iB4}$	−0.0150***	0.0009	−0.0183***	0.0011	−0.0040***	0.0005	0.0056***	0.0009	−0.0114***	0.0012
$\ln w_{i5}$	−0.0035***	0.0005	−0.0037***	0.0005	−0.0018***	0.0003	−0.0031***	0.0005	0.0054***	0.0006
$\ln w_{iB6}$	0.0323***	0.0008	−0.0016***	0.0006	0.0016***	0.0004	−0.0047***	0.0005	−0.0038***	0.0007
$\ln w_{iB7}$	−0.0016***	0.0006	0.0347***	0.0011	−0.0026***	0.0003	−0.0026***	0.0006	−0.0015*	0.0008
$\ln w_{iB8}$	0.0016***	0.0004	−0.0026***	0.0003	0.0164***	0.0004	−0.0003	0.0003	−0.0019***	0.0004
$\ln w_{iB9}$	−0.0047***	0.0005	−0.0026***	0.0006	−0.0003	0.0003	0.0291***	0.0007	−0.0027***	0.0006
$\ln w_{i10}$	−0.0038***	0.0007	−0.0015*	0.0008	−0.0019***	0.0004	−0.0027***	0.0006	0.0377***	0.0012
$\ln x_{i1}$	−0.0012	0.0008	0.0016	0.0010	−0.0004	0.0003	−0.0026***	0.0008	−0.0013	0.0012
$\ln x_{i2}$	−0.0022	0.0015	−0.0106***	0.0020	0.0005	0.0007	0.0001	0.0015	0.0036	0.0022
$\ln x_{i3}$	0.0002	0.0010	−0.0031**	0.0013	−0.0001	0.0004	−0.0009	0.0010	0.0021	0.0015
z_{i1}	0.0017	0.0029	−0.0025	0.0037	−0.0006	0.0013	0.0077***	0.0028	−0.0112***	0.0042
z_{i2}	−0.0081**	0.0033	−0.0017	0.0042	0.0000	0.0014	0.0040	0.0031	−0.0045	0.0048
z_{i3}	0.0075**	0.0031	0.0004	0.0040	0.0006	0.0013	−0.0050*	0.0029	−0.0001	0.0045
z_{i4}	0.0228	0.0175	0.0023	0.0227	0.0048	0.0077	−0.0408**	0.0168	−0.0024	0.0258
z_{i5}	−0.0044	0.0177	0.0203	0.0229	−0.0035	0.0078	−0.0203	0.0169	−0.0208	0.0260
z_{i6}	0.0065	0.0319	−0.0013	0.0414	0.0014	0.0140	−0.0064	0.0305	0.0100	0.0470
z_{i7}	−0.0174*	0.0096	0.0002	0.0124	−0.0014	0.0042	0.0095	0.0092	0.0155	0.0141
z_{i8}	−0.0072	0.0152	0.0024	0.0197	−0.0079	0.0067	0.0389***	0.0145	−0.0430*	0.0224
z_{i9}	−0.0149	0.0469	0.0357	0.0608	0.0017	0.0206	−0.0188	0.0449	−0.0110	0.0691
Constant term	0.1028***	0.0076	0.1952***	0.0097	0.0363***	0.0034	0.0682***	0.0072	0.0468***	0.0110

Notes: A full set of industry dummies is included. *, **, and *** signify statistical significance at the 10%, 5%, and 1% levels, respectively.

Appendix 2.3 Cost shares S_{ij}

S_{iA1}	S_{iA2}	S_{iA3}	S_{iA4}	S_{i5}	S_{iA6}	S_{iA7}	S_{iA8}	S_{iA9}	S_{i10}
0.029	0.359	0.012	0.320	0.024	0.027	0.087	0.009	0.057	0.077
S_{iB1}	S_{iB2}	S_{iB3}	S_{iB4}	S_{i5}	S_{iB6}	S_{iB7}	S_{iB8}	S_{iB9}	S_{i10}
0.033	0.354	0.011	0.320	0.024	0.036	0.078	0.010	0.056	0.077

Notes

1 Ekholm and Hakkala (2006) estimate the extent of factor-biased technology changes on labor demand induced by offshoring and employ the ratio of imported intermediate inputs to industry outputs as an index for offshoring. We regard this, however, as an argument about substitute and complementary workers with imported goods under a given production technology. Our interpretation of trade-induced factor-biased technology changes is one of changes in a firm's production function that are induced by the start of its trade activity.
2 As for the derivation of these elasticities, see the appendix of Ekholm and Hakkala (2006).
3 The original data sets of the Basic Survey on Wage Structure, the Basic Survey of Japanese Business Structure and Activities, and the Establishment and Enterprise Census are all unavailable to the public, since they include individual information on employees and employers. We applied to the Ministry of Health, Labor, and Welfare, the Ministry of Economy, Trade, and Industry, and the Ministry of Internal Affairs and Communications Statistics Bureau to obtain permission to use the original data set under strict conditions that ensure the confidentiality of the data and its academic use.

References

Ahn, S., Fukao, K., and Ito, K. (2008) "Outsourcing in East Asia and its impact on the Japanese and Korean labour markets," OECD Trade Policy Working Papers: 65.
Ekholm, K. and Hakkala, K. N. (2006) "The effect of offshoring on labor demand: evidence from Sweden," CEPR Discussion Papers: 5648.
Feenstra, R. C. and Hanson, G. H. (1999) "The impact of outsourcing and high-technology capital on wages: estimates for the United States, 1979–1990," *The Quarterly Journal of Economics*, 114: 907–40.
Frias, J. A., Kaplan, D. S., and Verhoogen, E. A. (2012) "Exports and within-plant wage distributions: evidence from Mexico," *American Economic Review*, 102: 435–40.
Krishna, P., Poole, J. P., and Senses, M. Z. (2011) "Trade liberalization, firm heterogeneity, and wages: new evidence from matched employer-employee data," The World Bank, Policy Research Working Paper Series: 5711.
Machikita, T. and Sato, H. (2011) "Temporary jobs and globalization: evidence from Japan," RIETI Discussion Paper Series: 11-E-029.
Tomiura, E., Ito, B., and Wakasugi, R. (2011) "Offshoring of tasks and flexible employment: Relationships at the firm level," *Economic Inquiry*, 49: 364–78.

3 The characteristics and perspective of FTAs in China

Yu Hong Sun

The development of FTAs in China

Similar to Japan and Republic of Korea (hereinafter referred to as Korea), China was relatively late in starting a bilateral FTA policy. In the light of an increasing tendency toward regionalism, and competitive liberalization all over the world, China has also embraced regional strategies by using FTAs as a policy option after its accession to the WTO (World Trade Organization) in 2001. The Chinese government regards FTAs as a new platform to further open up to the outside world and speed up domestic reforms, an effective approach to facilitate integration with the global economy and strengthen economic cooperation with other economies, and a particularly important supplement to the multilateral trading system.

China became a member of the Asia–Pacific Trade Agreement (APTA) in May 2001.[1] In addition to this, the first bilateral deal[2] was concluded with ASEAN in 2002. The following years witnessed the signing of two Closer Economic Partnership Arrangements with Hong Kong, China (June 2003) and Macau, China (October 2003) respectively. Based on this, FTAs with Chile (November 2005), Pakistan (November 2006), New Zealand (April 2008), Singapore (October 2008), Peru (April 2009) and Costa Rica (April 2010) have been signed and have entered in force. In addition to this, an Economic Cooperation Framework Agreement with Taipei was concluded in June 2010. China is also eager to sign FTAs with the GCC (Gulf Cooperation Council), Australia, Iceland and Norway, SACU (South African Customs Union) and Switzerland, and these FTAs are under negotiation. Currently, China has 16 FTA partners comprising 26 economies, among which ten agreements have been signed already and six agreements are under negotiation. At the same time, China is paying more attention to the relationship with its neighbouring powers, and China–India, China–Korea and China–Japan–Korea FTAs are under joint study.

The evidence above shows that China has been firmly embarking on the road towards FTAs and is constructing its own FTA network quickly.

The characteristics and problems of FTAs in China

When we take a look at the list of partners that have signed or are negotiating or making joint study FTAs with China, the pattern seems to be quite random.

Table 3.1 China's FTA network

In effect	Under negotiation	Under study
Mainland and Hong Kong CEPA	China–GCC FTA	China–India Regional Trade Arrangement Joint Feasibility Study
Mainland and Macao CEPA	China–Australia FTA	
China–ASEAN FTA	China–Iceland FTA	China–Korea FTA Joint Feasibility Study
China–Pakistan FTA	China–Norway FTA	
China–Chile FTA	China–SACU FTA	China–Japan–Korea Joint Study
China–New Zealand FTA		
China–Singapore FTA		China–Switzerland FTA
China–Peru FTA		
China–Costa Rica FTA		
ECFA		
APTA		

Source: Ministry of Commerce of the People's Republic of China. 'CHINA FTA WORKNET', 31 July 2012. See http://fta.mofcom.gov.cn/english/index.shtml.

Notes:

1 CEPA is the Closer Economic Partnership Arrangement.
2 APTA is the Asia–Pacific Trade Agreement, including members of China, Bangladesh, India, Lao, Republic of Korea and Sri Lanka.
3 GCC is the Gulf Cooperation Council, consisting of Saudi Arabia, United Arab Republic, Kuwait, Oman and Bahrain.
4 SACU is the Southern African Customs Union, consisting of South Africa, Botswana, Namibia, Lesotho and Swaziland.
5 ECFA means Economic Cooperation Framework Agreement (Across the Taiwan Straits).[3]

However, we can find the following characteristics and problems:

1 *Both regional and cross-regional FTAs have developed simultaneously, but FTA coverage rate is lower than other major countries.*

First, in terms of the geographic distribution of FTA partners, China selects these both from inside and outside the Asian region. The selected partners are located in almost every major region of the world, including Europe (Switzerland, Iceland and Norway; America (Chile, Peru and Costa Rica); the Middle East (GCC); Africa (SACU), East Asia (Korea, Japan, ASEAN, Singapore, Hong Kong and Macao); South Asia (Pakistan and India) and Oceania (New Zealand and Australia). The geographic distribution of China's FTA partners seems to indicate that China's structuring of a global FTA network is enabling it to pursue its strategy of engaging simultaneously in FTA negotiations with its neighbours and its extra-regional partners.

The geographical orientation of China's FTAs demonstrates a high degree of cross-regional orientation. However, the trend toward cross-regional FTAs is more

Table 3.2 The geographical orientation and coverage rate of exports and imports (CRE&I, %) of Japan's and South Korea's FTAs

Region	Country	Japan		South Korea	
		status	*CRE&I*	*status*	*CRE&I*
Asia	ASEAN	In effect	10.9	In effect	14.6
	Singapore	In effect	2.6	In effect	2.3
	Malaysia	In effect	1.8	In effect (ASEAN)	2.8
	Thailand	In effect	1.2	In effect (ASEAN)	3.8
	Indonesia	In effect	2.6	In effect (ASEAN)	3.0
	Brunei	In effect	0.2	In effect (ASEAN)	0.3
	the Philippines	In effect	1.0	In effect (ASEAN)	1.3
	Vietnam	In effect	1.5	In effect (ASEAN)	1.1
	India	In effect	1.9	In effect	1.0
	Japan–Korea	Suspended	10.4	Suspended	6.2
	China	–	25.1[5]	Under negotiation	19.4[4]
Oceania	Australia	Under negotiation	3.0	Under negotiation	4.2
	NZ	–	0.2	Under negotiation	0.3
North and Central and South America	US	–	10.1	In effect	12.7
	Canada	–	0.9	Under negotiation	1.4
	Mexico	In effect	1.2	Under negotiation	0.9
	Chile	In effect	0.8	In effect	0.7
	Peru	Under negotiation	0.2	In effect	0.2
	Colombia	–	0.2	Under negotiation	0.1

Table 3.2 Continued

		Japan	South Korea	
			CRE&I	CRE&I
Europe	EU	Under consideration	10.5	10.3
	EFTA	–	1.2	1.0
	Switzerland	In effect	1.0	0.3
Other	Turkey	–	0.2	0.5
	GCC	Under negotiation	8.4	8.9
	FTA cover percentage	Total in effect or signed	18.2	35.5

Notes:

1 Most percentages are calculated based on 2010 Trade Statistics. See Japan External Trade Organization (JETRO). '2011 JETRO Global Trade and Investment Report International Business as a Catalyst for Japan's Reconstruction' P56-7, http://www.jetro.go.jp/en/reports/white_paper/, 31 July 2012.

2 Percentages for China are from the WTO website and provide coverage rates for exports only.

Sources:

1 Ministry of Foreign Affairs and Trade Republic of Korea, 'FTA Status of ROK'. See http://www.mofat.go.kr/ENG/policy/fta/status/overview/index. jsp?menu = m_20_80_10, 31 July 2012.

2 Ministry of Foreign Affairs of Japan, 'Free Trade Agreement (FTA) and Economic Partnership Agreement (EPA)'. See http://www.mofa. go.jp/policy/economy/fta/index.html, 31 July 2012.

evident in Asia's proposed FTAs and those under negotiation. This pattern is also evident in the geographical orientation of Northeast Asian FTAs.

Japan, as a latecomer to FTAs, and the first developed economy in Asia, has rapidly implemented bilateral economic partnership agreements (EPAs) with 11 countries (see Table 3.2) and an agreement with ASEAN. It is negotiating an agreement with Australia, and is considering an agreement with the EU. Moreover, it is about to re-open negotiations with Korea and is in domestic discussion over participation in the Trans-Pacific Strategic Economic Partnership Agreement. The geographical orientation of Japan's FTAs indicates that it is paying more attention to negotiating FTAs with more powerful economies outside East Asia.

Although at first Korea seems not to have as many FTAs as China and Japan, it is now in the leading position. It has rapidly implemented bilateral FTAs with 13 countries (see Table 3.2), including some more powerful economies such as the US, EU, India, ASEAN and some hub economies such as Singapore, Chile, EFTA and Peru. Korea is negotiating FTAs with more economies including Canada, Mexico, GCC, Australia, New Zealand, Colombia and China. The geographical orientation of South Korea's FTAs indicates that Korea has agreements with members of APTA, ASEAN, Singapore and India within Asia, and that the main FTA partners are outside East Asia. Compared with Japan and China, Korea is in a leading position in the development of cross-regional FTAs.

Second, because Hong Kong, Macao and Taipei belong to China, while APTA is just a Preference Trade Arrangement, the latter covers limited items and does not get zero tariffs. With the exception of ASEAN, none of China's partners (concluded FTAs in Table 3.2) are major trade partners. Its top three trading partners, i.e. the EU, US and Japan, are not on the list. The 2011 JETRO Global Trade and Investment Report shows that the FTA coverage rate of China is 16.6 per cent. The figure for China excludes Hong Kong (7.7 per cent) and Macao (0.1 per cent).

According to the figures in Table 3.2, Japan's FTA coverage rate is 18.2 per cent, whilst South Korea's coverage rate is already up to 35.5 per cent. The FTA coverage rate of China is slightly lower than Japan's, but it is much lower than Korea's. However, even South Korea's coverage rate cannot compare with the EU (74.8 per cent), US (34.9 per cent), Mexico (80.9 per cent), Chile (89 per cent) and so on.[6]

2 *South–South and North–South FTAs have developed at the same time, but the development of North–South FTAs is slower than South–South FTAs.*

The most important characteristic of new regionalism in contemporary Asia is the North–South FTA, but most of the partners that China has selected are developing countries, and only a few of them are developed countries. The developed FTA partners include New Zealand, Australia, Singapore, Iceland, Norway, Switzerland and Japan–Korea, while the top trading partners and the main developed economic bodies (the EU and US and so on) are not on the list. If we only consider FTAs that are in effect, just two North–South agreements have been concluded – these are China–New Zealand and China–Singapore; the other concluded agreements are South–South FTAs.

3 *China usually selects a narrower type of FTA model, but, in recent years, it has sought a more comprehensive approach.*

In East Asia, FTAs can be broadly divided into two different models, according to Henry Gao (2011):[7]

> Within the NAFTA model, again there are two different sub-categories. The first is the Economic Partnership Agreement (EPA) approach advocated by Japan, which seeks to conclude comprehensive agreements that include trade in goods, services, and sometimes even environment protection and intellectual property rights. The other approach is much narrower and focuses on trade in goods only.

In particular, the 'narrower' agreements that China concluded prior to 2008 are typified by the China–ASEAN and China–Pakistan FTAs. According to Henry Gao (2011):[8]

> Normally, China would start with an agreement on trade in goods only and would only expand to trade in services and investment after the commitments on goods have been substantially implemented.

Take the FTA with ASEAN, for example: the agreement on goods was signed in November 2004, but the Early Harvest Program had been implemented in January 2004, while the agreement on service was only signed in February 2009, and the agreement on investment was signed in August 2009.[9]

However the typical representative, and more comprehensive, model that China is now pursuing is illustrated by the China–New Zealand FTA, which entered into force on 1 October 2008 and which covers areas such as trade in goods, services and investment.[10] This agreement is the first comprehensive FTA that China has ever signed, and it can, perhaps, be seen as a new landmark for the selection of China's model, for more and more comprehensive FTAs have been signed by China since then. However, as a big developing country, the question of how to deal with the non-trade clauses in FTA treaties is a critical issue for China to face.

4 *China enhances a partner country's political significance rather than strengthening economic ties with itself.*

First, political and diplomatic relationships seem to carry most weight, as almost all the partners do have good political and diplomatic relationships with China.[11] Second, according to most of its FTA partners, the volume of trade doesn't seem to be an important factor for China in its selection criteria. Third, all economies

Table 3.3 Growth in fruit imports from ASEAN after the Early Harvest Program

	2004	2005	2006	2007	2008	2009
Total imports (million $)	304.11	344.26	397.24	495.91	704.43	1008.57
Rate of growth (%)	22.66	13.20	15.39	24.84	42.11	43.11

Source: China Customs Statistics, see http://www.chinacustomsstat.com/aspx/1/Self_Search/Online Com.aspx.

that have entered, or are about to enter into FTAs with China have recognized its market economy status.

This is mainly concerned with a provision in China's WTO Accession Protocol. Section 15(a) of the Accession Protocol allows WTO Members to deem China a non-market economy in antidumping investigations. This mechanism is available to WTO Members for up to 15 years after China's accession.[12] In recent years, as more and more Chinese firms are subject to antidumping investigations abroad, people have started to realize the damaging effect of this provision. To solve the problem, China has chosen to negotiate with each of its trade partners. As of May, 2010, nearly 150 economies have recognized the market economy status of China.[13] However, the US and the EU etc. have still not followed this trend. To some extent, this situation has restricted the choice of FTA partners and affected the process of FTA development.

5 *In some South–South Free Trade Agreements (in which tariffs on non-processed agricultural products are reduced), consensus has usually been reached first.*

Some farmers' interests may be deprived by the promises, and the compensation system is not perfect.

All of us know that the Japanese and Korean governments usually seek to protect their agricultural sectors in spite of the spread of FTAs. By contrast, China, (especially for South–South contracts), used to start the Early Harvest Program before signing, so that the latter was called the 'fast track' or 'testing field' of the liberalization of goods. For example, in the negotiations between China and ASEAN, a key element in the 2002 FTA was an Early Harvest Program set to start in 2004.[14] The program cut tariffs ahead of the planned establishment of the CAFTA in 2010 (it was also called a 'trial move'). Since the implementation of the Early Harvest Program, the volume of fruit imports from ASEAN has been increasing substantially year-on-year, which has had a tremendous impact on the fruit industry in southern China.

In order to compensate for the farmers' losses, Korea has set up an effective compensation mechanism, while Japan has taken measures like exclusion, longer transition and renegotiation to protect its agricultural sector. China's agricultural liberalization comes first, but there is no related 'trade compensation mechanism' in China.

6 *The agreement with ASEAN has been criticized for a lack of stringency.*[15]

This mainly includes two aspects: the simple Rules of Origin and the flexibility allowed for reciprocal treatment.

One striking feature of China's emerging network of FTAs is the difference in the rules of origin. There are three criteria for defining ROO in FTAs. One of these criteria is Change in Tariff Classification (CTC) or 'tariff shift'; the second rule is the requirement of Regional (local) Value Contents (RVC); and the third rule is that of Technical Process (TP), which requires a specific production process for an item. It is worth mentioning that the ROO in the China–ASEAN FTA, which specifies a 40 per cent regional value of contents across all items are the simplest ROO in the world. The criterion of 40 per cent regional value contents was introduced by AFTA; China accepted the AFTA ROO and concluded the negotiation at the end of 2004. The uniform ROO of the China–ASEAN FTA and AFTA is simpler than the WTO recommends, and cannot be found in other FTAs. The ROO does not need the CTC criterion, since this requires only one criterion of 40 per cent RVC ratio. In fact, this criterion is simple in words, but very complicated in practice.

In the FTA negotiations between China and ASEAN, each country had a certain amount of flexibility during negotiations. According to the agreements on goods, all tariff lines shall be categorized as normal track and sensitive track products except for the tariff lines covered by the Early Harvest Program. All parties agreed to gradually reduce tariffs on products listed in the normal track, starting in July 2005, and remove them by 2010. In addition, they agreed to reduce tariffs on products in the sensitive track to 20 per cent by 2012 and to 0.5 per cent by 2018, but they also agreed to tariff reductions of 50 per cent on highly sensitive products by 2015.[16] This 'negative list' method meant that every party could independently decide which products it would consider as sensitive, so that all parties had a certain amount of flexibility in negotiations. In the case of bilateral negotiations between Japan and ASEAN, a request–offer list was exchanged, in which each country listed those products for which it wished to see tariff reductions. Thus, all tariffs on targeted products had to be discussed. Such a 'positive list' method meant that every party could be faced with episodes of serious bargaining.

7 *The lower rate of using FTA preference*

First, according to the statistics from the Ministry of Commerce, in the People's Republic of China, only 17.9 per cent of export preference has been used in exportation to ASEAN under the Early Harvest Program in 2004, while ASEAN's rate of export preference is up to 60 per cent. In addition, a survey by Zhang Yunling[17] of 232 exporters in leading sectors in October–December 2008 formed the basis for the first systematic study of the business impact of FTAs in China.

Among the firms that made use of FTAs, the ASEAN–PRC CECA was by far the most popular agreement (65.7 per cent). The PRC–Hong Kong, China CEPA had the second highest usage rate at 46.1 per cent (47 firms), followed

Table 3.4 Utilization rates of China FTAs

FTAs in effect	Use FTA		Use or plan to use FTA	
	No. of firms	*Rate (n = 102)*	*No. of firms*	*Rate (n = 226)*
China–ASEAN FTA	67	65.7%	50	22.1%
Mainland and Hong Kong CEPA	47	46.1%	32	14.2%
China–Pakistan FTA	33	32.4%	28	12.4%
China–Chile FTA	22	21.6%	31	13.7%
China–New Zealand FTA	15	14.7%	37	16.4%
Mainland and Macao CEPA	15	14.7%	25	11.1%

Source: Zhang Yunling (2010).[18]

by the PRC–Chile FTA (32.4 per cent). Among prospective users, 22.1 per cent of responding firms anticipated using the ASEAN–PRC CECA in the future; 16.4 per cent planned to use the PRC–New Zealand FTA; 14.2 per cent planned to use the PRC–Hong Kong, China CEPA; and 13.7 per cent planned to use the PRC–Pakistan FTA. The importance of the ASEAN–PRC FTA reflects the growing importance of regional markets to PRC exporters.

The above facts conclude the lower use of FTAs by Chinese firms, though we do not have specific data on certain FTAs or items. How to help firms make full use of the FTA preference is an important area, which will promote the realization of FTA interest and will need further study.

Conclusion and perspective

In summary, to make China's FTA strategy solid, the related problems shown above must be considered seriously. To achieve this goal, some recommendations or policy implications are put forward in the following.

1 In view of the 'competitive liberalization' of world-wide trade, It is necessary for China to take various measures to enlarge its FTA coverage rate, and especially, to make every effort to conclude FTAs with power economies, both within and outside the East Asian region.
2 At present, few developed economies have China as FTA partners. This is especially the case for the US and EU. Moreover, Japan is still not interested in making FTAs with China. North–South FTAs can bring the developing partner more advantages, including market access, FDI, technology spillover, economies of scale etc. Thus, it is a priority for China to intensify its program of FTA negotiation with developed economies.
3 Some FTAs all over the world include WTO-plus provisions, particularly the four Singapore issues that will be present in future agreements. As a developing

country, China needs to understand how to deal with these issues properly in future North–South FTA negotiations. This is a very important area and it requires professional study.

4 To promote the process of FTA development, in addition to paying attention to its political and diplomatic relationships, China should focus more on economic weight in its choice of FTA partner.

5 Learning from the experience of developed countries, China should construct a mechanism of its trade adjustment assistance in order to compensate FTA losers.

6 To tackle the Rules of Origin problem, China should encourage rationalization of ROO and upgrade administration to best practice levels.

7 China should improve the use of FTAs at firm level, through increased awareness and strengthened institutional support systems, particularly for SMEs.

Despite these issues, the Chinese government will try to implement its FTA strategy in the future. To overcome these problems and maximize the benefits of FTAs while minimizing their costs, several improvements can be made: paying more attention to economic interests, selecting scaled developed countries as FTA partners, using deeper integration models, balancing the interests of weak groups, making every effort to help firms to use the FTA preference, strengthening bargaining skills with FTA partners etc. With the development of FTAs in China, the government's strategy must be clear and effective.

This review of China's bilateral FTA networks, and comparison with those of Japan and Korea, has illustrated the degree of competitive liberalization in East Asia. The major political and economic driving force behind its approach towards bilateral FTAs remains, and results in East Asia forming a hub-and-spoke FTA network without a region-wide system. To some extent, such development of bilateral FTA networks may block the process of forming an East Asia region-wide FTA and has made the situation more complex.

Notes

1 The Bangkok Agreement, signed in 1975, is the predecessor of the 'Asia–Pacific Trade Agreement', and the predecessor of the 'Bangkok Agreement'. The 'Bangkok Agreement' was renamed the 'Asia–Pacific Trade Agreement' on 2 November 2005. See http://fta.mofcom.gov.cn/topic/enpacific.shtml.

2 China signed a Framework agreement on comprehensive economic cooperation with ASEAN in November 2002, and concluded negotiations on an FTA on goods in 2004. See http://fta.mofcom.gov.cn/topic/chinaasean.shtml.

3 Association for Relations Across the Taiwan Straits, 'Economic Cooperation Framework Agreement'. See http://www.arats.com.cn/xieyi/, 29 June 2010.

4 WTO. Home > Resources > Statistics > Statistics database > Trade profiles, http://stat. wto.org/CountryProfile/WSDBCountryPFView.aspx?Language = E&Country = JP.

5 WTO. Home > Resources > Statistics > Statistics database > Trade profiles, http://www. mofat.go.kr/ENG/policy/fta/status/overview/index.jsp?menu = m_20_80_10.

6 Japan External Trade Organization (JETRO), '2011 JETRO Global Trade and Investment Report International Business as a Catalyst for Japan's Reconstruction' P56-7. See http://www.jetro.go.jp/en/reports/white_paper/, 31 July 2012.

7 Gao, Henry (2011). 'China's strategy for free trade agreements: political battle in the name of trade'. In *East Asian Economic Integration: Law, Trade and Finance*, Cheltenham (u.a.): Elgar, pp. 104–120. See http://www.econbiz.de/en/search/detailed-view/doc/all/china-s-strategy-for-free-trade-agreements-political-battle-in-the-name-of-trade-gao-henry/10009313639/?no_cache = 1.

8 Ibid.

9 Ministry of Commerce of the People's Republic of China. 'Home Page > China's Free Trade Agreements > China-ASEAN FTA'. See http://fta.mofcom.gov.cn, 31 July 2012.

10 Ministry of Commerce of the People's Republic of China. 'Home Page > China's Free Trade Agreements > China-New Zealand FTA'. See http://fta.mofcom.gov.cn, 31 July 2012.

11 Gao, Henry (2011) 'China's strategy for free trade agreements: political battle in the name of trade'. In *East Asian Economic Integration: Law, trade and Finance*, Cheltenham (u.a.): Elgar, pp. 104–120. See http://www.econbiz.de/en/search/detailed-view/doc/all/china-s-strategy-for-free-trade-agreements-political-battle-in-the-name-of-trade-gao-henry/10009313639/?no_cache = 1.

12 Ibid.

13 Hu, J.Y. (2011) 'It is not far from being recognized the complete market economy status of China'. See http://www.people.com.cn/h/2011/0614/c25408-558977997.html, 31 July 2012.

14 Ministry of Commerce of the People's Republic of China. 'Home Page > China's Free Trade Agreements > China-ASEAN FTA'. See http://fta.mofcom.gov.cn, 31 July 2012.

15 Inkyo Cheong and Jungran Cho (2007) 'Market access in FTAs: assessment based on rules of origin and agricultural trade liberalization'. The Research Institute of Economy, Trade and Industry. See http:// www. riti.go.jp/en, p. 32.

16 'Agreement on trade in goods of the framework agreement on comprehensive economic co-operation between the People's Republic of China and the association of Southeast Asian nations'. See http://fta.mofcom.gov.cn/dongmeng/dm_hwmy.shtml.

17 Zhang, Y. (2010). 'The impact of free trade agreements on business activity: a survey of firms in the People's Republic of China'. ADBI Working Paper 251, Tokyo: Asian Development Bank Institute. See http://www.adbi.org/working-paper/2010/10/12/4088.impact.fta.business.activity.prc/.

18 Ibid.

4 The effect of regional trade agreements on technology spillovers through international trade[*]

Naoto Jinji, Xingyuan Zhang, and Shoji Haruna

Introduction

During the past two decades, the rapid proliferation of regional trade agreements (RTAs) has stimulated their economic analysis.[1] Most previous papers focus on the static effects of RTAs such as trade creation and trade diversion, whereas the dynamic effects of RTAs are addressed in relatively few studies. However, technology and production know-how play a crucial role in developing new products and reducing costs. Thus, the enhancement of technology spillovers may be an important effect of RTAs.

Empirical evidence that international trade works as a major channel of international technology spillovers is found in a number of studies (Coe and Helpman 1995; Xu and Wang 1999; Acharya and Keller 2009).[2] Because RTAs increase trade among member countries through the trade creation effect, they may facilitate technology spillovers among trade partners.

This chapter measures technology spillovers using data on patent citations. The study of technology spillovers based on patent citations was pioneered by Jaffe *et al.* (1993). Since then, the literature has been growing (e.g. Jaffe and Trajtenberg 1999; Hall *et al.* 2001; Maurseth and Verspagen 2002; MacGarvie 2006; Branstetter 2006; Haruna *et al.* 2010; Jinji *et al.* 2010, 2011).

An important issue in the literature on technology spillovers based on patent citations is whether they are hindered by geographical distance. Evidence of the localization of technology spillovers has been found both in the intranational context (Jaffe *et al.* 1993; Murata *et al.* 2010) and in the intraregional or international context (Maurseth and Verspagen 2002; Paci and Usai 2009).[3] Maurseth and Verspagen (2002) find that geographical distance negatively affects patent citations in 112 European regions and that such citations occur more frequently within countries than between regions located in separate countries. They also find

[*]We thank Akira Ishii and the participants of the International Symposium at the Otaru University of Commerce for their helpful comments and suggestions on an earlier version of this chapter. Financial support from the Japan Society for the Promotion of Science under the Grant-in-Aid for Scientific Research (B) No. 23330081 is gratefully acknowledged. The authors are solely responsible for any remaining errors.

that patent citations occur more frequently within regions that share the same language. Paci and Usai (2009) also examine the influence of geographical distance and spatial proximity on knowledge flows in Europe by extending their sample to cover the aggregate economies of 175 regions in Europe and by incorporating dynamics into the relationships. They confirm the previous findings, namely that knowledge flows (as measured by patent citations) decrease as geographical distance increases. Further, regions that share borders are more likely to mutually cite respective patents and patent citations are more frequent between two regions of the same country.

As discussed above, although the localization of technology spillovers has been well documented, the impact of "economic" distance on technology spillovers is underexplored. In particular, by fixing the geographical distance between two countries, it would be interesting to investigate the extent to which technology spillovers between two countries that are signatories to the same RTA differ from those between two countries that are not. To our knowledge, only Peri (2005) has investigated this issue. Using a sample of 147 subnational regions in Western Europe and North America, he estimates a gravity-type equation to examine the effect of several resistance factors on patent citations and finds that any borders (regional, national, or linguistic) have a significantly negative effect on technology spillovers. By contrast, the effect of trade blocs on technology spillovers is not significant. Thus, his result suggests that, unlike geographical distance and regional and national borders, trade bloc borders do not hinder technology spillovers.

This chapter thus examines whether RTAs enhance technology spillovers among RTA member countries. As explained above, we follow the literature on patent citations to measure technology spillovers by applying a version of the gravity model proposed by Rose (2004). In our gravity model, we include a dummy variable that indicates membership of the same RTA among trading partners as well as dummies for membership of the GATT/WTO and familiar control variables. Further, we estimate technology spillovers using a negative binomial (NB) model, which is the standard approach to estimation when one has count data on the dependent variable (Cameron and Trivedi 1998).

Our main finding is that RTAs have a positive and significant effect on technology spillovers, as measured by patent citations between trade partners. This finding contrasts with that of Peri (2005). The significantly positive effect of RTAs on technology spillovers remains even when we exclude the US from the sample. We also check the robustness of our results using a zero-inflated negative binomial (ZINB) model. The estimation results from this model indicate that most control variables in the gravity model, such as distance and land borders, have significant coefficients with the expected signs. A secondary finding is that the GATT/WTO enhances technology spillovers among member countries but hampers technology spillovers between member and non-member countries.

The remainder of this chapter is organized as follows. In the second section, we review the literature on the economic effects of regional integration. In the third section, we explain our approach to measuring technology spillovers using patent citation data. In the fourth section, we present the empirical framework. In the fifth section, we describe the data employed in our empirical analysis, and in the sixth section, we present our empirical results. The seventh section presents our conclusion.

Economic effects of regional integration: literature review

In this section, we briefly review the literature on the economic effects of RTAs.[4] The seminal work by Viner (1950) introduces the concepts of *trade creation* and *trade diversion*[5] and demonstrates that the welfare effects of RTAs based on static analysis are generally ambiguous. Although the terms trade creation and trade diversion are subject to several shortcomings, they "have remained central to policy debates" on RTAs because "economists have found these terms to be highly effective tools for focusing policy makers' attention on the ambiguous welfare effects" of RTAs (Panagariya 2000: 293).[6]

The various estimates of the trade creation and trade diversion effects of RTAs include those presented by Clausing (2001), Fukao *et al.* (2003), Trefler (2004), and Romalis (2007).[7] If countries in RTAs are large, then RTAs can induce terms-of-trade effects (Baldwin and Venables 1995; Panagariya 2000). Chang and Winters (2002) estimate the terms-of-trade gains of Mercosur, a customs union between Argentina, Brazil, Paraguay, and Uruguay. Moreover, the pro-competitive effects of regional trade liberalization are important for industries that exhibit economies of scale and face imperfect competition (Ethier and Horn 1984; Venables 1987; Haaland and Wooton 1992).

The manifold analyses of the welfare effects of RTAs using computable general equilibrium (CGE) models include those by Brown *et al.* (1992, 2003), Cox and Harris (1992), Philippidis and Snajuán (2007), Roland-Holst *et al.* (1994), and Sobarzo (1992).[8] These authors predict the changes in trade, prices, and welfare attributable to RTAs by incorporating complex interactions of various effects in the general equilibrium framework. In many cases, CGE models incorporate increasing returns and imperfect competition (e.g., Brown *et al.* 1992, 2003; Cox and Harris 1992; Roland-Holst *et al.* 1994; Sobarzo 1992).

More recently, the dynamic effects of RTAs, such as technology adoption and technology diffusion, have attracted much attention. Ben-David (1993) examines the issue of income convergence among European countries and finds significant convergence as economic integration proceeds. However, he does not specify the factors that induce convergence. Ederington and McCalman (2008) analyze a dynamic model of endogenous firm heterogeneity, in which RTAs affect the adoption rates of new technologies across firms. Bustos (2011) estimates the effects of Mercosur on technology adoption by Argentinian firms and finds that Brazil's tariff reduction has induced statistically significant increases in technology spending and the innovation (both process and product) indexes of Argentinian firms. Schiff and Wang (2003) estimate how the North American Free Trade Agreement (NAFTA) affects total factor productivity (TFP) in Mexico through its impact on trade-related technology transfers from OECD countries, as measured by trade-related foreign R&D stock. They find that Mexico's trade with its NAFTA partners (Canada and the US) has a statistically significant effect on Mexico's TFP, whereas trade with other OECD countries does not. Their simulation results indicate that NAFTA membership has led to a permanent increase in the TFP of the Mexican manufacturing industry of 5.6–7.5 percent, which implies a GDP increase of 1.2–1.6 percent.

Using a CGE model, Das and Andriamananjara (2006) analyze the welfare effects of FTAs in the Americas by incorporating technology spillovers. They compare a 'hub-and-spokes' (HAS)-type FTA with a more comprehensive regional FTA. In the HAS-type FTA, Chile becomes a hub by forming a bilateral FTA with the US and an FTA with Mercosur. The comprehensive regional FTA they consider is the Free Trade Area of the Americas. They find evidence of exogenous TFP improvement in high-technology sectors in the US. They also find that the technology embodied in intermediate inputs spills over both intranationally and internationally. As expected, according to their simulation, the hub (Chile) gains from the formation of HAS-type FTAs. Further, although moving from a HAS-type FTA to a more comprehensive regional FTA lowers the welfare gain for the hub, it benefits the laggard spoke (Mercosur). The flow of technological innovation thus reinforces the impact of FTA formation.

Technology spillovers and patent citations

How RTAs affect international technology spillovers is the main issue addressed in this chapter. However, it is challenging to measure technology spillovers.[9] One approach pioneered by Jaffe *et al.* (1993) is to utilize patent citation data as a proxy for the spillovers of technological knowledge.[10] The granting of a patent is "a legal statement that the idea embodied in the patent represents a novel and useful contribution over and above the previous state of knowledge" (Jaffe *et al.* 1993: 580). Patent citations serve "the legal function of delimiting the scope of the property right conveyed by the patent" (ibid.). Therefore, "a citation of Patent X by Patent Y means that X represents a piece of previously existing knowledge upon which Y builds" (ibid.). In the process of patent application, applicants are required to provide all references that may affect the patentability of the invention. In the US, applicants have a legal duty to list the patents that they cite on the front page of the application document. Examiners also identify the references that they consider to be relevant.

Compared with other approaches (such as analyzing the effects on TFP), the advantage of using patent citations is that it is a direct measure of technology spillovers (Hall *et al.* 2001). However, patent citation is a crude and noisy measure of knowledge flow, because not all inventions are patented and not all knowledge flows can be captured by patent citations (Jaffe *et al.* 1993). The range of technology spillovers that can be captured by patent citations is limited to "the process by which one inventor learns from the research outcomes of others' research projects and is able to enhance her own research productivity with this knowledge without fully compensating the other inventors for the value of this learning" (Branstetter 2006: 327–328).

Empirical framework

To estimate how FTAs affect international technology spillovers, we employ the gravity model, which is widely used to explain bilateral trade. Following Jaffe *et al.* (1993) and Jaffe and Trajtenberg (1999), we use patent citation data as a proxy for technology spillovers. Our approach is similar to that proposed by Peri (2005), which examines how various regional borders influence technology spillovers by employing a gravity-type model in which patent citation is the dependent variable. We modify the gravity model proposed by Rose (2004, 2005) as follows:

$$C_{ijt} = \beta_0 + \beta_1 \ln(P_{it} \times P_{jt}) + \beta_2 Border_{ij} + \beta_3 LDist_{ij} + \beta_4 ComLang_{ij}$$
$$+ \beta_5 ComCol_{ij} + \beta_6 Colony_{ij} + \gamma_1 Onein_{ijt} + \gamma_2 Bothin_{ijt}$$
$$+ \gamma_3 Regional_{ijt} + \gamma_4 GSP_{ijt} + \varepsilon_{ijt} \qquad (4.1)$$

where i and j denote trading partners $(i \neq j)$, t denotes time, and the variables are defined as follows:

- C_{ijt} denotes the number of US patent citations made by country i to country j or made by country j to country i.
- P_{it} and P_{jt} are the number of US patent applications by countries i and j, respectively.
- $Border_{ij}$ is a dummy variable that takes a value of unity if i and j share a land border and zero otherwise.
- $LDist_{ij}$ is the log of the distance between i and j.
- $ComLang_{ij}$ is a dummy variable that takes a value of unity if i and j have a common language and zero otherwise.
- $ComCol_{ij}$ is a dummy variable that takes a value of unity if i and j were ever colonies of the same colonizer after 1945 and zero otherwise.
- $Colony_{ij}$ is a dummy variable that takes a value of unity if i ever colonized j or vice versa and zero otherwise.
- $Onein_{ijt}$ is a dummy variable that takes a value of unity if either i or j was a GATT/WTO member at t and zero otherwise.
- $Bothin_{ijt}$ is a dummy variable that takes a value of unity if both i and j were GATT/WTO members at t and zero otherwise.
- $Regional_{ijt}$ is a dummy variable that takes a value of unity if i and j both belonged to the same RTA at t and zero otherwise.
- GSP_{ijt} is a dummy variable that takes a value of unity if i was a Generalized System of Preferences (GSP) beneficiary of j or vice versa at t and zero otherwise.[11]
- ε_{ijt} represents the effect of omitted influences on patent citations.

In our gravity equation, the coefficients of interest are γ_1, γ_2, γ_3, and γ_4. Of these coefficients, the most interesting is γ_3. This coefficient measures how RTAs affect technology spillovers under the assumption that all RTAs have the same effect on such spillovers. Following Rose (2004, 2005), the RTAs represented by the dummy variable *Regional* include the EEC/EC/EU, US–Israel FTA, NAFTA, CARICOM, PATCRA, ANZCERTA, CACM, Mercosur, and ASEAN.[12] We also estimate how individual RTAs affect technology spillovers by assigning a separate dummy to each agreement.

The coefficients γ_1 and γ_2 represent the effects of the GATT/WTO on technology spillovers. The coefficient γ_1 represents the corresponding effect if one country is a member and the other is not, while γ_2 represents the corresponding effect if both countries are GATT/WTO members. The coefficient γ_4 represents the effect of the GATT/WTO's GSP. Because we have counted data on our dependent variable (patent citations), we estimate the above gravity equation using the NB model presented by Cameron and Trivedi (1998), as is standard. In this model, the data are assumed to be generated by a GATT/WTO's GSP. Because we have counted data on our dependent variable (patent citations), we estimate the above gravity equation using the NB model presented by Cameron and Trivedi (1998), as is standard. In this model, the data are assumed to be generated by a Poisson process, but more flexible modeling of the variance is allowed to account for over-dispersion.

Moreover, there exist a large number of zero observations for patent citations (approximately 47 per cent), which raise two concerns. First, it causes a diversion from the normal distribution, which biases the estimated standard errors. More importantly, these zero observations might result from two quite different data-generating processes. In other words, countries that generate zero values for period t comprise those that never made a citation, whether they had patents or not, as well as those that, despite having made citations often in the past, did not make one at time t. To deal with these problems, we use the ZINB model. According to Cameron and Trivedi (1998), the ZINB model has the following distribution:

$$f(C_{ijt} \mid x_1, x_2, \theta_1, \theta_2)$$
$$= \begin{cases} f_1(0 \mid x_1, \theta_1) + [1 - f_1(0 \mid x_1, \theta_1)] \times f_2(0 \mid x_2, \theta_2) & \text{if } C_{ijt} = 0, \\ [1 - f_1(0 \mid x_1, \theta_1)] \times f_2(C_{ijt} \mid x_2, \theta_2) & \text{if } C_{ijt} \geq 1, \end{cases} \quad (4.2)$$

where $f_1(\cdot)$ represents the distribution of the zeros generated by the first data-generating process, $f_2(\cdot)$ represents the distribution of the data-generating process associated with both citations already made and those not yet made, x_i ($i = 1, 2$) denotes a vector of explanatory variables, and θ_i ($i = 1, 2$) denotes a vector of parameters. We suppose that $f_2(\cdot)$ follows a negative binomial distribution parameterized by $x_2'\theta_2$, in which x_2 includes all explanatory variables in equation (4.1); i.e. $\ln(P_{it} \times P_{jt})$, *Border*$_{ij}$, *LDist*$_{ij}$, *ComLang*$_{ij}$, *ComCol*$_{ij}$, *Colony*$_{ij}$, *Onein*$_{ijt}$, *Bothin*$_{ijt}$, *Regional*$_{ijt}$, and *GSP*$_{ijt}$. The distribution $f_1(\cdot)$ is logistic, and x_1 includes only $\ln P_{it}$ and $\ln P_{jt}$.

We use the maximum likelihood estimation technique to estimate the parameters θ_1 and θ_2 in the ZINB model. Having estimated the ZINB model, we report the Vuong (1989) test statistics. The test statistics for the ZINB model and the NB model have standard normal distributions under the null hypothesis.

Data

The data on patent applications and patent citations are taken from the National Bureau of Economic Research patent database at the United States Patent and Trademark Office. This dataset includes information on the application date, country name of the assignee, main US patent class, and citations made and received for each patent. We extract patent application and citation data from 1990 to 1999. The information used to construct the dummy variables in the gravity equation is taken from the webpage of Andrew K. Rose.[13] For details of the data, see Rose (2004, 2005).

Our sample period is 1990 to 1999. The sample includes trade partner countries between which there was at least one US patent citation during that period. Our sample covers 103 countries, which are listed in Table 4.1. Table 4.2 shows the descriptive statistics of the variables and Table 4.3 the correlations among the variables.

Empirical results

In this section, we first report our findings from the NB model and then those from the ZINB model. The estimation results from the NB model are reported in Table 4.1. Columns (1) to (3) report the estimation results for the whole sample, and columns (4) to (6) those for the sample that excludes the US. Because the number of patent citations made or received by the US is unevenly larger than those of other countries, it is worth examining how the results are affected by excluding the US.

As shown in Table 4.1, most control variables have highly significant coefficients with the expected signs in all regressions. The coefficient of the log of the product of US patents held by both trade partners ($\ln(P_i \times P_j)$) is positive and significant. This means that trade partners that hold more patents experience higher technology spillovers. The land border dummy (*Border*) and common language dummy (*ComLang*) have positive and significant coefficients in all regressions. The log of the distance between trade partners (*LDist*) has a negative and significant coefficient in many cases, but the coefficient is not significant in columns (1) and (2). As shown in Table 4.2, the non-significant coefficient in the regression for the whole sample occurs because of the strong effect of the US.

The presented results imply that countries that share a language or land border exchange technological knowledge more, whereas geographical distance tends to reduce knowledge spillovers. These results suggest that technology spillovers have similar determinants to internationally traded goods. The latter result is consistent with the findings of previous studies (Jaffe and Trajtenberg 1999; Peri 2005), but

Table 4.1 NB estimates of US patent citations between trade partners

Variable	(1)	(2)	(3)	(4)	(5)	(6)
$\ln(P_i \times P_j)$	0.70***	0.70***	0.73***	0.83***	0.83***	0.85***
	(12.08)	(12.06)	(16.19)	(124.53)	(124.59)	(128.49)
Border	0.40***	0.40***	0.29***	0.20***	0.20***	0.20***
	(7.11)	(7.00)	(5.42)	(5.52)	(5.53)	(5.47)
LDist	0.00	0.00	−0.09***	−0.14***	−0.14***	−0.18***
	(0.06)	(0.07)	(−3.65)	(−13.03)	(−13.00)	(−17.75)
ComLang	0.46***	0.46***	0.45***	0.18***	0.18***	0.20***
	(4.42)	(4.44)	(4.66)	(6.47)	(6.50)	(6.98)
ComCol	−0.97***	−0.94***	−0.69***	−0.23	−0.22	−0.20
	(−2.76)	(−2.73)	(−2.77)	(−1.15)	(−1.11)	(−1.04)
Colony	0.01	0.01	0.08	0.24***	0.24***	0.23***
	(0.14)	(0.14)	(0.86)	(5.47)	(5.47)	(5.17)
Onein	−0.30**			−0.11***		
	(−2.42)			(−2.78)		
Bothin		0.29**			0.10**	
		(2.35)			(2.52)	
GSP	−0.46***	−0.47***		−0.28***	−0.28***	
	(−4.39)	(−4.38)		(−14.01)	(−14.03)	
Regional	0.18***	0.18***		0.05*	0.05**	
	(2.98)	(2.99)		(1.94)	(1.98)	
EEC/EC/EU			0.08			0.04
			(1.37)			(1.62)

Table 4.1 Continued

Variable	(1)	(2)	(3)	(4)	(5)	(6)
US–Israel			1.33*** (9.26)			0.41*** (3.54)
NAFTA			1.03*** (6.31)			6.56*** (4.05)
CARICOM			5.24* (1.99)			0.81*** (5.87)
PATCRA			0.18 (0.79)			4.02*** (3.72)
CACM			2.56** (2.13)			0.23 (0.71)
Mercosur			−0.59 (−1.42)			0.85*** (2.61)
ASEAN			0.43 (1.12)			
No. of Obs.	19,854	19,854	19,854	18,464	18,464	18,464
log likelihood	−53,555.2	−53,557.0	−53,762.8	−36,348.1	−36,349.3	−36,451.5

Notes:

a The sample covers the period between 1990 and 1999 and includes trade partner countries that have at least one US patent citation between them in the sample period.

b ***, **, and * denote 1%, 5%, and 10% significance levels, respectively.

c The values in parentheses are *t*-statistics.

d The regressions include year dummies.

Table 4.2 ZINB estimates of US patent citations between trade partners

Variable	(1)	(2)	(3)	(4)	(5)	(6)
ln($P_i \times P_j$)	0.23***	0.23***	0.26***	0.81***	0.81***	0.83***
	(86.50)	(86.56)	(105.44)	(223.79)	(223.75)	(230.90)
Border	0.48***	0.54***	0.66***	0.21***	0.22***	0.22***
	(4.30)	(4.82)	(5.25)	(5.04)	(5.07)	(4.96)
LDist	0.25***	0.26***	0.39***	-0.14***	-0.14***	-0.18***
	(9.58)	(9.75)	(12.31)	(-12.88)	(-12.86)	(-16.87)
ComLang	0.86***	0.84***	0.57***	0.17***	0.17***	0.20***
	(12.42)	(12.16)	(7.30)	(6.72)	(6.74)	(7.52)
ComCol	-4.30***	-3.97***	-3.54***	-0.28**	-0.28**	-0.24*
	(-17.20)	(-15.22)	(-12.30)	(-2.09)	(-2.04)	(-1.69)
Colony	-0.27**	-0.25**	0.29**	0.23***	0.23***	0.23***
	(-2.24)	(-2.12)	(2.28)	(4.97)	(4.98)	(4.91)
Onein	-1.78***			-0.13***		
	(-28.22)			(-4.26)		
Bothin		1.77***			0.12***	
		(28.11)			(3.93)	
GSP	-1.55***	-1.55***		-0.29***	-0.29***	
	(-34.54)	(-34.45)		(-15.96)	(-15.98)	
Regional	0.17**	0.16**		0.06**	0.06**	
	(2.22)	(2.07)		(2.24)	(2.27)	
EEC/EC/EU			0.41***			0.06**
			(4.50)			(2.07)

Table 4.2 Continued

Variable	(1)	(2)	(3)	(4)	(5)	(6)
US–Israel			1.77*** (3.40)			0.40* (1.83)
NAFTA			2.18*** (5.94)			
CARICOM			2.23 (0.90)			19.12*** (15.56)
PATCRA			−2.13*** (−4.04)			0.77*** (4.16)
CACM			−1.70 (−0.84)			3.81*** (3.62)
Mercosur			−4.08*** (−6.48)			0.11 (0.30)
ASEAN			0.70 (1.06)			0.79*** (2.74)
No. of Obs.	19,854	19,854	19,854	18,464	18,464	18,464
log likelihood	−55,527.9	−55,528.8	−56,371.6	−37,428.5	−37,429.8	−37,541.4
Vuong test	8.58***	8.58***	7.95***	4.81***	4.81***	3.98***

Notes:
a The sample covers the period between 1990 and 1999 and includes trade partner countries that have at least one US patent citation between them in the sample period.
b ***, **, and * denote 1%, 5%, and 10% significance levels, respectively.
c The values in parentheses are t-statistics.
d The Vuong test denotes a test of the ZINB model against the NB model. The test statistics are standard normally distributed under the null hypothesis.
e The regression equation for zero counts includes $\ln(P_i)$ and $\ln(P_j)$. The estimates are available upon request.
f The regressions include year dummies.

60 *N. Jinji et al.*

Table 4.3 Sample countries

No.	Country	No.	Country	No.	Country	No.	Country
1	Antigua and Barbuda	27	El Salvador	53	Korea, South (R)	79	Russia
2	Argentina	28	Estonia	54	Kuwait	80	Saudi Arabia
3	Armenia	29	Fiji	55	Latvia	81	Senegal
4	Australia	30	Finland	56	Lebanon	82	Singapore
5	Austria	31	France	57	Lithuania	83	Slovenia
6	Azerbaijan	32	Germany	58	Luxembourg	84	South Africa
7	Bahrain	33	Ghana	59	Madagascar	85	Spain
8	Barbados	34	Greece	60	Malaysia	86	Sri Lanka
9	Belarus	35	Guatemala	61	Malta	87	Suriname
10	Belgium	36	Guinea	62	Mauritius	88	Sweden
11	Bermuda	37	Guyana	63	Mexico	89	Switzerland
12	Bolivia	38	Haiti	64	Morocco	90	Syria
13	Brazil	39	Honduras	65	Netherlands	91	Tanzania
14	Bulgaria	40	Hungary	66	New Zealand	92	Thailand
15	Canada	41	Iceland	67	Nicaragua	93	Tunisia
16	Chile	42	India	68	Niger	94	Turkey
17	China	43	Indonesia	69	Nigeria	95	Uganda
18	Colombia	44	Iran	70	Norway	96	Ukraine
19	Costa Rica	45	Ireland	71	Oman	97	United Kingdom
20	Croatia	46	Israel	72	Pakistan	98	United States
21	Cyprus	47	Italy	73	Panama	99	Uruguay
22	Czech Republic	48	Jamaica	74	Paraguay	100	Uzbekistan
23	Denmark	49	Japan	75	Peru	101	Venezuela
24	Dominica	50	Jordan	76	Philippines	102	Vietnam
25	Ecuador	51	Kazakhstan	77	Poland	103	Zimbabwe
26	Egypt	52	Kenya	78	Portugal		

the former is new to the literature. The effects of colonial history on technology spillovers, represented by *ComCol* and *Colony*, are mixed. The coefficient of *ComCol* is negative and significant in the regressions for the whole sample but not significant when the US is excluded from the sample. By contrast, the coefficient of *Colony* is not significant in the regressions for the whole sample but is positive and significant when the US is excluded. These results imply that the effects of colonial history on technology spillovers are different from those on internationally traded goods.

In columns (1) and (2) of Table 4.1, *Regional* has a significantly positive coefficient. This implies that RTAs have a positive and significant effect on technology spillovers in the sense that trade partners that belong to the same RTA have more patent citations. The results in columns (4) and (5) show that this positive and significant effect of RTAs on technology spillovers remains when the US is excluded from the sample, although the coefficient is significant at a slightly higher level than before (i.e. 5 percent or 10 percent rather than 1 percent). The coefficient of *Regional* captures the effect of RTAs under the assumption that all agreements have the same effect.

Table 4.4 Descriptive statistics

Variable	No. of Obs.	Mean	Std. Dev.	Min	Max
C	19,854	232.46	2,908.22	0.00	134,135.00
$\ln(P_i \times P_j)$	19,854	8.44	6.16	−6.91	21.88
Border	19,854	0.03	0.18	0.00	1.00
LDist	19,854	8.15	0.90	4.80	9.42
ComLang	19,854	0.16	0.37	0.00	1.00
ComCol	19,854	0.01	0.09	0.00	1.00
Colony	19,854	0.03	0.18	0.00	1.00
Regional	19,854	0.07	0.25	0.00	1.00
GSP	19,854	0.52	0.50	0.00	1.00
Onein	19,854	0.15	0.36	0.00	1.00
Bothin	19,854	0.85	0.36	0.00	1.00

We also estimate the effects of eight individual RTAs by including a separate dummy for each. The results are shown in columns (3) and (6). The coefficients are positive and significant for the US–Israel FTA, NAFTA, CARICOM, and CACM. Moreover, although they are not significant for PATCRA and ASEAN in the whole sample, they are positive and significant when the US is excluded. We also find that the effects of EEC/EC/EU and Mercosur on technology spillovers are not significant.

We further estimate the effect of the GATT/WTO.[14] The significantly negative coefficient of *Onein* (in columns (1) and (4)) and the significantly positive coefficient of *Bothin* (in columns (2) and (5)) indicate that the GATT/WTO enhances technology spillovers if both trade partners are GATT/WTO members but hinders them between member and non-member countries. *GSP* also affects technology spillovers negatively, as shown by the results in columns (1), (2), (4), and (5). These effects of the GATT/WTO and GSP on technology spillovers differ from their effects on trade. Rose (2004) finds that the effects of *Onein* and *Bothin* are not significant in a number of econometric specifications, whereas *GSP* has a strongly positive effect on trade. Although our sample period is shorter than that used by Rose (2004), we find that *Bothin* has a significantly positive effect on technology spillovers, whereas *Onein* and *GSP* have significantly negative effects.

Table 4.2 reports the estimation results of the ZINB model. As in Table 4.1, the estimation results for the whole sample are reported in columns (1) to (3) and the results excluding the US are reported in columns (4) to (6). Although these results are generally consistent with those derived from the NB model, there are some differences. First, the coefficient of *LDist* is positive and significant in the whole sample (see columns (1) to (3)), because the number of patent citations made or received by the US is unevenly larger than those of other countries. Consequently, excluding the US has a strong effect on the estimated coefficient of *LDist*. Excluding the US from the sample (as in columns (4) to (6)) gives the coefficient of *LDist* its expected sign.

Second, although the positive and significant coefficient of *Regional* is unchanged, the coefficients of some of the dummies for the individual RTAs

Table 4.5 Correlations of the variables

	$\ln(P_i \times P_j)$	Border	LDist	ComLang	ComCol	Colony	Regional	GSP	Onein	Bothin
$\ln(P_i \times P_j)$	1.000									
Border	0.084	1.000								
LDist	-0.102	-0.421	1.000							
ComLang	-0.030	0.110	0.045	1.000						
ComCol	-0.044	-0.005	-0.023	0.145	1.000					
Colony	-0.012	0.043	-0.027	0.313	-0.017	1.000				
Regional	0.174	0.214	-0.437	-0.021	0.006	0.010	1.000			
GSP	-0.227	-0.172	0.331	-0.049	-0.096	0.012	-0.205	1.000		
Onein	-0.154	-0.055	-0.005	-0.128	-0.023	-0.054	-0.114	-0.004	1.000	
Bothin	0.157	0.049	0.005	0.130	0.018	0.055	0.115	0.009	-0.992	1.000

change sign. For example, the estimated coefficient of the EEC/EC/EU dummy is positive and significant, which implies that Europe's RTA facilitates technology spillovers between major European countries. Further, the coefficients of CARICOM and CACM are not significant in the whole sample (see column (3)), whereas they are positive and significant when the US is excluded as before (see column (6)). Moreover, the coefficients of PATCRA and Mercosur are negative and significant in the whole sample (see column (3)), whereas their estimated effects in column (6) are consistent with those in Table 4.1. Finally, the significantly positive Vuong test statistics in all regressions indicate that the ZINB model is superior to the NB model.

The coefficient of *Regional* in Table 4.2 is positive and significant, regardless of whether the US is included. The coefficients of the variables that represent RTAs of which the US is a member (i.e. the US–Israel FTA and NAFTA) are positive and significant in the whole sample. In addition, the estimated coefficients of the other RTAs (except for Mercosur) are also positive and significant when the US is excluded from the sample. These results indicate that RTAs generally have positive effects on technology spillovers between trade partners.

Conclusions

This chapter investigated empirically whether RTAs enhance technology spillovers among member countries. We used patent citation data from the US Patent and Trademark Office as a proxy for technology spillovers. Using the NB model, we found that technology spillovers, as measured by patent citations between trade partners, are higher if these countries are members of the same RTA. We also found that most individual RTAs have significantly positive effects on technology spillovers. Our major findings were confirmed by the estimates obtained from the ZINB model, which addresses the econometric issue that arises from a large number of countries recording a value of zero for current patent citations. We also found that the GATT/WTO positively affects technology spillovers among member countries, whereas it negatively affects technology spillovers between members and non-members. Finally, the GSP negatively affects technology spillovers, which contrasts with its effect on international trade in goods.

As did Peri (2005), we found that the gravity model performs well in analyzing technology spillovers. Thus, we suggest that further studies of technology spillovers based on a gravity-type approach are worthwhile.

Notes

1 In this chapter, we use the terms RTAs and free trade agreements (FTAs) interchangeably. A more precise term is preferential trade agreements. To emphasize the aspect of regional integration, we mainly use the term RTAs.
2 See Keller (2004) for a survey of the literature.
3 However, the evidence of localized knowledge spillovers remains inconclusive; see Thompson and Fox-Kean (2005) and Henderson *et al.* (2005).

4 For a survey of the literature, see, for example, Baldwin and Venables (1995), Bhagwati and Panagariya (1996), Panagariya (2000), and Krishna (2005).

5 "The former is the substitution in the importing country of a lower cost source of supply within the area for a more costly source and is, therefore, beneficial to the member countries and the world as a whole. In contrast, trade diversion is the substitution of a more costly source of supply within the area for a less costly source outside the area" (Lloyd and MacLaren 2004: 446).

6 Detailed discussions of trade creation and trade diversion are provided by Panagariya (2000) and Baldwin and Wyplosz (2009, Chapter 5). Baldwin and Wyplosz (2009: 171) argue that "these terms have become quite standard, so much so that one really cannot talk about preferential liberalization without mentioning them."

7 Using plant- and industry-level data for Canada and the US, Trefler (2004) estimates the effects of the Canada–US FTA on productivity and employment.

8 Baldwin and Venables (1995) and Lloyd and MacLaren (2004) provide surveys of empirical studies of the effects of RTAs based on CGE models.

9 The most popular approach in the literature is to examine the correlation between the TFPs of domestic firms and the R&D of foreign firms. See Keller (2004) for a survey of the literature.

10 There is a growing empirical literature on the study of international technological spillovers based on patent citations (e.g. Jaffe and Trajtenberg 1999; MacGarvie 2006; Haruna *et al.* 2010; Jinji *et al.* 2010, 2011).

11 The GSP is a system of exemption from the rules of the WTO designed to promote economic growth in developing countries. Under the GSP system, developed countries provide preferential duty-free entry to their domestic markets for products exported from designated beneficiary countries.

12 Besides NAFTA (already defined above), the formal names of these RTAs are: EEC/EC/EU: the European Economic Community/the European Community/the European Union; US–Israel FTA: the United States–Israel Free Trade Agreement; CARICOM: the Caribbean Community; PATCRA: the Agreement on Trade and Commercial Relations between Australia and Papua New Guinea; ANZCERTA: Australia New Zealand Closer Economic Agreement; CACM: Central American Common Market; Mercosur: Mercado Común del Sur; and ASEAN: the Association of Southeast Asian Nations.

13 Available at http://faculty.haas.berkeley.edu/arose/.

14 As shown in Table 4.5, the correlation between *Onein* and *Bothin* is very high. Thus, we estimate the effects of *Onein* and *Bothin* in separate regressions.

References

Acharya, Ram C. and Wolfgang Keller (2009) "Technology transfer through imports." *Canadian Journal of Economics* 42(4): 1411–48.

Baldwin, Richard E. and Anthony J. Venables (1995) "Regional economic integration." In Grossman, Gene M. and Kenneth Rogoff, (eds.) *Handbook of International Economics, Vol. 3.* Amsterdam: North-Holland, 1597–644.

Baldwin, Richard and Charles Wyplosz (2009) *The Economics of European Integration, Third Edition.* Berkshire, UK: McGraw-Hill Higher Education.

Ben-David, Dan (1993) "Equalizing exchange: Trade liberalization and income convergence." *Quarterly Journal of Economics* 108(3): 653–79.

Bhagwati, Jagdish and Arvind Panagariya (1996) "The theory of preferential trade agreements: Historical evolution and current trends." *American Economic Review, Papers and Proceedings* 86(2): 82–7.

Branstetter, Lee (2006) "Is foreign direct investment a channel of knowledge spillovers? Evidence from Japan's FDI in the United States." *Journal of International Economics* 68(2): 325–44.

Brown, Drusilla, Alan V. Deardorff, and Robert M. Stern (1992) "A North American Free Trade Agreement: Analytical issues and computational assessment." *World Economy* 15(1): 11–29.

Brown, Drusilla, Alan V. Deardorff, and Robert M. Stern (2003) "Multilateral, regional and bilateral trade-policy options for the United States and Japan." *World Economy* 26(6): 803–28.

Bustos, Paula (2011) "Trade liberalization, exports, and technology upgrading: Evidence on the impact of MERCOSUR on Argentinian firms." *American Economic Review* 101(1): 304–40.

Cameron, A. Colin and Pravin K. Trivedi (1998) *Regression Analysis of Count Data.* Cambridge: Cambridge University Press.

Chang, Won and L. Alan Winters (2002) "How regional blocs affect excluded countries: The price effects of MERCOSUR." *American Economic Review* 92(4): 889–904.

Clausing, Kimberly A. (2001) "Trade creation and trade diversion in the Canada–United States Free Trade Agreement." *Canadian Journal of Economics* 34(3): 677–96.

Coe, David T. and Elhanan Helpman (1995) "International R&D spillovers." *European Economic Review* 39(5): 859–87.

Cox, David and Richard G. Harris (1992) "North American free trade and its implications for Canada: Results from a CGE model of North American trade." *World Economy* 15(1): 31–44.

Das, Gourange Gopel and Soamiely Andriamananjara (2006) "Hub-and-spokes free trade agreements in the presence of technology spillovers: An application to the Western Hemisphere." *Review of World Economics* 142(1): 33–66.

Ederington, Josh and Phillip McCalman (2008) "Endogenous firm heterogeneity and the dynamics of trade liberalization." *Journal of International Economics* 74(2): 422–40.

Ethier, Wilfred and Henrik Horn (1984) "A new look at economic integration." In Kierzkowski, H., (ed.) *Monopolistic Competition and International Trade.* Oxford: Oxford University Press, 207–29.

Fukao, Kyoji, Toshihiro Okubo, and Robert M. Stern (2003) "An econometric analysis of trade diversion under NAFTA." *North American Journal of Economics and Finance* 14(1): 3–24.

Haaland, Jan I. and Ian Wooton (1992) "Market integration, competition, and welfare." In Winters, W. A., (ed.) *Trade Flows and Trade Policy after "1992".* Cambridge: Cambridge University Press, 125–47.

Hall, Bronwyn H., Adam B. Jaffe, and Manuel Trajtenberg (2001) "The NBER patent citations data file: Lesson, insights and methodological tools." NBER Working Paper No. 8498.

Haruna, Shoji, Naoto Jinji, and Xingyuan Zhang (2010) "Patent citations, technology diffusion, and international trade: Evidence from Asian countries." *Journal of Economics and Finance* 34(4): 365–90.

Henderson, Rebecca, Adam Jaffe, and Manuel Trajtenberg (2005) "Patent citations and the geography of knowledge spillovers: A reassessment: Comment." *American Economic Review* 95(1): 461–64.

Jaffe, Adam B. and Manuel Trajtenberg (1999) "International knowledge flows: Evidence from patent citations." *Economics of Innovation & New Technology* 8(1/2): 105–36.

Jaffe, Adam B., Manuel Trajtenberg, and Rebecca Henderson (1993) "Geographic localization of knowledge spillovers as evidenced by patent citations." *Quarterly Journal of Economics* 108(3): 577–98.

Jinji, Naoto, Xingyuan Zhang, and Shoji Haruna (2010) "Trade patterns and international technology spillovers: Theory and evidence from patent citations." Graduate School of Economics, Kyoto University, Research Project Center Discussion Paper Series No. E–10–006.

Jinji, Naoto, Xingyuan Zhang, and Shoji Haruna (2011) "Does the structure of multi-national enterprises' activity affect technology spillovers?" Discussion Paper Series No. 11–E–027, Research Institute of Economy, Trade and Industry (RIETI).

Keller, Wolfgang (2004) "International technology diffusion." *Journal of Economic Literature* 42(3): 752–82.

Krishna, Pravin (2005) "The economics of preferential trade agreements." In Choi, E. Kwan and James Harrigan, (eds.) *Handbook of International Trade, Vol.* 2. Oxford: Blackwell Publishing, 294–312.

Lloyd, Peter J. and Donald MacLaren (2004) "Gains and losses from regional trading agreements: A survey." *Economic Record* 80(251): 445–67.

MacGarvie, Megan (2006) "Do firms learn from international trade?" *Review of Economics and Statistics* 88(1): 46–60.

Maurseth, Per Botolf, and Bart Verspagen (2002) "Knowledge spillovers in Europe: A patent citations analysis." *Scandinavian Journal of Economics* 104(4): 531–45.

Murata, Yasusada, Ryo Nakajima, Ryosuke Okamoto, and Ryuichi Tamura (2010) "Localized knowledge spillovers and patent citations: A distance-based approach." Unpublished manuscript.

Paci, Raffaele and Stefano Usai (2009) "Knowledge flows across European regions." *Annals of Regional Science* 43(3): 669–90.

Panagariya, Arvind (2000) "Preferential trade liberalization: The traditional theory and new developments." *Journal of Economic Literature* 38(2): 287–331.

Peri, Giovanni (2005) "Determinants of knowledge flows and their effect on innovation." *Review of Economics and Statistics* 87(2): 308–22.

Philippidis, G. and A. I. Snajuán (2007) "An analysis of Mercosur's regional trading Arrangements." *World Economy* 30(3): 504–31.

Roland-Holst, David W., Kenneth A. Reinert, and Clinton R. Shiells (1994) "A general equilibrium analysis of North American economic integration." In Francois, J. F. and C.R. Shiells, (eds.) *Modeling Trade Policy: Applied General Equilibrium Assessments of North American Free Trade.* Cambridge: Cambridge University Press, 47–82.

Romalis, John (2007) "NAFTA's and CUSFTA's impact on international trade." *Review of Economics and Statistics* 89(3): 416–35.

Rose, Andrew K. (2004) "Do we really know that the WTO increases trade?" *American Economic Review* 94(1): 98–114.

Rose, Andrew K. (2005) "Which international institutions promote international trade?" *Review of International Economics* 13(4): 682–98.

Schiff, Maurize and Yanling Wang (2003) "Regional integration and technology diffusion: The case of the North American Free Trade Agreement." World Bank Policy Research Paper No. 3132.

Sobarzo, Horacio E. (1992) "A general equilibrium analysis of the gains from trade for the Mexican economy of a North American Free Trade Agreement." *World Economy* 15(1): 83–100.

Thompson, Peter and Melanie Fox-Kean (2005) "Patent citations and the geography of knowledge spillovers: A reassessment." *American Economic Review* 95(1): 450–60.

Trefler, Daniel (2004) "The long and short of the Canada–U.S. Free Trade Agreement." *American Economic Review* 94(4): 870–95.

Venables, Anthony J. (1987) "Customs Union and tariff reform under imperfect competition." *European Economic Review* 31(1): 103–10.

Viner, Jacob (1950) *The Customs Union Issue.* New York: Carnegie Endowment for International Peace.

Vuong, Quang H. (1989) "Likelihood ratio tests for model selection and non-nested hypotheses." *Econometrica* 57(2): 307–33.

Xu, Bin and Jianmao Wang (1999) "Capital goods trade and R&D spillovers in the OECD." *Canadian Journal of Economics* 32(5): 1258–74.

5 Currency cooperation between ASEAN countries and China, Japan, and Korea*

A reality check

Chan-Guk Huh

Introduction

The integration of the European currency has generated a large body of literature. During early discussions, the adoption of a common currency was regarded as a daring venture to the point of almost defying the gravity of skepticism rooted in the economic reasoning of optimal currency area (OCA) theories. Along with the OCA, the optimal sequence of economic and currency integration in Europe was also debated throughout the 1960s and 1970s: "The 'economists' considered economic convergence should happen before actual monetary integration. The 'monetarists' ... believed just the contrary: monetary integration would act as a trigger for economic convergence in the EEC/EU."[1] Although the preconditions for monetary integration seemed to be insufficient from the economists' viewpoint and according to many OCA criteria, the European monetary system (EMS) initiative that yielded the common currency of the euro formally started in 1999 – and it quickly became a success story. Indeed, it rapidly ascended to become a strong contender to the US dollar as the reserve currency for central banks.

This European undertaking has prompted economists both within and outside the region to ponder the desirability and feasibility of a similar venture in East Asia. The shockingly negative crisis experiences of many East Asian countries in 1997, namely the collapses of managed dollar peg systems in the face of large and rapid capital outflows, have provided a real catalyst for change. Further, these experiences have made searching for a stability-enhancing currency arrangement in East Asia an undertaking with a large potential payoff.

Active research on currency cooperation in East Asia (particularly in the so-called ASEAN + 3 nations) has picked up pace since the 1997 financial crisis.[2] Most previous studies have relied on OCA theories and European experiences to assess the various aspects of any potential East Asian currency cooperation arrangement, namely feasibility, costs and benefits, candidate groupings, and so forth.[3] One strand of the views based on endogenous OCA theories (i.e. the

*An earlier draft of this chapter was presented at the Otaru University of Commerce "Globalism and Regional Economies," Symposium in Otaru, Japan in August 2011. Helpful comments by Professor Eiji Ogawa are gratefully acknowledged. Any remaining errors are my own.

"monetarist" school of thought) went as far as to emphasize the beneficial spillover effects of currency cooperation (e.g. alleviating the inadequacies of participating countries) and, by implication, argued for a speedier establishment of such an arrangement.[4] However, recent developments in the wake of the 2008 global financial crisis seem to warrant a more measured assessment of these issues. In the eurozone, for instance, the lack of an enforcement mechanism in the area of fiscal policy among member states, an apparent inadequacy that had been pointed out by skeptics (Tanzi 2004) early on, is threatening the integrity as well as continued existence of the eurozone in its current guise.

In light of the foregoing, this chapter critically examines some of the issues surrounding currency cooperation in East Asia from an economist's point of view and suggests reasons why the pursuit has gained traction in the region. Growing intra-regional trade and increasing multinational production networks between ASEAN and the "plus 3" countries have been pointed out as the key factors that make regional currency cooperation both desirable and feasible. At the same time, however, East Asian countries seem to lack not only comparable historical and economic momentum, but also attendant support institutions such as multinational policymaking, consultation bodies, and fiscal resources, compared with the European project. Thus, a closer examination of factors that are important for a workable regional cooperative arrangement is needed.

Two issues are examined herein. The first concerns the expected costs and benefits of regional exchange rate cooperation. Despite the absence of a developed framework to make quantitative assessments, we could explore the desirability of such an arrangement based on economic theories and previous empirical results. Although many studies have based their investigations on a broad project involving ASEAN + 3, it remains unclear what less developed countries would gain from such an arrangement. Exchange rate coordination implies the supremacy of exchange rate-oriented monetary policy, and this might not be the most suitable policy focus compared with getting help from a weak real exchange rate in order to pursue economic growth, such as Korea during its rapid growth period and China more recently.

The second area of examination is to assess the degree of the economic integration of the region through a comparative study of the trade structures of ASEAN + 3 and major EMS countries. Examinations of recent trends suggest that intra-European Union trade is more important in Europe, whereas ASEAN + 3 trade patterns seem rather outward-oriented.[5] If this were the case, then a deeper intra-regional integration via enhanced trade flow would be called for.

Finally, this chapter offers a speculative explanation of why efforts to strengthen regional cooperation such as the Chiang Mai Initiative (CMI) are still ongoing despite the relative paucity of supportive findings in the related literature. Since early 2000, ASEAN + 3 countries have maintained a substantial trade surplus in their external trade with the rest of world, including the US and EU. Hence, adopting a currency cooperation regime that would stabilize intra-regional exchange rates but provide flexibility against the US dollar and euro might be an acceptable policy option. If this conjecture holds, then some form of East Asian currency cooperation arrangement might be realized sometime in the future despite the overwhelming skepticism that presently persists. That said, many hurdles need to be overcome and details of the mechanism further worked out, which are serious challenges for regional economists and policymakers.

Detailed arguments on the above points are presented in the remainder of this chapter. The second section overviews the Asian Monetary Unit (AMU) and other basket peg proposals, and critically examines their rationales, policy implications, and applicability to ASEAN + 3 exchange rate cooperation. The third section examines some of the important economic statistics and trade patterns of ASEAN + 3 and compares and contrasts them with those of Euro-11,[6] and the final section discusses implications and concludes.

Exchange rate-centered approach to ASEAN + 3 currency cooperation

Exchange rate cooperation in East Asia

A large body of literature has dealt with currency cooperation in Europe and subsequently in East Asia. European exchange rate cooperation, which provides the template for any potential East Asian project, was a direct offshoot of the Bretton Woods managed peg exchange rate regime that broke down in the early 1970s. European countries had continued to maintain and reinforce a managed peg system in the form of the "snake in the tunnel" (1971–3), the "snake in the lake" (1973–6), and the exchange rate mechanism (ERM) of the EMS that followed. The gestation period lasted more than 40 years before the birth of the euro in 1999.[7] Until then, various collective and bilateral efforts to maintain exchange rate stability were tried amid a number of small and large crises. Separate from currency-related developments, from the late 1950s and early 1960s intra-regional trade grew and general economic cooperation deepened, facilitated by the establishment of customs union, the Common Agricultural Policy, and the European Commission (Baldwin and Wyplosz 2009).

In comparison, the 1997 breakdown of an implicit US dollar peg system was the key catalyst in East Asia. Despite the lack of a formal cooperation agreement, many countries followed the implicit peg, which collapsed under the weight of rapid capital flows during the 1997 Asian financial crisis. Some economists interpreted the crisis as a prima facie evidence of the fundamental difficulty of maintaining an exchange rate regime other than a hard peg (e.g. euro) or free-floating (e.g. US dollar) regime.[8] Others, who were not convinced by the bipolar view, have pointed to the absence of the Japanese yen (the currency of the largest regional trading partner) from the pre-1997 regional basket peg system as a major flaw. Thus, much attention has since been paid to how to construct a balanced basket to improve the pre-crisis soft dollar peg (Ogawa and Ito 2002; Rajan 2002). In addition, East Asian countries began to consider regional cooperation in areas such as foreign exchange reserves and exchange rates.

These initiatives materialized in the form of the technical mechanisms of exchange rate cooperation per se, with the stated purpose of stabilizing regional exchange rates. The CMI proposed by ASEAN + 3 is the most significant embodiment of East Asian regional economies, while the AMU is the most visible representation of efforts to provide meaningful content to the CMI. Rationales for the AMU, modeled after the European Currency Unit (ECU), are thus explained as follows:

> This monetary cooperation after the crisis resulted in the Chiang Mai Initiative (CMI), which was established by the ASEAN + 3 ... as a network of bilateral and multilateral swap arrangements to deal with a currency crisis in member countries. Under the CMI, the monetary authorities should conduct surveillance to prevent a currency crisis in the future. As one of the new surveillance criteria, we propose the creation of an Asian Monetary Unit (AMU) and AMU Deviation Indicators for East Asian currencies.
>
> (RIETI 2007: http://www.rieti.go.jp/users/amu/en/index.html)

The AMU, proposed and calculated by Ogawa and other economists (Mori *et al.* 2002; Ogawa and Kawasaki 2006), uses a basket that combines the US dollar and euro with weights of 65 percent and 35 percent, respectively (Figure 5.1). The value of the AMU has gone down roughly 15 percent against the euro, while it has gone up approximately 25 percent against the US dollar since 2000. Based on the AMU, Ogawa and Shimizu (2006) thus calculate "AMU deviation indicators" for each currency, which can measure the amount of deviation of each if the AMU were taken as defining the central parities for currencies in the basket in a common basket peg system.

The AMU is not the only basket peg system that has been proposed for East Asia.[9] The so-called "basket, band, crawl" system proposed by Williamson (1999) predates the AMU. Subsequently, Williamson (2005) demonstrates that the proposed system can considerably reduce the volatility of regional currencies measured in terms of nominal effective exchange rate variability for East Asian currencies. Further, many researchers have proposed a basket pegging arrangement for exchange rates in East Asian countries as a suitable open-ended volatility reduction mechanism. Park and Wyplosz (2008) and Wyplosz (2010) both suggest that a basket peg system in which individual East Asian countries choose weights based on their trade structures could also bring about exchange rate stability, similar to the case of the AMU.

In principle, any differences between these various peg systems are unlikely to be substantial because of the similarities in how they were constructed. However, there are nuances in how they should be used. The AMU has closer cooperation among regional countries within the existing CMI framework. The AMU's deviation indicators, for example, could be used to define a parity grid that determines the details of coordinated foreign exchange market interventions by participating countries, as in the EMU. Following the path of the EMU, closer currency cooperation is implicitly assumed in this vein. By contrast, Williamson (2005) emphasizes the utility of the basket system as a neutral halfway house. In other words, the short-term effects of reducing regional exchange rate volatility

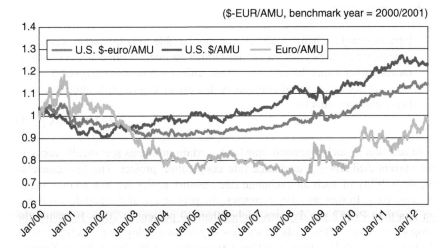

Figure 5.1 AMU exchange rates.

Source: AMU-related data can be found on the RIETI website. See http://www.rieti.go.jp/users/
amu/en/index.html#figures, accessed on July 4, 2011.

is a desirable goal, as the basket peg system "would constitute a useful transi-
tional device, pending [the] adoption of either full floating or monetary union"
(Williamson 2005, p. 1).

However, there is little difference in policy implications between these basket
peg systems for participating countries. Selecting an exchange rate system that
requires a central bank to manage the currency's exchange rate always involves a
policy authority's intervention in the foreign exchange market in the short run and
a particular ordering of monetary policy priorities in the long run, as interventions
in the foreign exchange market would have ramifications on domestic monetary
conditions.

The cost of the ASEAN + 3 basket peg

The incompatibility of an exchange rate peg, free international capital flow, and
monetary policy autonomy, the so-called impossible trinity (or trilemma), is a
well-understood proposition in the literature. The adoption of a peg means not
only ceding unilateral control over the exchange rate value of a country, but also
committing to maintain a monetary policy stance that is aligned with key members of the cooperation arrangement. For example, Wyplosz (2002) suggests that
the relative success of the soft peg in Europe was at least partly because of capital
control (see also Andrews 1994), and that the comparatively freer flow of capital
in East Asia would complicate any such attempt. Further, Fischer (2001) expresses
reservations about a basket peg such as Williamson's "basket, band, crawl" system
in emerging countries because of this tension between capital flow and the viability

of a soft peg. There are also well-understood problems with regional exchange rate stability arrangements:

> Intra-regional exchange stability may not be able to help react to economic shocks, which then places a greater burden on internal price and cost adjustments within a specific economy. Also, unless a system is designed to allow some flexibility ... misalignments or distortions can result leading to speculative currency attacks.
>
> (ADB 2010, p. 51)

In addition to such a general drawback, certain problems specifically apply to the current ASEAN + 3 exchange rate cooperation project. The first concerns the desirability of such an exchange rate stability policy for low-income member countries. In four member countries, the percentage of the population living on less than PPP$2 per day was higher than 40 percent in 2006–10, while the proportion of agriculture, fishery, and forestry sector employment was higher than 30 per cent in all but three countries (Association of Southeast Asian Nations, 2012, p. 58, Table 50). For these less developed low-income countries, exchange rate stability might not be the top priority. Though it is not a sufficient condition for fostering growth by itself, an extensive review by Eichengreen (2008b) offers some evidence to support real depreciation as an important facilitator of economic growth, or a "development-relevant policy tool" (ibid., p. 2).[10] For example, the experiences of Japan since World War II, those of Singapore, Korea, and Taiwan during their rapid growth periods, and the current policy of China, are cases in point. Indeed, there are indications that some ASEAN countries are following a strategy of real devaluation. According to the monthly real AMU deviation indicators, the real exchange rates of Indonesia and Laos compared with the AMU have been weakening (depreciating) since 2001. The Philippines and Vietnam have also joined since 2007.

Second, the so-called "Nth" country problem is well known in any collective exchange rate agreement. Since there can be only $N - 1$ bilateral exchange rates in an N-country collective arrangement, one country will always act as an anchor for determining the bilateral rate between external currencies and member countries. In the European case, Germany played such a role, as the Deutschmark's weight in the ECU had been more than 30 percent, much larger than that of the second largest economy France's franc of less than 20 percent. However, it is hard to think of a system where one particular country could play a similar role due to the rapid growth of China and Japan, which could have assumed such a role only a decade ago. Further, although smaller than these two countries, Korea is also much larger than most ASEAN members.

Recognizing such a reality, ADB (2010) suggests some alternatives:

> From an economic viewpoint, there is nothing inherently wrong with this arrangement, but the political aspects are bound to be delicate. If, as likely, the PRC, Japan and Korea [CJK hereafter] elect to stay out, then the AMU,

and the exchange rates of ASEAN countries, would be driven by the average evolution of the Japanese yen, the PRC renminbi, and Korean won. The principle of averages implies that ASEAN exchange rates would not deviate much from the three 'outs'.[11]

The question remains why the exchange rates of ASEAN countries should follow an average of these three "outs." Based on recent trends and extant pressures for them to revalue, the currencies of China and Korea are likely to be on an appreciating trend vis-à-vis the US dollar and euro, regardless of the economic conditions of ASEAN members. That would be detrimental to ASEAN countries' economic growth prospects because the EU and US still feature prominently in the trade structure of ASEAN. Growing intra-East Asia trade notwithstanding, CJK individually falls short of the dominant position of Germany compared with Euro-11 countries.

There is an additional issue on the "cost" side. ERM countries saw frequent unilateral as well as bilateral interventions in the face of speculative attacks in foreign exchange markets, which required standby financial resource pools such as the short-term and very short-term financing facilities for weak-currency countries. Similar reserve resources would be needed for ASEAN + 3 basket peg members, and although the financial resources available under the CMI and CMI multilateralization could be used for such purposes, it would be a big leap from viewing the resource pool as a fire-truck to be used in emergencies, to using it as a regional exchange rate stabilization fund.[12]

The benefits of an ASEAN + 3 basket peg system are not transparent

Broadly speaking, the easier trade flow of goods and FDI is one important advantage of a fixed exchange rate regime, but there other kinds of benefits such as a credible commitment mechanism for countries that lack macroeconomic stabilization credibility. Further, such a rate regime can help solve the high inflation problem that is worsened by a lack of policy credibility and unmoored inflation expectations. However, this is not the situation of most ASEAN + 3 countries, and thus the enhancement of policy credibility through a basket peg exchange regime is not relevant at the moment.

Proponents of ASEAN + 3 exchange rate cooperation argue as follows:

> Achieving greater intra-regional exchange rate stability promotes intra-regional trade, reduces exchange rate policy tension and improves the allocation of regional resources.... The objective of regional exchange rate cooperation should be to stabilize *intra-regional* exchange rates, while allowing for sufficient *inter-regional* exchange rate flexibility.
>
> (ADB 2010, p. 51)

According to the literature, the important cost of entering currency integration is mostly macroeconomic in nature, such as maintaining exchange rate stability over other domestic monetary priorities. Consequently, the gains are mostly microeco-nomic, such as businesses engaging in more international trade in response to a decrease in exchange rate risk. However, how exchange rate stability influences trade over time remains subject to theoretical ambiguity (De Grauwe 2005).

It is hard to find robust estimates of the positive effects of a fixed exchange rate regime. Earlier studies using data from industrialized countries tended to find non-significant positive effects on trade flow. More recently, Rose (2000) offers large estimates of the trade-enhancing effects of exchange rate stability;[13, 14] however, in a series of related papers, Baldwin and co-authors critically reviewed previous empirical estimates of the so-called "Rose effect," and found smaller estimates of trade enhancement effect. Moreover, Eichengreen (2008b, p. 10) concludes that the link between real exchange rate volatility and growth is "less than definitive." After comparing volatility measures against growth rates for various countries, he further states that "the appearance of a negative relationship is derived by a few outliers, China and Argentina in the emerging market subsample, Ukraine and the Baltics in the developing country subsample" (ibid., p. 14).[15]

If one were to take these estimates at the higher end seriously, countries that are not part of an exchange rate arrangement must be enjoying larger counter-vailing welfare gains based on having currency freedom. By contrast, there is the distinct possibility that these low estimates do not measure the important benefit of being in a currency union, namely avoiding having occasional exchange rate crises. In other words, the potential disruptions that a country could experience in the face of a sudden disruptive change in its currency value, or those of its regional competitors (which might necessitate a competitive devaluation response), might comprise the major benefit of entering an exchange rate arrangement.

Implications of trade patterns

Comparison of ASEAN + 3 and Euro-11 countries

Many previous studies have compared the sets of common quantitative indicators related to OCA criteria from East Asia with those of European countries to find varying results. Despite the multiplicity of comparative studies, however, previous researchers have paid insufficient attention to certain areas. For example, Wyplosz (2002) raises similar issues under the heading of "real convergence," which refers to the stage of development by means of comparing the GDP per capita dispersion of Asian and European countries.

Table 5.1 shows a set of simple statistics to compare ASEAN + 3 and inaugural eurozone countries over a 10-year period. It is easy to see some glaring dissim-ilarities. Dispersions in economy size as well as average income level are much larger for ASEAN + 3 countries. For example, the largest Euro-11 economy in 1995 was approximately 7.2 times larger than the median-sized economy, which in turn was approximately 5.2 times larger than the smallest. In terms of GDP per capita, an average citizen of the highest income country earned approximately 1.1 times his/her counterpart in the country with a median per capita income, which, in turn, earned 1.5 times more than the lowest income country citizen.

Table 5.1 Comparison of key indicators for Euro-11 and ASEAN + 3 countries (maximum, minimum, and median values for each category)

Indicator	Euro-11 (1995)	ASEAN + 3 (2005)
GDP (current million US$)		
Max	2,522,792	4,552,200
Min	67,060	2,723
Med	351,556	137,848
GDP per capita, PPP		
Max	23,480	45,374
Min	13,471	1,453
Med	20,659	4,115
General government expenditure (percentage of GDP)		
Max	61.66	34.20
Min	39.83	12.32
Med	53.47	18.75
Money and quasi money (M2) as a percentage of GDP		
Max	165.43	207.24
Min	66.87	17.95
Med	107.31	68.16
Market capitalization of listed companies (percentage of GDP)		
Max	85.09	252.48
Min	13.64	0.87
Med	33.20	70.80
Trade (percentage of GDP)		
Max	140.88	428.46
Min	44.41	27.28
Med	63.33	99.30

Source: World Bank, IMF.

Notes:

a Euro-11: except Luxembourg.

b ASEAN + 3: except Brunei (for GDP and GDP per capita), Myanmar, and Cambodia. Laos was not included in "Market capitalization of listed companies."

In comparison, the largest economy of ASEAN + 3 in 2005 was approximately 33 times the median-sized economy, which, in turn, was approximately 51 times larger than the smallest. In terms of income, a citizen in the highest income country earned 11 times more than his/her median country counterpart, whereas the ratio between the median country and the poorest country was only 2.8.

Government budget is also an interesting area to look at, because it reflects not only the size of the government and a country's spending propensity, but also the fiscal infrastructure of the country, such as tax collection, presence of a functioning government debt security market, and the extent of public domain economic activities (in contrast to a shadow economy). Large fiscal resources also imply the availability of an alternative policy instrument to counter an idiosyncratic shock that affects only that particular country in the currency union. Table 5.1 shows that government expenditure as a share of GDP for Euro-11 countries is approximately three times larger than that for ASEAN + 3.

Financial development indicators such as money, and quasi money and stock market capitalizations, also convey a similar impression. Euro-11 countries in 1995 were positioned much more closely together compared with their ASEAN + 3 counterparts in 2005. Although these indicators look less diverse in the case of trade, a closer examination shows this appearance to be superficial, as discussed below. Further, there are significant differences in the initial conditions of the pre-currency integration periods for ASEAN + 3 and Euro-11 countries. As such, assigning top priority to maintaining the exchange value of a country's currency through internal and external shocks might be neither feasible nor desirable for certain low-income countries.

External trade and exchange rates in the 1980s EMS[16]

The EMS of the 1980s characterized a group of countries that were already economically integrated through a customs union reattempting to establish a higher degree of currency cooperation. The EMS that started with eight countries[17] and the accompanying ERM was designed to be a more resilient arrangement built on earlier tumultuous experiences of the immediate post-Bretton Woods era, and the precursor system that eventually led to the birth of the euro in 1999. However, the system endured many volatile periods. We limit our examination in this chapter to the trade and exchange rate developments of the 1980s, when interactions between external imbalances and adjustments in bilateral exchange rates were notable.

The share distributions of key export destinations/import sources out of total trade in 1985 are shown in Figure 5.2. Two points are noteworthy. First, approximately 55 percent of total trade was intra-ERM, which rose to 70 percent when trade with non-ERM European partners was added. This share of intra-EU trade has remained stable over time. Second, the ERM's trade levels with key trading blocks and partners were evenly balanced, despite small imbalances in its trade with the US and Japan.

Next, the trade structure of the exports and imports of the top six ERM countries is examined based on Euro-11 data (Table 5.2). The dominance of regional countries as both destinations and sources of Euro-11 member countries is clear. Of the top six, the US, third in the ranking, is the only non-regional country. This pattern remains almost unchanged. The sources of imports also show a similar ranking.

ASEAN + 3 trade patterns and exchange rates

In terms of openness, as measured by the ratio of trade to GDP, both East Asian and EU countries are highly open; the median for ASEAN + 3 countries is almost 100 percent in the mid-2000s, somewhat larger than that for Euro-11 countries in the mid-1990s (70 percent). The trade breakdowns for ASEAN and ASEAN + 3 countries in 2005 are shown in Figures 5.3 and 5.4, respectively. Two points

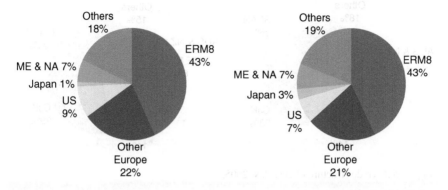

Exports (total: USD 513,944 mil.)

Others 18%
ERM8 43%
ME & NA 7%
Japan 1%
US 9%
Other Europe 22%

Imports (total: USD 507,320 mil.)

Others 19%
ERM8 43%
ME & NA 7%
Japan 3%
US 7%
Other Europe 21%

Figure 5.2 Trade structure of the ERM, 1985.

Source: DOT, IMF.

Note: ME & NA: Middle East and North Africa.

Table 5.2 Top five export and import partners of Euro-11 (million USD, percentage)[1]

	Exports	*Imports*		*Exports*	*Imports*
	1985			*1990*	
Total	557,676	560,935	Total	1,208,270	1,215,475
DEU	12.28%	13.32%	DEU	13.50%	15.45%
FRA	10.18%	8.22%	FRA	11.46%	9.46%
USA	8.92%	7.18%	GBR	8.93%	7.42%
GBR	8.89%	8.14%	ITA	7.47%	7.15%
ITA	6.44%	5.66%	LUX	6.55%	6.46%
	2000			*2010*	
Total	1,854,922	1,809,610	Total	3,765,792	3,720,663
DEU	12.40%	12.70%	DEU	12.38%	12.74%
FRA	10.09%	8.05%	FRA	9.59%	6.51%
GBR	9.28%	7.88%	GBR	6.79%	5.17%
USA	8.46%	7.51%	ITA	5.53%	4.52%
ITA	6.29%	5.35%	USA	5.43%	4.04%

Note:

1 Countries ordered by export values (DOT, IMF).

are noteworthy. First, the intra-regional trade concentration is much smaller for ASEAN and ASEAN + 3 compared with the ERM case. Indeed, the share of intra-ASEAN trade is approximately a quarter of the total, roughly equal to the share of trade with CJK. Thus, CJK is the largest trading partner for ASEAN members. However, the combined share of the US and EU is also approximately a quarter of the total. For ASEAN + 3, given that the total trade of CJK is approximately three

Exports (total: USD 653.224 mil.)   Imports (total: USD 582,920 mil.)

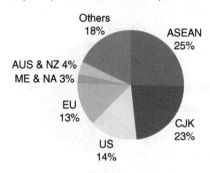 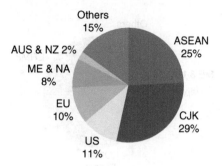

Figure 5.3 Trade structure of ASEAN, 2005.

Source: DOT, IMF.

Note: AUS & NZ and ME & NA: Australia and New Zealand, and Middle East & North Africa, respectively.

Exports (total: USD 2,296,494 mil.)   Imports (total: USD 2,019,605 mil.)

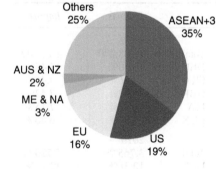 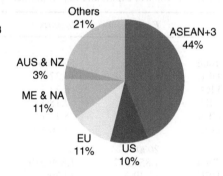

Figure 5.4 Trade structure of ASEAN + 3, 2005.

Source: DOT, IMF.

Note: AUS & NZ and ME & NA: Australia and New Zealand, and Middle East & North Africa, respectively.

times larger than that of ASEAN, the pattern of ASEAN + 3 is largely influenced by the composition of CJK trade. The share of ASEAN + 3 intra-regional trade (35 percent) is matched by the combined share of the total exports of the US and EU, whereas the comparison becomes more lopsided for total imports.

Second, notable mismatches between the exports and imports of the key blocks of the three groupings are seen (Figure 5.3). For ASEAN's trade with CJK, the share of imports from the latter exceed that of exports by six percentage points, while for the US and EU, the gap is approximately three percentage points. For

ASEAN + 3, these mismatches are much larger. For example, the US share of total ASEAN + 3 exports exceeds that of total imports by nine percentage points (Figure 5.4). The comparable gap is five percentage points for the EU. The share of intra-ASEAN + 3 trade (35 percent) is the same as the sum of the US/EU share of total exports, whereas ASEAN + 3's share of total imports is approximately twice the size of that of US/EU. ASEAN + 3 also has large deficits in its trade with oil producers of the Middle East and North Africa.

Next, Tables 5.3 and 5.4 show for selected years (1990, 2000, and 2010) the total values of exports and imports as well as the top six countries for both categories and their respective shares for ASEAN and CJK. In each table, countries are ranked in terms of the size of exports. We see that the US has mostly been the top export destination between the early 1990s and 2006, followed by the EU and Japan. China's significance as an export destination has grown since the early 2000s, when its share was close to that of Korea. In 2010, China became the top destination, albeit following the downturn in the US and EU in the wake of the 2008 global financial crisis. In terms of imports, Japan was the dominant top

Table 5.3 Top six trading partners of ASEAN countries (million USD, percentage)[1]

	1990			*2000*			*2010*	
	Exports	*Imports*		*Exports*	*Imports*		*Exports*	*Imports*
Total	144,488	163,276	Total	426,785	369,001	Total	1,094,591	1,022,623
USA	19.38%	14.44%	USA	18.97%	13.99%	CHN	12.68%	14.36%
JPN	18.89%	23.13%	EUA	14.98%	11.08%	EUA	10.79%	8.70%
EUA	16.03%	15.69%	JPN	13.44%	19.08%	USA	9.70%	8.14%
SGP	7.60%	5.79%	SGP	8.20%	6.80%	JPN	9.35%	11.69%
MYS	5.46%	6.18%	MYS	7.43%	8.02%	HKG	6.68%	1.76%
HKG	4.58%	2.41%	HKG	5.29%	2.51%	MYS	6.02%	6.11%

Note:

1 Countries ordered by export values (DOT, IMF). EUA, SGP, MYS, and HKG are respectively EU-27, Singapore, Malaysia, and Hong Kong.

Table 5.4 Top six trading partners of CJK (million USD, percentage)

	1990			*2000*			*2010*	
	Exports	*Imports*		*Exports*	*Imports*		*Exports*	*Imports*
Total	418,577	363,575	Total	900,457	765,281	Total	2,813,733	2,512,003
USA	27.68%	21.01%	USA	25.98%	16.23%	USA	16.00%	8.51%
EUA	18.29%	15.73%	EUA	16.28%	12.38%	EUA	15.73%	10.78%
HKG	10.52%	4.78%	HKG	9.15%	1.62%	HKG	9.81%	0.74%
DEU	5.46%	4.92%	JPN	6.90%	9.58%	CHN	9.78%	9.12%
JPN	5.22%	7.21%	CHN	5.42%	8.88%	JPN	5.20%	9.75%
KOR	4.28%	3.29%	KOR	4.66%	5.71%	KOR	4.42%	6.64%

source until 2007, when China overtook it. The crisis year of 1998 was the only time when the US was the top import source.

Next, we turn to the trend in CJK trade (Table 5.4). As in the ASEAN case, the US has remained the largest export destination, although its share has fallen from above 30 percent in 1985 to below 20 percent in 2010. However, the combined share of the US and EU is still above 30 percent. The main contributor to this is China, close to 30 percent of whose exports went to the US in 2005. Although regional countries' exports to China have risen considerably in recent years, they have not overturned the overwhelming US bias in China's exports. Within CJK, Japan's position as the center of northeast Asia has been overtaken by China as the top destination since the early 2000s.

Trends in ASEAN + 3 trade have been accompanied by similarly concentrated trade balance patterns, as shown in Table 5.5. Its share of global trade has risen from below 20 percent in the 1990s, to over 24 percent in 2010; however, its overall trade balance with the world has consistently been positive. The most striking feature is its persistent and growing trade surpluses vis-à-vis the US and EU. Indeed, the size of ASEAN + 3's trade surpluses with the US has been more than 30 percent of total trade since 2002, although that with the EU has been slightly smaller (i.e. approximately 20 percent).

In summary, ASEAN + 3 has been running trade surpluses with the rest of the world, including disproportionately large ones with the US and EU. Within the group, ASEAN has run trade deficits with CJK, especially China, since 2009. ASEAN typically runs trade deficits with CJK (mainly with Japan until 2006 and with China since then), but surpluses with non-ASEAN + 3 partners, especially the US, the EU, Australia, and Hong Kong in that order. However, its external trade balance has shown a distinct shift around 1997, the year of the Asian financial crisis. ASEAN had a trade deficit with the rest of the world until 1997, but has had a surplus ever since. A somewhat similar pattern is seen in the case of Korea. Judging solely from its external trade balances, the magnitude of exchange rate adjustments in the aftermath of the 1997 crisis was enough to turn ASEAN and Korean trade balances positive, after being in deficit for most of the 1990s.

Policy implications and conclusion

The foregoing suggests that a currency cooperation arrangement that comprises ASEAN + 3 might take a long time to materialize. The policy choice for participating members implied by adopting such an arrangement would be to place exchange rate stability ahead of all other economic considerations. Member countries are too diverse in terms of their key economic characteristics (or initial conditions), and economic integration in the form of trade linkage has not yet deepened sufficiently. This observation stands out when the key aspects of ASEAN + 3 are compared with those of the eurozone states.

There have been some suggestions to begin a currency cooperation arrangement among ASEAN countries first (Wyplosz 2002; ADB 2010).[18] In principle, however, the order of who goes first might make little difference. There are two

Table 5.5 Trade values and trade balances of ASEAN + 3 (billion USD, percentage)[1]

	1990	1995	2000	2005	2010
Global total trade	6,900.7	10,229.1	12,982.0	21,120.9	30,512.6
ASEAN + 3 trade with world	1,089.9	2,020.6	2,461.5	4,316.1	7,443.0
(share of global total)	(15.8%)	(19.8%)	(19.0%)	(20.4%)	(24.4%)
Trade surplus as a percentage of total trade	3.3%	3.9%	7.8%	6.4%	5.0%
ASEAN + 3 trade with the US	243.8	403.7	490.7	641.0	853.3
ASEAN + 3 trade surplus	43.9	58.2	139.1	228.6	259.4
(as a percentage of trade with the US)	(18.0%)	(14.4%)	(28.4%)	(35.7%)	(30.4%)
ASEAN + 3 trade with the EU	156.1	255.8	309.7	509.8	785.5
ASEAN + 3 trade surplus	13.1	14.6	74.3	120.8	161.3
(as a percentage of trade with the EU)	(8.4%)	(5.7%)	(24.0%)	(23.7%)	(20.5%)

Note:

1 Trade values are exports + imports (DOT, IMF).

reasons why launching the CJK arrangement seems to be preferable. First, because ASEAN includes a substantially diverse group of economies in terms of size and development, prioritizing exchange rate stability might not be advisable for certain member countries. This concern could be overlooked in favor of maintaining exchange rate stability if the prospect of serious competitive devaluation was threatening; however, the utility of an ASEAN-only AMU does not seem to be significant. Second, if an arrangement that involved all ASEAN + 3 members were a secondary goal, then the internal coordination of CJK could not be avoided. In particular, the issue of what kind of anchor (individual or collective) to offer the pan-ASEAN + 3 exchange rate arrangement would emerge.

Solely based on economic similarities, it might be more realistic for CJK to initiate an arrangement. Indeed, there are some supporting results for a more segmented approach in the East Asian OCA literature. Some studies have suggested that currency cooperation arrangements are more suitable for segmented groups of East Asian countries. For example, Bayoumi *et al.* (2000) and Wyplosz (2002) both find that different groups of East Asian countries present different levels of OCA readiness. More recently, Han and Lee (2010) draw a similar conclusion regarding how wide an optimal OCA grouping should be. CJK share some characteristics, such as greater economic proximity and rapidly growing intra-regional trade. However, compared with Europe, the nature of intra-regional trade is different in that it is still undergirded by exports to the US.

Finally, the presented analysis has demonstrated that it is straightforward to understand the scarcity of support for an ASEAN + 3 currency cooperation project. However, some economic rationale seems to exist and thus this project is not likely to be abandoned completely, despite neglect by regional countries and complicating developments such as the rapid rise of China and its implication on the leadership of the project. Many East Asian economies adopted an exchange rate regime of implicitly pegging to the US dollar until the late 1990s, when many were forced to change their policies as a consequence of the 1997 Asian crisis. While it lasted, an implicitly coordinated or uncoordinated regional dollar peg served many countries well for their export-oriented growth policies.[19] Indeed, since early 2000, ASEAN + 3 has maintained a substantial trade surplus with the rest of the world including the US and EU. Hence, adopting a currency cooperation regime that stabilizes intra-regional exchange rates, but allows flexibility against the US dollar and euro, might be an acceptable policy option. In summary, one cannot discount the likelihood of some form of East Asian currency cooperation in the future, although many serious hurdles need to be overcome first.

Notes

1 For historical accounts, see Willett, Permpoon, and Srisorn (2010), Mourlon-Druol (2011), and Truman (2011).
2 This includes the ten ASEAN member countries (Brunei, Cambodia, Indonesia, Laos, Malaysia, Myanmar, the Philippines, Singapore, Thailand, and Vietnam) and China, Japan, and Korea.

3 Numerous studies have offered similar observations. For views based on general historical and institutional developments, see Wyplosz (2002), Mundell (2003), Ruffini (2006),
Eichengreen (2007), Nicolas (2011), and Willett, Permpoon, and Srisorn (2010). For
an OCA criteria view, see Bayoumi, Eichengreen, and Mauro (2000), Ngiam and Yuen
(2001), Wyplosz (2002), Zhang, Sato, and McAleer (2004), Chow and Kim (2003), Rhee
(2004), Ahn, Kim and Chang (2006), and Han and Lee (2010).

4 See Willett, Permpoon, and Srisorn (2010) for a critical review of endogenous OCA
views in this context.

5 There is evidence that the nature of intra-industry trades, which have contributed significantly to intra-regional trade, is different in Europe compared with East Asia. It is more
horizontal based on differentiated products in the former, whereas it is vertical seeking
efficiency gains through, for example, lower wage costs in the latter (Kimura, Takahashi,
and Hayakawa 2007).

6 Euro-11 includes all the eight inaugural ERM members plus Finland, Portugal, and
Spain.

7 The "tunnel" refers to the exchange rate band that existed during the Smithsonian
Agreement period of 1971–3. For more discussion, see Eichengreen (2008a).

8 See Fischer (2001) for a definitive explanation of this the so-called "bipolar view". Also
see Willett (2007) for a somewhat different view.

9 See Wyplosz (2002) for a general discussion of the viability of a soft peg for East Asia.
For specific comparisons of different peg systems including the AMU, see Ogawa and
Shimizu (2007).

10 Even in Europe, control over monetary policy autonomy had been guarded closely
throughout periods of exchange rate cooperation. The first country to give up monetary policy independency, the Netherlands, did so in 1982, and "in a large number of
countries, monetary policy was not only seen as a macroeconomic tool, but also as an
instrument to support fiscal policy through the financing of budget deficits, and even to
conduct industrial policies" (Wyplosz 2002, p. 137).

11 The policy implications would be similar to an alternative approach to the common basket that targets the AMU in the form of each country using individual baskets based
on their respective trade structures, as proposed by Park and Wyplosz (2008). "If these
are similar across the region, the region's economies are in effect adopting the same
basket. ... By leaving each country free both to define its own basket and to decide on
the degree of stabilization vis-à-vis the basket, this approach greatly simplifies political issues while achieving similar economic goals. It also removes the $N − 1$ problem
once non-regional currencies are included in individual baskets" (ADB 2010, p. 54).
While this might work for loose and non-binding exchange rate cooperation among
ASEAN + 3, once tighter cooperation with an eye towards currency union becomes the
goal, the Nth country problem will resurface.

12 In addition, Wyplosz (2002) points out two crucial differences between the CMI and
EMS arrangements. "First, the exchange rate mechanism (ERM) of EMS provided for
automatic and unlimited support of bilateral pegs." Thus, conveying to the market that
speculative attacks on any one currency "is bound to face strong official resistance" from
the strong currency central bank with an unlimited supply of its currency (pp. 143–4).
Nicolas (2011) summarizes three weaknesses. "Firstly, the CMIM is still faced with
a leadership issue, with Japan and China competing for leadership without necessarily wanting to openly overtake the responsibility. ... A second problem pertains to the
strength of the participating countries' commitment to the cooperative mechanism. ... A
third issue relates to the persistent problem of size: for example, in the absence of IMF
support, Indonesia could merely access 20 percent of its total, namely US$2.28 billion,
which is far from what was required in 1997 for instance." (pp. 29–30).

13 Additional estimates range from a one s.d. increase in exchange rate volatility reducing bilateral trade by 13 percent (Rose 2000) to raising trade by 2 percent (Dell'Ariccia

1998; Tenreyro 2007). Some econometric flaws in Rose's (2000) method were pointed out and addressed in Glick and Rose (2002). For a detailed discussion of these methodological issues, see Baldwin and Taglioni (2008).

14 However, Micco, Ernesto, and Guillermo (2003) and Baldwin and Taglioni (2008) attribute earlier estimates of large positive effects to be disproportionately influenced by developments in very small Caribbean countries that were in a currency union arrangement.

15 See Clark, Tamirisa, and Wei (2004) for a similar study by the IMF.

16 Parts 2 and 3 borrow heavily from Huh (2012).

17 The inaugural eight countries in the ERM were Belgium, Denmark, France, Germany, Ireland, and Italy, Luxembourg, and the Netherlands.

18 "Undoubtedly, the Asian experience so far suggests the absence of political will towards the kind of cooperation that Europe has nurtured over several decades of increasing regional integration. One possibility is that only a subgroup of Asian countries undertake to deepen cooperation. Such a subgroup would probably not include initially the three largest economies. . . . This again would be the opposite of the European experience" (ADB 2010).

19 See Huh and Kasa (2001) for an example of such an interpretation of the Asian exchange rate arrangement before the 1997 Asian crisis.

References

Ahn, C., Kim, H., and Chang, D. (2006) "Is East Asia fit for an optimum currency area? An assessment of the economic feasibility of a higher degree of monetary cooperation in East Asia," *The Developing Economies*, 44: 288–305.

Andrews, D. (1994) "Capital mobility and monetary adjustment in Western Europe, 1973–1991," *Policy Science*, 27: 425–45.

Asian Development Bank (ADB) (2010) "Exchange rate cooperation: Is East Asia ready?" *Asia Economic Monitor December 2010*, pp. 46–58.

Association of Southeast Asian Nations (ASEAN) (2012), *Asean Community in Figures 2011*, http://www.asean.org/documents/ASEAN%20community%20in%20figures.pdf.

Baldwin, R. and Taglioni, D. (2008) "The Rose effect: the euro's impact on aggregate trade flows," Chapter 2, Study on the Impact of the Euro on Trade and Foreign Direct Investment, Economic Paper 321, Economic and Financial Affairs, European Commission.

Baldwin, R. and Wyplosz, C. (2009) *The Economics of European Integration*, 3rd ed., McGraw-Hill, Higher Education.

Bayoumi, T., Eichengreen, B., and Mauro, P. (2000) "Is Asia an optimum currency area? Can it become one? Regional, global and historical perspectives on Asian monetary relations," in *Exchange Rate Policies in Emerging Asian Countries*, Stefan Collignon, Jean Pisani-Ferry, and Yung Chul Park (eds), London: Routledge.

Chow, H. and Kim, Y. (2003) "A common currency peg in East Asia? Perspectives from Western Europe," *Journal of Macroeconomics*, 5: 331–50.

Clark, P., Tamirisa, N., and Wei, S. (2004) "A new look at exchange rate volatility and trade flows – some new evidence," Occasional Paper 235, IMF.

De Grauwe, P. (2005) *Economics of Monetary Union*, 6th ed., Oxford: Oxford University Press.

Dell'Arricia G. (1998) "Exchange rate fluctuations and trade flows: Evidence from the European Union," IMF Working Paper WP98/107.

Eichengreen, B. (2007) "Fostering monetary and exchange rate cooperation in East Asia," mimeo, Berkeley, CA: University of California.

Eichengreen, B. (2008a) *Globalizing Capital: A History of the International Monetary System*, 2nd ed., Princeton, NJ: Princeton University Press.

Eichengreen, B. (2008b) "The real exchange rate and economic growth," Working Paper No. 4 Commission on Growth and Development, The World Bank.

Fischer, S. (2001) "Exchange rate regimes: Is the bipolar view correct?," *Journal of Economic Perspectives*, 15: 3–24.

Glick, R. and Rose, A. (2002) "Does a currency union affect trade? The time series evidence," *European Economic Review*, 46: 1125–51.

Han, K. and Lee, Y. (2010) "East Asian monetary integration and the composite index of OCA criteria," *Korea and the World Economy*, 11: 297–339.

Huh, C. (2012) "Exchange rate cooperation in ASEAN + 3: Implications from comparison of trade patterns of East Asia and ERM countries," mimeo, http://www.akes.or.kr/eng/papers(2012)/18.full.pdf.

Huh, C. and Kasa, K. (2001) "Dynamic model of export competition, policy coordination, and simultaneous currency collapse," *Review of International Economics*, 9: 68–80.

Kimura, F., Takahashi, Y., and Hayakawa, K. (2007) "Fragmentation and parts and components trade: Comparison between East Asia and Europe," *North American Journal of Economics and Finance*, 18: 23–40.

Micco, A., Ernesto, S., and Guillermo, O. (2003) "The currency union effect on trade: Early evidence from EMU," *Economic Policy*, 37: 315–56.

Mori, J., Kinukawa, N., Nukaya, H., and Hashimoto, M. (2002) "Integration of the East Asian economies and a step by step approach towards a currency basket regime," IIMA Research Report no. 2, Institute for International Monetary Affairs.

Mourlon-Druol, E. (2011) "The Euro crisis: A historical perspective," mimeo, London School of Economics and Political Science, http://www2.lse.ac.uk/IDEAS/publications/reports/SU007.aspx.

Mundell, R. (2003), "Prospects for an Asian Currency Area," *Journal of Asian Economics*, 14: 1–10.

Ngiam, K. and Yuen, H. (2001) "Monetary cooperation in East Asia: A way forward," *Singapore Economic Review*, 46: 211–46.

Nicolas, F. (2011) "East Asian regional economic integration: A post-crisis update," Asie.Visions 43, Center for Asian Studies, French Institute of International Relations (Ifri).

Ogawa, E. and Ito, T. (2002) "On the desirability of a regional basket currency arrangement," *Journal of Japan and International Economies*, 16: 317–34.

Ogawa, E. and Kawasaki, K. (2006) "Adopting a common currency basket arrangement into the 'ASEAN + 3'," RIETI Discussion Paper 06–E–028.

Ogawa, E. and Shimizu, J. (2006) "AMU deviation indicator for coordinated exchange rate policies in East Asia and its relation with effective exchange rates," RIETI Discussion Paper 06–E–002.

Ogawa, E. and Shimizu, J. (2007) "Progress toward a common currency basket system in East Asia," RIETI Discussion Paper 07-E-002.

Park, Y. and Wyplosz, C. (2008) "Exchange rate cooperation in East Asia: A European view and a simple solution," mimeo, www.nomurafoundation.or.jp/data/20081111-12_C_Wyplosz-Y-C_Park.pdf

Rajan, R. S. (2002) "Exchange rate policy options for post-crisis Southeast Asia: Is there a case for currency baskets?" *The World Economy*, 25: 137–63.

Research Institute of Economy, Trade and Industry (RIETI) (2012) "AMU and AMU Deviation Indicators," http://www.rieti.go.jp/users/amu/en/.

Rhee, Y. (2004) "East Asian monetary integration destined to fail?" *Social Science Japan Journal*, 7: 83–102.

Rose, A. (2000) "One money, one market: Estimating the effect of common currencies on trade," *Economic Policy*, 30: 9–45.

Ruffini, P.-B. (2006) "Regional integration in East Asia: Which lessons to draw from the European experience?" Paper presented at the Asia–Pacific Economic Association Conference, University of Washington, Seattle, USA, July 29–30.

Tanzi, V. (2004) "The stability and growth pact: Its role and future," *Cato Journal*, 24: 57–69.

Tenreyro, S. (2007) "On the trade impact of nominal exchange rate volatility," *Journal of Development Economics*, 82: 485–508.

Truman, E. (2011) "The future of the euro area," Speeches and Papers, Peterson Institute for International Economics, http://www.iie.com/publications/papers/print.cfm?researchid=1846&doc=pub.

Willett, T. (2007) "Why the middle is unstable: The political economy of exchange rate regimes and currency crises," *The World Economy*, 30: 709–32.

Willett, T., Permpoon, O., and Srisorn, L. (2010) "Asian monetary cooperation: Perspectives from the optimum currency area analysis," *Singapore Economic Review*, 55: 103–24.

Williamson, J. (1999) "The case for a common basket peg for East Asian currencies," in S. Collignon, J. Pisani-Perry, and Y. Park (eds), *Exchange Rate Policies in Emerging Asian Countries*, London and New York: Routledge.

Williamson, J. (2005) "A currency basket for East Asia, not just China," Policy Briefs, PB05, Institute for International Economics.

Wyplosz, C. (2002) "A monetary union in Asia? Some European lessons," in *Future Direction for Monetary Policies in East Asia*, Reserve Bank of Australia: 124–55.

Wyplosz, C. (2010) "An Asian monetary unit?," Paper prepared for the International Monetary Advisory Group of the Asian, aric.adb.org/grs/papers/Wyplosz.pdf.

Zhang, Z., Sato, K., and McAleer, M. (2004) "Is a monetary union feasible for East Asia?," *Applied Economics*, 36: 1031–43.

Part II
Tourism

6 Events and networking in tourism marketing destinations

The America's Cup case study

Juergen Gnoth, Luisa Andreu and
Rafael Currás-Pérez

Introduction

Attracting and managing major events has grown into an internationally competitive activity for city councils and governments. Events are effective in creating publicity for the destination through media exposure (Goldblatt 2000), investment through new facilities and infrastructure (Sakai 2006), income through tourism (Long and Perdue 1990; Uysal and Gitelson 1994) and boosting industries downstream (Frechtling and Horvath 1999). The event organisers and primary stakeholders (Reid and Arcodia 2002) thereby offer local tourism operators long-term opportunities to consolidate the destination brand as well as to increase revenues for themselves and the destination in the short term, through integrated marketing initiatives. In return, the secondary stakeholders who provide for tourists and facilitate the visit to the event need to provide a match between the event's theme and aspirations, and the destination's long-term strategic goals that stem from holding events.

Little is known about how operators rise to the challenge of tackling opportunities of value creation as a result, and in support, of events. In this chapter we analyse how the celebration of the America's Cup yachting event in two tourism destinations, Auckland (New Zealand) and Valencia (Spain) provided benefits to tourist operators. The research question is, therefore, how do tourism operations make use of the opportunities offered by events, in this case, the America's Cup yachting spectacle, a race that has been held every four years since 1871?

In order to answer the research question, we first undertake a literature review of event tourism and networking in tourism destinations. Second, accounting for the importance of networking behaviour in tourism events based on previous research literature, we offer research propositions that are analysed by using the America's Cup as a case study. Third, the case study is analysed by means of both qualitative and quantitative approaches. The fourth part highlights the main issues again in the discussion and conclusion section.

Literature review

Events in tourism destinations

Events are an important motivation of tourism, and they figure prominently in the development and marketing plans of most destinations (Getz 2008). Many events market themselves to tourists, and that is the beginning of event tourism. Event tourism must be viewed from both demand and supply sides. A consumer perspective refers to an analysis of who travels for events, or can be motivated to attend events while travelling. On the supply side, for destinations, event tourism is the development and marketing of planned events to achieve desired benefits (Getz 2008). This chapter focuses on the supply perspective regarding a planned event for sport competitions such as the America's Cup.

Events can have multiple purposes for destinations and their stakeholders. In the short term, they increase local revenues, while in the long term they help develop and market the destination. According to Getz (2005, 2007), the five main economic and tourism roles of events are attraction, animator, catalyst, place marketer and image-maker. These are all destination marketing functions embodying the concepts of 'product' (events as tourist attractions and animators) and 'communications' (events as image-makers or conveyors of messages about destinations and sponsors).

Sport events have played a key role in the growth of the events industry. One reason is that sport events have been seen to be an effective addition to the economic development mix of cities and regions. It has also been argued that sport events can: stimulate planning to improve the amenities and business activities in a city or region, improve a city's or region's position in the market, increase the aggregate number of visitors a city or region attracts, and reduce the seasonality of tourist visits (Chalip and McGuirty 2004). Although these benefits are sometimes intangible and are often realised over time that extends beyond the period of the event itself, the value of an event to the local economy is typically evaluated in terms of its immediate economic impact. It is not uncommon for studies to find that the aggregate economic benefit from an event is positive, even if the event itself was not profitable (see Chalip and McGuirty 2004 for a review). As an illustration, Table 6.1 shows the grand totals of the economic impact of the 32nd America's Cup, Valencia 2007.

Hosting mega sporting events potentially offers both direct and indirect economic benefits as illustrated in Table 6.1. Direct benefits include capital and infrastructure construction related to the event, long-term benefits such as lower transportation costs, thanks to an improved road or rail network, and spending by tourists who travel from out of town to attend the games. Indirect benefits may include advertising effects that showcase the host city or country as a potential tourist destination. But there is also a potential downside, resulting from possible cost overruns, poor land use, inadequate planning and underutilised facilities (Zimbalist 2010). Thus, previous research from Australia (Chalip and Leyns 2002), the United Kingdom (Weed 2003) and the United States (Ahmed *et al.* 1996) demonstrates ineffective cross-leverage of events with their host destinations. These reports are somewhat surprising, given the degree to which event marketers and destination marketers both stand to gain from a robust marketing alliance. There has been substantial discussion in the tourism literature about the need for collaboration among stakeholders in the management and marketing of destinations (Chalip and McGuirty 2004).

Table 6.1 Grand total of the economic impact of the 32nd America's Cup, Valencia 2007

- Holding the America's Cup in Valencia signified an injection of 2,768 million euros (approx NZ$ 5,126m at the time) expenditure over the period 2004–7.
- 74% of the expenditure necessary to hold the event in Valencian waters has been investment in infrastructures (E 2,048m; NZ$ 3,793m).
- The total impact of the America's Cup on the revenue (value added) of the Valencian economy is 2,274m euros while in terms of output, the impact is 5,748m euros (NZ$ 10,644m).
- In employment terms, the America's Cup led to the creation/maintenance of 73,859 jobs from 2004 to 2007.
- The cumulative impacts for the period 2004–7 represent 2.67% of the GDP and 3.29% of the employment of the Valencia Region; an annual growth of about 1% of GDP and employment in the years 2005, 2006 and 2007.
- The agents most directly involved in the competition (participating teams, organising company, visitors, super-yachts and the media) generated 1,150m in output, 599m euros in value added and 14,665 jobs in the Valencian economy.

Source: IVIE (2007).

Table 6.2 Economic impact to the build-up of the Cup for Auckland and New Zealand, 2000–2

Sector	Direct expenditure ($m)	Direct value added ($m)	Total value added ($m)	Direct employment (FTE yrs)	Total employment (FTE yrs)
Auckland					
2001–2	60	21	46	700	1,110
2000–2	71	26	55	830	1,320
New Zealand					
2001–2	62	22	55	710	1,240
2000–2	73	27	65	840	1,470

Source: Market Economics Ltd. (2002).

In New Zealand, the expenditures surrounding the erection of facilities around Auckland and New Zealand as a whole created an economic impact of around (NZ$ 62m) (Market Economics Ltd. 2002), and as shown in Table 6.2.

The sectors which benefited most were the Accommodation and Hospitality, and the Marine sector followed by the Construction and Retail/Wholesale sectors, creating an estimated 710 full-time equivalent jobs. While the above figures relate to the build-up phase to the second regatta, held in New Zealand, the overall estimates for the 2003 regatta were NZ$ 528 million (see Table 6.3).

It should be noted, however, that New Zealand had also won the Cup in 1995, and therefore was able to hold the Cup in Auckland in 1999. The impact analysis for the 1999 America's Cup Challenge reported some NZ$ 495 million. It may be argued that the increase of about NZ$ 33 million in total impact,

Table 6.3 Total economic impact of the 2003 America's Cup Challenge for New Zealand

Total event impacts	New Zealand
Economic impacts ($m)	523.4 NZ$
Expenditure	212.7 NZ$
Direct value added	528.6 NZ$
Total value added	
Employment impacts (FTE yrs)	1,210
Direct employment	2,350
Total employment	

Source: Market Economics Ltd. (2003).

that is, less than 10 per cent, is surprising if not disappointing. Reasons offered range from higher leakage of profits to overseas companies, to a lack of New Zealand's tourism sector and its leaders to learn from past lessons and collaborate more intensively and effectively. Understanding the mechanisms of collaboration better, as well as developing tools by which it can be measured in relation to benefits for participating firms, may therefore help encourage higher value creation.

Collaboration and networking in tourism destinations

The emerging theory of destination management (e.g. Gretzel *et al.* 2006; Wang and Fesenmaier 2007) and branding (e.g. Hankinson 2005) ideally favours cooperative (Beritelli 2011) and network approaches (Wassermann and Faust 1994), all of which pay tribute to the fact that tourism businesses are embedded in functional relationships without which the tourism product could not emerge (e.g. Leiper 1990; Kaspar 1986). The network approach as an analytical tool (Baggio *et al.* 2010; Bramwell and Sharman 1999; Dredge 2006; Pavlovich 2001) highlights structures and opportunities rendering business activities more efficient. As an activity, networking enhances destination capabilities (Haugland *et al.* 2011) and thereby builds the destination's brand (Gnoth 2002; Gnoth and Anwar 2000). Yet, as the cited tourism network literature also highlights, there is a clear difference between theoretical approaches or ideal conditions for efficient destination management, and the realities 'on the ground', as it were, that determine the success of the network.

Comprising mostly SMEs, collaborative networking helps tourism operations to lower their high transaction costs, both in terms of the procurement of resources and in capturing customers (Bieger and Wittmer 2006; Powell 1990). However, destination networks are inherently dynamic, as they evolve in a cyclical fashion (Butler 1980) and are influenced by multiplex geographic, social, institutional and contractual contingencies (Haugland *et al.* 2011). Ontologically, destinations comprise both collaborators as well as competitors that cause these networks to exhibit certain 'messiness' (Dredge 2006: 279). In the first instance, destinations exist only in the eyes of the tourist; it is not until the opportunity is realised, and the destination is marketed actively, that the idea of a destination as a potentially managed network emerges. Hence, when destinations hold events, cooperation amongst stakeholders is necessary, but this does not mean that collaboration occurs, or that it is formally established (Beritelli 2011).

The theory of marketing has evolved from transaction marketing (Williamson 1975) to relationship marketing (Grönroos 2000) and has recently been enhanced further through the concept of co-creation (Ramaswamy 2009). Transaction marketing corresponds to a chaotic market organisation, in which operators fend for themselves targeting individual, discrete transactions, whereas, in relationship marketing, marketers attempt to create lasting ties with their customers. Not only does this lower transaction costs, but it also tends to satisfy the selected markets more effectively. A consequence of this latter approach is that often firms also create more formal ties with their suppliers, resulting in network relationships. This suits particularly SMEs, as networks of strong and loose ties generate efficiencies on the supply side and ease resource procurement. In contrast, hierarchically organised firms are said to have the lowest transaction costs and highest levels of efficiencies because their networks are internalised or consolidated, and under clear ownership and management structures (Powell 1990).

However, the ownership structure of destinations differs from integrated firms such as theme parks. Destinations usually act as virtual firms; in the first instance, heterogeneous producers create the tourist experience independently from each other. Their services may be activated totally by the tourist (Gnoth 2007). In this case, no service provider knows whom the tourist chooses next. The compound tourism-experience would thereby be supplied by chaotically organised firms, with no (or only little) commonality between suppliers other than their geographical proximity or contiguity in supply channels (Leiper 1990). Conversely, if the destination operated like a consolidated firm, it could manage the tourist's experience far more efficiently and effectively as it would control the value propositions of service processes and attributes (e.g. offerings, prices, quality, atmosphere, the fit between brand experiences and event, etc.). Destinations offer opportunities for SMEs and community-based firms. They usually exist somewhere between these extremes of chaotic and consolidated firms. Events offer the opportunity to celebrate and consolidate the destination as a virtual firm, but require tourism operators to 'continuously integrate resources and competencies distributed across a number of different actors' (Haugland *et al.* 2011: 273).

Ideally, the destination brand proposition provides the context for a coherent experience of the place, whereby each service provider independently recreates some or all of the essence of the place. In turn, the tourist integrates these propositions in his/her own experience-creating processes and evaluates them as value-in-context (Vargo and Lusch 2008). The essence of the destination is thus contained in and contextualised through its culture (Geertz 1973) whereby it is expressed, that is, continuously re-invented and rejuvenated in 'the continuity of praxis' (Giddens 1984: 171).

Networking behaviour in tourism events: research propositions

Several inter-related management theories – stakeholder theory and social network theory – have important implications for destinations and event tourism. A number of studies have taken a stakeholder management perspective on festivals and events. Stakeholders are those people or groups who can influence a firm or destination, and are also those impacted by the destination's actions or non-actions (Freeman 1984). Reid and Arcodia (2002) proposed a conceptual model showing how events are linked to primary and secondary stakeholders. 'Primary' stakeholders were defined as those on whom the festival is dependent (namely, employees, volunteers, sponsors, suppliers, spectators, attendees and participants) while 'secondary' stakeholders include the host community, government, essential services, media, tourist organisations and businesses. As an illustration, Figure 6.1 shows the different stakeholders on whom the America's Cup event is dependent.

Social network theory views organisations as a system of objects within society. Objects can be individuals, groups or organisations, and they are joined by a variety of relationships such as friendships, exchange of resources like funds or information, or overlapping memberships (Tichy *et al.* 1979). Network analysts examine the pattern of relationships between members of the relevant network, arguing that one's position in networks influences their opportunities, constraints and behaviours (Wasserman and Galaskiewicz 1994). Within the network, nodes or actors are entities, persons, organisations or events that define the network. Links are the relationships, of any kind, between the actors. Links may be money

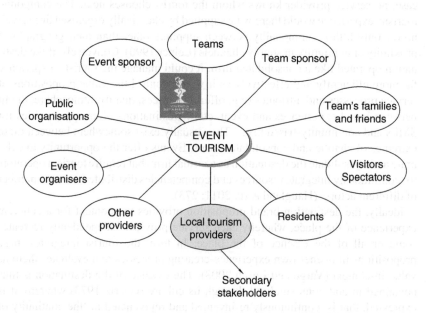

Figure 6.1 Primary and secondary stakeholders in the America's Cup event.

transfers, communications, publications sent to subscribers, friendships and so on (Cobb 1988). Networks are the patterns formed from the combination of all the actors and links within the system.

Taking into account the above-mentioned theories that can be applied in event tourism, our research analyses how stakeholders are joined by a variety of relationships with different actors and the level of involvement of a firm with other partners or actors. In the context of a sport event, links may be between companies within the same industry sector (i.e. collaborations between hotels during the event), within companies of their neighbourhood (i.e. collaboration between different firms), or within the industry association (e.g., association of restaurants). These itemised links to the construct represent the most common types of relationships businesses enter into to create leverage and efficiencies. They are thus reflective of a network-culture, representing mechanisms by which economic capital can be managed and created (Bourdieu 1986; Gnoth 2007).

Unfortunately, destination marketers and event organisers often fail to work together in a manner that enables an event to be cross-leveraged with other attractions at its host destination (Ahmed *et al.* 1996; Chalip and Leyns 2002; Weed 2003). One core reason for this failure seems to be that destination marketers and event organisers have not explored the means to cross-leverage (Chalip and McGuirty 2004). However, it is important to analyse how firms collaborate with other partners during the event and to establish if different groups can be identified based on their collaboration patterns. Consequently, our first research proposition is formulated as follows:

RP1: The level of involvement of a firm with other partners during the event can be used as segmentation criteria to identify firms using different levels of networking (high/low network group).

Transaction oriented tourism firms generally would not care about the generation of a sense of destination in these terms, as this would lie outside of its immediate purpose during the interaction with tourists. Collaboration with other firms in the production of a memorable and cohesive destination experience would therefore go beyond the features of their servicescape (Bitner 1992). There would be no acknowledgment of the event in their service offerings and processes, nor any atmospheric or thematic tie-in with the destination or event. In contrast, collaboratively networking firms would show attitudes and behaviour indicating their belief in the benefits of exchanging information, generating common understandings, and service attributes and processes that reflect the unity and sense of place, that is, a cohesive destination image (Hosany *et al.* 2006) and brand (Hankinson 2005). In the context of event tourism, we suggest that collaboratively networking firms would show stronger positive beliefs in networking than transaction-oriented firms. Similarly, collaboratively networking firms would show a behaviour indicating higher industry collaboration. Consequently, a set of propositions has been formulated as follows:

RP2: The different levels of networking behaviour by companies can be explained by their beliefs in networking. In other words, it is expected that those companies with higher networking behaviour also have stronger positive beliefs in network-ing in tourism.

RP3: The different levels of networking behaviour by the companies can be explained by their industry collaboration. In other words, it is expected that those companies with higher networking behaviour have a stronger industry orientation.

Following Fishbein and Ajzen's (1975) behavioural model of intention forma-tion, we argue that if operators have a positive attitude towards collaboration, they will also be committed to act upon it. This collaboration creates opportunities for the exchange of information and other resources by which familiarity and, fol-lowing Giddens (1984) and Swidler (2001), from which we deduce that a sense of identity is generated that is anchored in the praxis of the place (i.e. Auckland, New Zealand and Valencia, Spain). This sense of place is further enhanced by the firm linking its value propositions directly to the event, by developing a dedicated marketing plan, collaborative activities, and products. Such collaborative and tar-geted marketing activity is proposed to lead to higher satisfaction with staging the event. The literature motivates the following propositions:

RP4: A positive belief in networking is related to industry collaboration. In other words, higher positive belief in networking is related to higher industry collaboration.

In order to measure the overall impact networking may have on operators' success, the following proposition was developed:

RP5: The more tourism operators collaborate, the more satisfied they are with the event financially, in terms of exposure to the market and overall.

Case study: the America's Cup in tourism destinations

Case study context and objectives

Description of the America's Cup

The America's Cup is one of the longest-running sporting events in the world, and its media coverage is comparable to that of the Olympics. It is a competition deter-mined by precision, technological development and strategy; a historic milestone in the professional careers of the competitors; and a tremendous source of prestige for champions and challengers alike.

The international sailing competition of the America's Cup took this name when, in the year 1851, an American schooner beat the best British boats and won the 100 Guineas Cup of the New York Yacht Club. Since then the chal-lenge has been repeated on 32 occasions. The New York Yacht Club acted as defender for many years, winning all the encounters until the year 1983. The vic-tory of the Swiss team, Alinghi, in New Zealand in the year 2003, brought the America's Cup to Europe for the first time, since the winning team has the right to organise the following competition and to defend the title against the different challengers.

Switzerland is a landlocked country, and, in facing the impossibility of competing in a lake in the Alpine country, a process of selection was called for, to which around 70 candidates presented themselves. After passing the different phases, the city of Valencia was finally chosen as the venue for celebrating the 32nd America's Cup. Hosting the America's Cup consolidated Valencia's status as a city open to the Mediterranean Sea, with infrastructures capable of holding an event on such a grand scale.

Objectives of the case study

The specific research objectives to be analysed in the case study with regard to the America's Cup are as follows:

1 To analyse the level of collaboration and networking of different stakeholders in the America's Cup event.
2 To analyse the profile of firms with high propensity to cooperate with other firms during the America's Cup. Specifically, their actual networking behaviour (considering the number of associations that they are involved with), their intention to maintain the relationships not only during the event, but in the future, and their adoption of cooperative initiatives during the event.
3 To analyse how different levels of networking behaviour are related to beliefs and attitudes towards networking and industry collaboration.
4 To measure the relationship between beliefs in networking and industry collaboration.
5 To evaluate the perceived satisfaction of firms with the America's Cup.

The first and second objective will help to analyse the first research proposition. The third objective is related to the second and third research proposition. The fourth and fifth objectives are related to the fourth and fifth research propositions, respectively. In order to analyse the research objectives, we explain the case study methodology in the following section.

Case study methodology

The present research was executed in two stages, a qualitative one and a quantitative one. It found a base on which to build its understanding of collaboration at destinations in a number of case studies (e.g. Bramwell and Sharman 1999; Dredge 2006; Gangsjo 2003; Pavlovich 2001). As a first step, the methodology involved an exploratory qualitative step of convergent interviewing (Dick 1990; Jepsen and Rodwell 2008). According to Dick (1990) this involves procedures for designing, conducting and analysing in-depth interviews that establish an understanding of phenomena with the purpose of refining questions for further interviews. Once the set of questions produces the required understanding in both interviewees and researcher, and leads to redundancy in the information obtained, the research can enter the phase of scale development. During that phase, researchers can gain an idea of the size of phenomena. This will be explained in the second part of this section.

Qualitative approach

Events are often subsidised by government departments and public tax funds signalling a communal effort which, by rising to the occasion, creates benefits through synergies otherwise not obtainable. Given the dearth of knowledge about targeted networking in tourism networks, we sought to understand how the potential network of secondary event providers actually develops. In other words, how do tourism operators generate extra revenue over and above the income brought into the destination by the additional tourists?

The researcher applied theoretical sampling and selected 12 tourism-related businesses in a 1.5 kilometre radius around Auckland's Viaduct Harbour where, apart from the races themselves, most of the 2003 America's Cup regatta activities took place. This area is approximately the city's CBD (central business district), the largest in the country, and it contains high-rise office buildings, retail shopping malls, hotels, restaurants and entertainment facilities, as well as plenty of residential accommodation. It is also a traffic hub, with several ferry and land transport terminals serving locals and international tourists, most of whom use Auckland and its airport as a gateway to New Zealand.

Following standard tourism theory that describes the destination tourism system (attractions, accommodation, transport and hospitality; Kaspar 1986; Leiper 1990; Gnoth 2002) the sample comprised attractions (3), accommodation (2), hospitality (3) and tour providers (2), as well as retailers selling arts and crafts, and souvenirs (2). The selection was based on shop-front impressions signalling the target of international tourists, which was then later confirmed through more intensive and detailed study. Similar to a multi-sited case study (Marcus 1998), the researcher observed activities, lived at the accommodation, ate at the restaurants and visited the shops international tourists frequent. While on these premises, the researcher also conducted *ethnography of marketing* research (Arnould and Wallendorf 1994) involving the observation of staff and including formal and informal interviews (taking notes and some recordings) over five consecutive days at the height of the races in 2003. The formal study involved studying, price lists, brochures and other marketing communications, web-pages and the foot traffic to gain an idea of the ratio of tourists versus locals frequenting these places. Observations focused on service delivery to customers, overhearing the general conversations and specific sales talk, and noting the presence or absence of mentioning the regatta. The semi-structured interviews then established business and supplier profiles, information on the types of markets these firms target and serve, product mixes, and the substance of marketing plans, before the researcher moved to the focal concern: collaborative networking. Interviewees were mostly managers, but also the staff as they rotated through the shifts across the five days. They included chefs, bar personnel, receptionists, shop assistants, cleaners and bus drivers.

After five days of intensive study, collating data and analysing the material every night at the hotel, the researcher was consistently disappointed. There were no themes of collaboration, and in the bars and restaurants right by the regatta boat-sheds, there were few or no America's Cup promotions that would link the service (operation) to the event. All firms under observation primarily catered for international tourists (apart from the restaurants, which had a noticeable mixture of locals and tourists); however, event tourists were treated as any international tourists and served as usual. These could frequently be identified by their sturdy weather gear, as worn aboard boats, or by Cup mementoes worn on clothing. Although the opportunities existed for special products and promotions, these interviews revealed that none of the businesses had developed a special marketing plan to benefit from the event, other than through the extra foot traffic ending up in an increase of sales.

All in all, there was very little talk about collaboration other than referrals. Only one accommodation provider collaborated with a tour operator targeting event visitors, and another one had decorated the hotel lobby with some sailing paraphernalia; none of the other selected firms revealed any networking activity other than a slight increase in contact with suppliers. One of the accommodation providers also allowed the restaurant and bar next door to let its tables and chairs flood the hotel's entrance area to cater for its customers, many of whom had come for the event and stayed at the hotel.

Discussing with managers and staff who they work with, where they receive their marketing intelligence from and how they made decisions appertaining to their product and price policy, most talked about their relationships with immediate business neighbours and suppliers, and some mentioned industry organisations, including the regional tourism organisation. Asked whether they thought networking was important, they all maintained that it was very important but, when probed, revealed that most of it occurred casually at trade events, through industry communications, or chats with competitors and colleagues at suppliers' premises. Discussion revealed that industry organisations were either perceived to be potential and/or important sources and some operators offered some criticism as to the amount of marketing support these organisations were providing.

The results thus appeared to indicate that the potential networking opportunities were not taken up and New Zealand's taxpayers, together with the event organisers, were creating totally underutilised opportunities. This in itself would be an important finding, as it implicates industry and tourism organisations and their failure to mobilise and train their constituency. Their role appeared to be even more important as about half of the managers (and some staff) who were interviewed had university degrees, indicating a high level of education; however, only a few had business and marketing skills. Due to these findings and their potential importance for future event organisation and funding decisions by public rather than corporate sponsors, it was decided to add a quantitative research effort in order to be able to generalise these results. Such quantitative research is important, as the literature indicates that those who network and communicate with a variety of sources are both more adaptable (Luhmann 1995) and more innovative

(Granovetter 1973; Hjalager 2002). Such skills add to the resilience of both firms and business sectors and raise the capabilities of the destination and its brand (Haugland *et al.* 2011).

Quantitative research

Based on the literature review, and using the previously reported convergent interviews for substance, multi-scale items were developed (Churchill 1979) that became part of a structured questionnaire as detailed in the results. The data gathered were entered and analysed with a statistical software package (SPSS 19.0).

Four years after the Auckland event, the America's Cup regatta was taking place in Valencia, Spain. Valencia, though smaller, is similar to Auckland as an event venue, not only because it is by the sea and has an established and substantive tourism sector, but also because the lay-out of the harbour, its proximity to hotels, hospitality, and entertainment, are somewhat similar. In contrast to Auckland however, Valencia is far closer to many population centres. The original researcher found that collaborators and the instruments developed were replicated in Spanish and applied in Valencia as well. The reasoning behind this, and the consequences this has for the interpretation of the results, will be discussed later. First we describe the sampling and instrument development for Auckland, before the results are presented together with those of Valencia.

DATA COLLECTION IN AUCKLAND AND VALENCIA

Auckland dataset.   The research applied a stratified random sampling technique. The targets of the Auckland research effort were the tourism businesses in and around the Viaduct Harbour Basin in the Central Business District of down-town Auckland, New Zealand. Despite the ubiquitous use of multi-sited business case studies reported on previously, little is known about issues surrounding networking and productivity in tourism. This study therefore uses a proficient means of raising the major reasons impacting productivity through a mixed method approach (Creswell 2003), by adding quantitative research to gain further evidence on previous findings. Auckland is New Zealand's largest city, with approximately 1.2 million people. Counting advertisements in the yellow (business) pages, the national telephone company listed some 1,800 tourism companies in Auckland, of which 400 businesses operated in the CBD (as later confirmed by the company which categorises its business customers according to sectors). The categories from which the 400 addresses were selected included accommodation, transport and attraction providers (e.g. bungee jumping, diving, sailing), as well as tourism retail shops (including souvenir shops and galleries), and entertainment and hospitality providers, such as cafes and restaurants.

These addresses were entered into a spreadsheet and 100 were randomly chosen, following the aims similar to a previous study that probed network activities during the 1999 America's Cup (Gnoth and Anwar 2000). A short survey with an accompanying letter was then sent to these businesses six months after the final race had taken place. After one week, reminders were sent out. After three weeks, 21 questionnaires had been returned, some not fully completed, 2 marked as 'not applicable' and one 'sorry, we're out of business'. The other non-returns were followed up by a telephone call to firms that had not replied. The usual reason for non-response was that they were too busy. Consequently, telephone interviews for those businesses that had not replied were arranged and conducted. Only one firm declined. While the covering letter to the questionnaire (as well as the phone interview) asked for the manager or CEO to respond, it was frequently the duty manager or administrative manager that did so. The final Auckland sample was 89.

Valencia dataset. The last sailing regatta of the 32nd America's Cup was in July 2007. From October 2007 to June 2008, 320 companies were contacted, using the following procedure. First, we sent the questionnaire by email to companies within the city of Valencia that belong to the tourist sector. Second, due to a low response, we asked for collaboration from tourism institutions (associations of hotels and associations of restaurants). They emailed the questionnaire to their own members. Third, we phoned hotels and restaurants that were near to the harbour. Finally, 68 questionnaires were received (21 per cent response rate), and 66 were considered suitable for analysis.

RESEARCH QUESTIONNAIRE

In order to deal with the above-mentioned research objectives, and to analyse the research propositions, the research instrument for the quantitative study comprises the following variables: perceived level of involvement between the firm and partners during the event, actual networking behaviour, intention to maintain the relationship after the event, adoption of cooperative initiatives during the event, beliefs in networking, industry collaboration and perceived level of satisfaction with the event.

To measure the *perceived level of involvement between the firm and partners during the event*, we used four items and five-point scales (1 = never; 5 = very often): 'During the America's Cup I networked with (1) my industry association/s, (2) companies within my industry sector, (3) companies in different industry sectors and (4) companies within my neighbourhood.'

To measure *actual networking behaviour* we asked to state the list of associations that firms were involved with. Later on, we sum the number of associations.

To measure the *intention to maintain the relationship after the event* (1 = 'No, we will not maintain'; 2 = 'It's probable that we will maintain'; 3 = 'Yes, we will maintain'), four items were analysed: relationships (1) with industry associations, (2) with companies within the same industry sector, (3) with companies in different industry sectors and (4) companies within my neighbourhood.

To measure the *level of adoption of cooperative initiatives during the event*, we used a five-point scale (1 = no, not at all; 5 = yes, very much) for the following initiatives: strategic alliances with other firms, package deals with other companies, joint promotions, sharing information, referring customers to other business and formal commercial network.

Previous research in tourism networking used the construct *Beliefs in network-ing* to analyse general attitudes and beliefs by tourism organisations towards networking. Initially, we used the nine-item scale proposed by Gnoth (2007) to measure beliefs in networking. However, a principal component analysis with varimax rotation was conducted with the aim of identifying potential factors regarding these general beliefs toward networking. The optimal final solution explained 55.16 per cent of the initial variance. The basic indicators to apply factor analysis were positive: the KMO index (0.811) was higher than 0.63, which is the minimum value recommended for exploratory research, and the Bartlett sphericity test, which was highly significant (0.000). Factor one, explaining 36.87 per cent of the variance refers to positive beliefs in networking. This factor possessed inter-nal consistency (α Cronbach = 0.82). For our measurement instrument, we use the mean of these items to calculate an index. Consequently, to measure *beliefs in networking*, we used a five-point scale (1 = no, not at all; 5 = yes, very much) for the following five items: my business success depends very much on networking, networking helps me to understand my business better, I intend to increase my involvement in tourism networks, I am very much committed to networking, and our tourism network is strong on strategy development and industry collaboration.

To measure *industry orientation*, we used an adaptation of nine items from Gnoth (2007). To identify potential factors regarding the actual orientation toward the industry, we conducted a further principal component analysis with vari-max rotation. The EFA provided a solution of three factors with 65.6 per cent of explained variance. Again, the indicators to apply factor analysis were also positive: KMO index was near 0.7 (0.689), which is considered adequate for exploratory research. The Bartlett sphericity test was also significant. Factor one, explaining the higher percentage of the variance (32.05 per cent) refers to the gen-eral orientation toward networking. This factor was reliable (α Cronbach = 0.76), which permitted us to aggregate the items. So, to measure *industry orientation*, we used a five-point scale (1 = no, not at all; 5 = yes, very much) for the following four items: we often use business advice and information from tourism industry organi-sations, we collaborate with industry organisations regarding upcoming events, we purposely (re)designed our organisational structure in response to the America's Cup (e.g. dedicated marketing manager with special budget), and tourism industry organisations provide us with strategic information on major events.

The *perceived level of satisfaction with the event* was measured using a five-point scale (1 = no, not at all; 5 = yes, very much) for the following items: overall satisfaction, satisfaction in terms of economic benefits, and satisfaction with the awareness and exposure that has been created.

Research findings

Sample characteristics

Of the Auckland sample ($n = 89$), 52 per cent of the companies belonged to the hospitality sector, 20 per cent to the accommodation sector, 12 per cent to the retail sector, 8 per cent to the entertainment and 4 per cent to the transport sector. As for the staff, 60 per cent had 7 or fewer staff, 30 per cent had up to 30 staff, while the last 10 per cent had up to 95 full- and part-time staff. Finally, of the firms, three had been set up specifically for the 31st America's Cup, but only one had been operating for less than one year, 7 per cent for between one and two years, 27 per cent for two to five years, 24 per cent for five to ten years and 37 per cent for more than ten years.

Of the Valencia sample ($n = 66$), 38 per cent of the firms belonged to the accommodation sector, 23 per cent to the event organisation sector, 17 per cent to the hospitality sector, 8 per cent to the entertainment and leisure sector, 6 per cent to the transport sector and 3 per cent to the retail sector. Of the sample, 32 per cent had seven or fewer staff, 27 per cent had up to 30 staff, while the last 41 per cent had more than 30 full- and part-time staff. Of the firms, 8 per cent were aged less than two years old, 30 per cent were aged between two to five years, 20 per cent five to ten years and 42 per cent were more than ten years in operation. In Valencia, just 6 per cent of the business sample (four firms) were created specifically for the celebration of the 32nd America's Cup, in 2007.

Study findings

LEVEL OF INVOLVEMENT OF A FIRM WITH OTHER PARTNERS DURING THE EVENT:
HIGH AND LOW NETWORK GROUP

According to the first research proposition of this study (*RP1*), the level of involvement of a firm with other partners during the event can be used as segmentation criteria to identify firms with different levels of networking (high/low network group). High level of relationships between a firm and other partners during the event (i.e. considering the perceived level of networking with industry associations, within the industry sector, in different industry sectors and within the firm's neighbourhood) means that the firm is active in terms of networking. On the contrary, low levels of relationship between a firm and other partners during the event means that the firm is passive in terms of networking. Under this premise, we conducted a cluster analysis (Punj and Stewart 1983) taking into account the perceived level of involvement during the America's Cup. Thus, we differentiated those firms with higher/lower levels of relationships.

The cluster analysis was performed following a two-step process (hierarchical and non-hierarchical methods) in order to improve results (Hair *et al.* 2005). By means of hierarchical cluster analysis using Ward's method and the Euclidean distance, the agglomeration schedule was obtained. Because the largest increases were observed in going from two clusters to one, the two-cluster solution was selected. The second step uses non-hierarchical techniques (the K-means algorithm) to adjust the results from the hierarchical procedures. Using the initial seed points from the results in the hierarchical cluster, the K-means cluster defined two groups. Information essential to the interpretation and profiling stages is provided in Table 6.4, which shows the final cluster centres. For each cluster, the mean value (centroid) of each of the four items (the perceived level of involvement with four

Table 6.4 Cluster analysis of business depending on the level of relationships during the event

Cluster	X_1	X_2	X_3	X_4
LN ($n = 110$)	2.07	2.09	1.99	2.35
HN ($n = 53$)	2.98	4.30	2.96	4.42
t value	4.30*	12.73*	4.82*	11.34*

Notes:
Total ($n = 155$)
X_1 = Level of cooperation with industry associations.
X_2 = Level of cooperation with companies within the same industry sector.
X_3 = Level of cooperation with companies in different industry sector.
X_4 = Level of cooperation with companies within the same neighbourhood.
LN: Low networked group.
HN: High networked group.
*$p < 0.01$.

different partners) is provided. Similar to the hierarchical method, the four-cluster variables showed differences between the clusters confirming the hierarchical results.

Looking at the final cluster centres, it can be concluded that cluster 1 ($n = 105$) presents lower values than those of cluster 2 ($n = 50$), so it is possible to confirm that the former is characterised by organisations that showed passive behaviour with regard to relationships during the America's Cup event in Auckland and Valencia. In contrast, the latter is characterised by an active behaviour in the generation of relationships with sector associations, companies within its industry sector, companies in different industry sectors, and companies within its neighbourhood. Overall, it was considered appropriate to interpret the first group as 'a Lowly Networked group' (cluster 1, LN) and the second as a 'Highly Networked group' (cluster 2, HN).

To better understand the networking behaviour of both groups, we analysed (1) the actual behaviour (considering the number of associations that they are involved with), (2) the intention to maintain the relationships in the future and (3) the adoption of networking initiatives.

Actual networking behaviour.   Respondents were asked to list the associations or institutions that their companies belong to. Considering the global sample ($n = 155$), 49 businesses (30.1 per cent) did not mention any industry affiliation that they are involved with, 42.8 per cent were affiliated with one or two organisations and 30.3 per cent were affiliated with three or more organisations. However, as expected, it is interesting to highlight the differences between both clusters. Results show that the firms in the HN group are significantly involved in more affiliations (mean value = 1.47) than the companies in the LN group (mean value = 1.29) ($t = 2.71$; $p < 0.05$).

Intention to maintain the relationships.   Firms with higher levels of relationships during the event not only network for the event, but they also intend to maintain

Table 6.5 Differences between clusters depending on the intention to maintain the relationships

	LN (n = 105)			HN (n = 50)			
Type of relation	N	P	Y	N	P	Y	$\chi 2$
Industry associations	17%	26%	57%	2%	7%	81%	17.60*
Companies within the same industry sector	16%	34%	49%	4%	14%	82%	13.80*
Companies in different industry sector	39%	31%	28%	19%	30%	48%	7.54*
Companies within the same neighbourhood	27%	27%	44%	2%	22%	76%	17.03*

Notes: N, no relationship is maintained; P, probably will keep the relationship; Y, maintains the relationship.
* $p < 0.01$.

Table 6.6 Differences between clusters depending on the level of cooperation initiatives undertaken

	LN (n = 105)	HN (n = 50)	
	m	m	t
Strategic alliances with other firms	1.90	2.58	2.56*
Package deals with other companies	1.93	2.71	3.10**
Joint promotions	1.65	2.51	3.84**
Sharing information	2.09	3.15	4.36**
Referring customers to other business	2.53	3.59	3.98**
Formal commercial network	1.77	1.95	0.76

Notes: Five-point scale with (1 = Not at all, 5, Very much) * = <0.05; ** = <0.01.
m = mean value.

the relationship in the future, even after the conclusion of the event. As expected, cross tabulation results (see Table 6.5) show that the businesses in the HN group maintain their relationships with other companies for a longer term than in the LN group, particularly in their dealings with companies in the same sector and with industry associations.

Adoption of cooperative initiatives during the event. In order to make tangible the networking behaviour, firms with higher levels of relationships during the event are expected to undertake more cooperative initiatives during the event. To test the differences between HN and LN groups in terms of the adoption of cooperative initiatives, we analyse the mean values of each group with a series of *t*-tests. As shown in Table 6.6, there are significant differences between both groups. Those businesses in the high networking group used significantly more intensively all the analysed initiatives, except the creation of a formal commercial network.

In order for an event and its host destination to be brought together into a joint package, the event and the host destination's attractions need to be appropriately bundled (Chalip and McGuirty 2004). Interestingly, research findings reveal that the practice of bundling (package deals with other companies) is significantly higher for the HN group than the LN group. However, in both groups, there is a need to work together in a manner that enables an event to be cross-leveraged with other attractions.

To sum up, our research shows that companies with more relationships and with different partners (industry associations, within the industry sector, in different sectors or within the neighbourhood) are active companies in terms of networking and not only in terms of the intensity of *perceived* networking with those partners. Findings show that the HN group in comparison to the LN group: (1) are involved with a higher number of industry associations, (2) are planning to maintain the relationship in the future with their partners and (3) are applying cooperative measures during the event. Consequently, the highly consistent networking behaviour of the HN group allows us to confirm that the 'level of involvement of a firm with other partners during the event can be used as segmentation criterion to identify firms with different levels of networking (high/low network group)'.

LEVELS OF NETWORKING BEHAVIOUR AND BELIEFS IN NETWORKING IN TOURISM

Following the second research proposition *(RP2)*, *it is expected that those companies with higher networking behaviour have stronger positive beliefs in networking in tourism.* In order to test *RP2*, we analysed the significant differences between the HN and LN groups with regard to their beliefs in networking. Results show that the firms in the HN group have significantly higher positive beliefs in networking (mean value = 3.67) than the companies in the LN group (mean value = 3.20) ($t = 2.38$; $p < 0.05$).

LEVELS OF NETWORKING BEHAVIOUR AND INDUSTRY COLLABORATION

With regard to the third research proposition *(RP3)*, *it is expected that those companies with higher networking behaviour have a stronger industry orientation.* In order to analyse *RP3*, we analysed the significant differences between the HN and LN groups with regard to the level of industry collaboration. Results show that the firms in the HN group have significantly higher levels of industry collaboration (mean value = 2.69) than the companies in the LN group (mean value = 2.39) ($t = 2.70$; $p < 0.05$).

BELIEFS IN NETWORKING AND INDUSTRY COLLABORATION

In order to analyse the fourth research proposition, we analysed the correlation between the factors positive beliefs in networking (mean value = 3.35; Std Dev = 1.00) and industry collaboration (mean value = 2.51; Std Dev = 0.96). We used the Pearson Correlation. It is interesting to note that positive beliefs in networking are significantly correlated (0.453; $p < 0.05$) with industry collaboration. Therefore, higher positive belief in networking is related to higher industry collaboration.

LEVELS OF NETWORKING BEHAVIOUR AND PERCEIVED SATISFACTION WITH THE EVENT

This research makes the general assumption that those who collaborate and network are more likely to benefit from a major event such as the America's Cup. Indeed, our final research proposition (*RP5*) analysed whether those who collaborated, also showed higher levels of satisfaction with holding the event.

We use the *t*-test of independent samples to analyse whether there were different levels of satisfaction with the event among firms with different levels of business networking (HN and LN segments). As expected (see Table 6.7), the test was significant, with the three indicators of satisfaction, demonstrating that firms with low networking activities reported a lower satisfaction level in comparison to the firms with a high networking level. This finding shows that, despite the low levels of actual cooperation and networking occurring before and during the event, those companies that were actively committed to collaboration strategies are those who are significantly more satisfied with the results obtained after the celebration of the America's Cup, and this is in terms of economic and marketing effectiveness.

Discussion and conclusion

Events in tourism destinations provide opportunities not only to the destination but also to tourist operators. This statement is analysed in this chapter and, specifically, we analyse how tourist operators make use of the opportunities offered by the America's Cup regatta in two destinations: Auckland (New Zealand) and Valencia (Spain).

Drawing from previous studies, this chapter analyses the benefits of sport events in tourism destinations and the need for collaboration among stakeholders in the management and marketing of destinations (Chalip and McGuirty 2004). Taking into account the stakeholder and social network theory that can be applied in event

Table 6.7 Differences between clusters depending on the perceived level of satisfaction with the event

	LN (n = 105)	HN (n = 50)	
	m	m	t
Overall, to what extent did the Cup benefit your business?	3.36	3.92	2.33*
How successful was the Cup financially to you?	3.22	3.82	2.46*
How much exposure did your business get due to the Cup?	2.94	3.54	2.45*

Notes: Five-point scale with (1 = Not at all; 5, Very much) * = <0.05.
m = mean value.

tourism, our research analyses how stakeholders are involved with other partners in the tourist destination, and how different levels of involvement of operators with other partners allows us to segment tourism firms and explain the networking behaviour that is needed to obtain benefits from the event.

Using the level of involvement of a firm with other partners during the America's Cup event as segmentation criteria, our chapter identifies two main stakeholder groups: high versus low networking groups. As analysed in the first research question, in comparison with the low network group, the high network group is characterised by higher actual networking behaviour (i.e. more affiliations to associations or institutions), higher intentions to maintain the relationships even after the conclusion of the event and higher adoption of cooperative initiatives (i.e. strategic alliances with other firms, package deals with other companies, joint promotions, sharing information and referring customers to other business).

With regard to the second and third research propositions, we confirm that those with higher networking behaviour also have stronger positive beliefs in networking in tourism (i.e. a perception of how business success depends on networking) and a stronger industry orientation (i.e. collaboration with industry organisations regarding upcoming events), respectively. Both these beliefs and attitudes towards industry orientation are correlated, supporting the fourth research proposition.

Interestingly, the findings show that the celebration of an event is not perceived as beneficial by all tourism operators. Despite the low levels of actual cooperation and networking occurring before and during the America's Cup event in Auckland and Valencia, those companies that were actively committed to collaboration strategies are those who are significantly more satisfied with the results obtained after the celebration of this event, and this is in terms of economic and marketing effectiveness.

References

Ahmed, Z.U., Krohn, F.B. and Heller, V.L. (1996) 'World University Games – 1993 at Buffalo (New York): Boosting its tourism industry or missing an opportunity. An international marketing perspective', *Journal of Professional Services Marketing*, 14(2): 79–97.

Arnould, E. J. and Wallendorf, M. (1994) 'Market-oriented ethnography: Interpretation building and marketing strategy formulation', *Journal of Marketing Research*, 31: 484–504.

Baggio, R., Scott, N. and Cooper, C. (2010) 'Network science: A review focused on tourism', *Annals of Tourism Research*, 37(3): 802–27.

Beritelli, P. (2011) 'Cooperation among prominent actors in a tourist destination', *Annals of Tourism Research*, 38(2): 607–29.

Bieger, T. and Wittmer, A. (2006) 'Air transport and tourism – perspectives and challenges for destinations, airlines and governments', *Journal of Air Transport Management*, 2(1): 40–6.

Bitner, M.J. (1992) 'Servicescapes: the impact of physical surroundings on customers and employees', *Journal of Marketing*, 56(2): 57–71.

Bourdieu, P. (1986) 'The forms of capital', in Richardson, J.G. and Bourdieu, P. (eds), *Handbook of Theory and Research for the Sociology of Education*. New York: Greenwood Press.

Bramwell, B. and Sharman, A. (1999) 'Collaboration in local tourism policy-making', *Annals of Tourism Research*, 26(2): 392–415.

Butler, R.W. (1980) 'The concept of a tourist area cycle of evolution: implications for the management of resources', *The Canadian Geographer*, 24(2): 5–12.

Chalip, L. and Leyns, A. (2002) 'Local business leveraging of a sport event: Managing an event for economic benefit', *Journal of Sport Management*, 16(2): 132–58.

Chalip, L. and McGuirty, J. (2004) 'Bundling sport events with the host destination', *Journal of Sport Tourism*, 9: 267–82.

Churchill, G.A. (1979) 'A paradigm for developing better measures of marketing constructs', *Journal of Marketing Research*, 16(1): 64–73.

Cobb, M. (1988) *Influence and exchange networks among tourism oriented business in four Michigan communities*. Doctoral Dissertation, East Lansing: Michigan State University.

Creswell, J.W. (2003) *Research Design: Qualitative, Quantitative, and Mixed Methods Approaches* (2nd edn). Thousand Oaks: Sage Publications.

Dick, R. (1990) *Convergent Interviewing* (3rd edn). Chapel Hill Q.: Interchange.

Dredge, D. (2006) 'Policy networks and the local organisation of tourism', *Tourism Management*, 27(2): 269–80.

Fishbein, M. and Ajzen, I. (1975) *Belief, Attitude, Intention, and Behavior: An Introduction to Theory and Research*. Reading, MA: Addison-Wesley.

Frechtling, D.C. and Horvath, E. (1999) 'Estimating the multiplier effects of tourism expenditures on a local economy through a regional input–output model', *Journal of Travel Research*, 37: 324–32.

Freeman, R. E. (1984) *Strategic Management: A Stakeholder Approach*. Boston: Pitman.

Gangsjo, Y. (2003) 'Destination networking: co-opetition in peripheral surroundings', *International Journal of Physical Distribution and Logistics Management*, 33(5): 427–48.

Geertz, C. (1973) *The Interpretation of Cultures*. New York: Basic Books.

Getz, D. (2005) *Event Management and Event Tourism* (2nd edn). New York: Cognizant.

Getz, D. (2007) *Event Studies: Theory, Research and Event Tourism* (2nd edn). New York: Cognizant.

Getz, D. (2008) 'Event tourism: Definition, evolution, and research', *Tourism Management*, 29(3): 403–28.

Giddens, A. (1984) *The Constitution of Society. Outline of the Theory of Structuration*. Cambridge: Polity Press.

Gnoth, J. (2002) 'Leveraging export Brands through a tourism destination brand', *Journal of Brand Management*, 9(4–5): 262–80.

Gnoth, J. (2007). 'Destinations as Networking Virtual Service Firms', *International Journal of Excellence in Tourism, Hospitality and Catering*, 1(1): 1–18.

Gnoth, J. (2007) 'Networking amongst tourism operators during the America's Cup, Auckland, New Zealand, 2003: Who profited the most?', in Andreu, L., Gnoth, J. and Kozak, M. (eds), *Proceedings of the 2007 Advances in Tourism Marketing Conference*. Valencia: Publicacions de la Universitat de València.

Gnoth, J. and Anwar, S.A. (2000) 'New Zealand bets on event tourism', *Cornell Hotel and Restaurant Administration Quarterly*, 41(4): 72–83.

Goldblatt, J. (2000) *The International Dictionary of Event Management*. New York: John Wiley & Sons.

Granovetter, M. (1973) 'The strength of weak ties', *American Journal of Sociology*, 78(6): 1360–80.

Gretzel, U., Fesenmaier, D.R., Formica, S. and O'Leary, J.T. (2006) 'Searching for the future: Challenges faced by destination marketing organizations', *Journal of Travel Research*, 45(2):116–26.

Grönroos, C. (2000) 'Creating a relationship dialogue: Communication, interaction and value', *The Marketing Review*, 1(1): 5–14.

Hair, J., Black, W., Babin, B., Anderson, R. and Tatham, R. (2005) *Multivariate Data Analysis*. Englewood Cliffs, NJ: Prentice Hall.

Hankinson, G. (2005) 'Destination brand images: a business tourism perspective', *Journal of Services Marketing*, 19(1): 24–32.

Haugland, S.A., Ness, H., Grønseth, B.-O. and Aarstad, J. (2011) 'Development of tourism destinations: An integrated multilevel perspective', *Annals of Tourism Research*, 38(1): 268–90.

Hjalager, A. M. (2002) 'Repairing innovation defectiveness in tourism', *Tourism Management*, 23(5): 465–74.

Hosany, S., Ekinci, Y. and Uysal, M. (2006) 'Destination image and destination personality: An application of branding theories to tourism places', *Journal of Business Research*, 59(5): 638–42.

IVIE (2007) *Impacto económico de la 32nd America's Cup Valencia 2007*. Valencia: Instituto Valenciano de Investigaciones Económicas, available at: http://www.ivie.es/downloads/ws/2008/ac1/informe_ac2007.pdf

Jepsen, D. M. and Rodwell, J. (2008) 'Convergent interviewing: A diagnostic technique for researchers', *Management Research News*, 31(9): 650–58.

Kaspar, C. (1986) *Die Fremdenverkehrslehre im Grundriss*, Bern.

Leiper, N. (1990) 'Tourist attraction systems', *Annals of Tourism Research*, 17(3): 367–84.

Long, P.T. and Perdue, R.R. (1990) 'The economic impact of rural festivals and special events: Assessing the spatial distribution of expenditures', *Journal of Travel Research*, 28(4): 10–14.

Luhmann, N. (1995) *Social Systems*. Palo Alto: Stanford University Press.

Marcus, G.E. (1998) *Ethnography through Thick and Thin*. Princeton, NJ: Princeton University Press.

Market Economics Ltd. (2002) *The America's Cup Build-up to the 2003 Defence. Economic Impact Assessment*. Wellington: Ministry of Tourism.

Market Economics Ltd. (2003) *The Economic Impact of the 2003 America's Cup Defence*. Wellington, Ministry of Tourism.

Pavlovich, K. (2001) 'The evolution and transformation of a tourism destination network: The Waitomo Caves, New Zealand', *Tourism Management*, 24: 203–16.

Powell, W. W. (1990) 'Neither market nor hierarchy: Network forms of organizations', *Research in Organizational Behavior*, 2: 295–336.

Punj, G. and Stewart, D. (1983) 'Cluster analysis in marketing research: Review and suggestions for application', *Journal of Marketing Research*, 20: 134–48.

Ramaswamy, V. (2009) 'Leading the transformation to co-creation of value', *Strategy & Leadership*, 37(2): 32–7.

Reid, S. and Arcodia, C. (2002) 'Understanding the role of the stakeholder in event management', *Journal of Sport & Tourism*, 7(3): 20–2.

Sakai, M. (2006) 'Public sector investment in tourism infrastructure', in Dwyer, L. and Forsyth, P. (eds), *International Handbook on the Economics of Tourism*. Cheltenham: Edward Elgar, 266–82.

Swidler, A. (2001) 'What anchors cultural practices', in Schatzki, T. R., Cetina, K. and von Savingy, E. (eds), *The Practice Turn in Contemporary Theory*. London: Routledge.

Tichy, N.M., Tushman, M.L. and Fombrun, C. (1979) 'Social network analysis for organizations', *The Academy of Management Review*, 4(4): 507–19.

Uysal, M. and Gitelson, R. (1994) 'Assessment of economic impacts: festivals and special events', *Festival Management & Event Tourism*, 2(1): 3–10.

Vargo, S.L. and Lusch, R.F. (2008) 'From goods to service(s): divergence and convergences of logics', *Industrial Marketing Management*, 37(3): 254–59.

Wang, Y. and Fesenmaier, D.R. (2007) 'Collaborative destination marketing: A case study of Elkhart county, Indiana', *Tourism Management*, 28(3):863–75.

Wasserman, S. and Faust, K. (1994) *Social Network Analysis: Methods and Applications*. Cambridge: Cambridge University Press.

Wasserman, S. and Galaskiewicz, J. (1994) *Advances in Social Network Analysis: Research from the Social and Behavioral Sciences*. Newbury Park, CA: Sage Publications.

Weed, M.E. (2003) 'Why the two won't tango: Explaining the lack of integrated policies for sport and tourism in the UK', *Journal of Sport Management*, 17(3): 258–83.

Williamson, O. (1975) *Markets and Hierarchies: Analysis and Antitrust Implications*. New York: Free Press.

Zimbalist, A. (2010) 'Is it worth it?', *Finance & Development*, 47(1): 8–11.

7 The status of e-tourism in Hokkaido and Austria

A comparative study

Alfred Taudes and Akiko Tanaka

Introduction

Hokkaido and Austria have many similarities. They have a similar land area, are at the same northern latitude and are rich in tourism resources like nature and culture throughout the year. Also, since they have been hosts to the Winter Olympic Games, they have become well known worldwide as winter leisure destinations. However, while Austria is a global player in the tourism industry, the Hokkaido government (2010a) estimates that approximately 85 per cent of its visitors come from Hokkaido, but foreign visitors account for only 6.4 per cent of overnight stays on average. So, why is Hokkaido not as successful as Austria with regards to inbound tourism?

We conjecture that the physical and digital tourism infrastructures of Hokkaido are not yet optimized for international tourism. To investigate this hypothesis, the tourism and e-tourism competence of Hokkaido is compared to that of Austria. At first, the chapter compares the size and structure of Hokkaido's tourism industry with the Austrian sector. Then a quantitative assessment of the touristic internet contents of the two areas is conducted and the official tourism websites of Hokkaido and Austria are compared via qualitative and quantitative approaches. On this basis suggestions are made for improvements to local governments and destination management organizations (DMOs) in Hokkaido that enable a better participation of this region in global tourism growth.

Comparison of the tourism industry in Hokkaido and Austria

Let us at first examine the development of tourism in Hokkaido as shown in Figure 7.1. In fiscal year (FY) 2009, Hokkaido welcomed 46,820 thousand visitors (see Hokkaido Government 2010b). Around 85 per cent of visitors came from Hokkaido, of which approximately 80 per cent made a day trip, but did not stay overnight. Naturally, visitors from outside Hokkaido, including foreign visitors, stayed overnight. After the peak in 2006, however, the number of overnight visitors was shrinking. As shown in Figure 7.2, the foreign market for Hokkaido consists mainly of the Asian neighbouring countries such as Taiwan, Hong Kong,

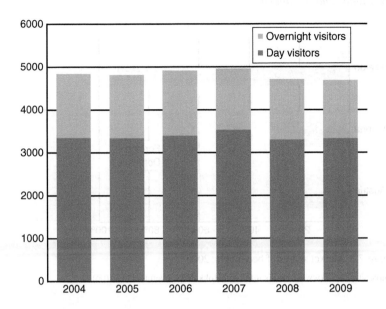

Figure 7.1 Development of day and overnight visitors in Hokkaido (Unit/ten thousand).

Source: Hokkaido Government (2010b).

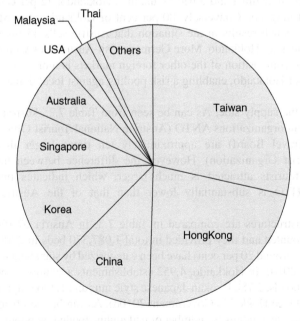

Figure 7.2 Guest mix by bed nights, 2009.

Source: Hokkaido Government (2010c).

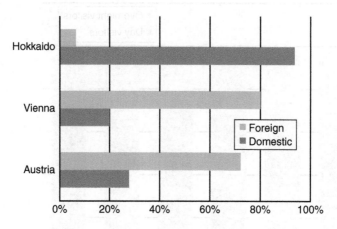

Figure 7.3 Market shares of bed nights, 2009.

Source: TourMIS (www.tourmis.info) and Hokkaido Government (2010c).

China, Korea, Singapore and Australia. Only very few visitors come from Europe or the USA.

As shown in Figure 7.3 and Table 7.1, the situation is completely different in Austria. Austria attracts four times more bed nights than Hokkaido, 72 per cent of which are sold to foreigners. Conversely, 80 per cent of Hokkaido's tourists come from Hokkaido, which results in the situation that Austria sells 45 times more foreign bed nights than Hokkaido. More Germans visit Austria and Vienna than Austrians, and the composition of the other foreign markets is more evenly distributed than those of Hokkaido, enabling a risk pooling against local demand fluctuations.

Let us now turn to the supply side. As can be seen from Table 7.2, Austria's destination management organizations ANTO (Austrian National Tourist Office) and VTB (Vienna Travel Board) are approximately ten times larger than HTO (Hokkaido Tourist Organization). However, the difference between the numbers of foreign tourists attracted is much larger, which indicates that the productivity of HTO is substantially lower than that of the Austrian counterparts.

The two hotel infrastructures are compared in Table 7.3. In Austria 67,166 establishments were counted and they provided in total 1,087,370 beds in 2009. Thereof, 13,600 hotels (around 20 per cent) have been categorized by star standard (see Statistics Austria 2010). In Hokkaido, 4,952 establishments accommodated 327,471 beds and 668 hotels, 2,788 Ryokan-Japanese style inns and 1,496 lodging houses were registered (see Hokkaido Government 2010d). As can be seen from Table 7.3, in Austria the travel intensity (number of bed nights divided by population) is three times as high as that of Hokkaido, indicating a stronger competitive position.

Table 7.1 Top source Markets 2009 in Austria, Vienna and Hokkaido (bed nights)

Austria		Share %	Vienna		Share %	Hokkaido		Share %
Germany	48,856,862	39.3	Germany	2,076,866	21.1	*Japan*	*28,940,000*	*93.6*
Austria	*34,400,000*	*27.7*	*Austria*	*1,970,301*	*20.0*	Taiwan	564,102	1.8
Netherlands	9,451,747	7.6	Italy	560,469	5.7	Hong Kong	436,155	1.4
UK	3,263,866	2.6	USA	507,905	5.2	China	240,184	0.8
Switzerland	3,641,860	2.9	UK	358,630	3.6	Korea	230,804	0.7
Italy	3,015,873	2.4	Spain	308,079	3.1	Singapore	144,577	0.5
Belgium	2,530,232	2.0	France	284,871	2.9	Australia	130,052	0.4
Czech	1,955,027	1.6	Switzerland	284,148	2.9	USA	45,205	0.1

Source: TourMIS (www.tourmis.info) and Hokkaido Government (2010c).

Table 7.2 Comparison of organizational structure (as of 2009)

	ANTO	VTB	HTO
Budget 2009	€ 52 mil.	€ 23.7 mil.	¥691,439,000 ≈ € 5.7 mil.
	75%: Austrian Government	47%: Accommodation Tax	75%: Hokkaido Government
	25%: Austrian Chamber of Commerce	22%: City Government	Others: Memberships, Sponsors
		Others: Vienna Chamber of Commerce, Sponsors	
Employees	230	106	27
Arrivals by foreigners	21,355,439	3,349,738	675,350
Bed nights by foreigners	89,864,164	7,872,526	1,979,431

Source: ANTO, VTB, Bureau of Tourism-Department of Economic Affairs, Hokkaido Government.

Table 7.3 Accommodations comparison, 2009

	Austria	Hokkaido
Population (a)	8,281,295	5,600,000
No. of establishments category	67,166	4,952
	5–4 star 2,400	Hotel 668
	3 star 5,500	Ryokan 2,788
	2–1 star 5,700	Lodging 1,496
Subtotal of hotel category	(13,600)	(4,952)
Other establishments	53,566	–
Total supplied beds (b)	1,087,370	327,471
Total no. of bed nights (c)	124,307,317	30,921,700
Ratio (c/b)	114.3	94.4
Travel intensity (c/a)	15.0	5.5

Source: Statistics Austria, Japan Tourism Agency (2010a).

Let us now turn to the comparison of the transportation systems in Table 7.4. The transportation system in Austria is highly developed and efficient for public convenience. The rail provider in Austria is Austrian Federal Railways (ÖBB), which has an extensive countrywide network. Compared to Austria, Hokkaido has a less organized traffic network. The railway is fairly developed and is a popular mode of travel, but many cities are still accessible only by roads and the Austrian track covers 2.5 times more than that in Hokkaido.

Table 7.4 Comparison of transport infrastructure between Austria and Hokkaido

	Austria	*Hokkaido*
Area	83,859 km^2	78,000 km^2
No. of airports	6	13
Railway provider	ÖBB	JR Hokkaido
Area of service	6,600 km	2,500 km
Bus providers	Postbus: countrywide operation	Chuo Bus, JR Bus, and many locals: urban and local operators
Network system	Integrated	Not integrated

Source: Wikipedia (2010), ÖBB-Postbus (2010), Japan Railways Hokkaido (2010) and Hokkaido Chuo Bus (2010).

Table 7.5 Turnover by Japanese leading travel agencies and size of tourism

	FY 2009		*FY 2008*
Overseas travel turnover	1,954,169,770	35%	2,421,349,432
Inbound turnover	52,225,441	1%	62,057,630
Domestic travel turnover	3,533,888,285	64%	3,954,239,101
Total (unit in thousand Yen)	5,540,283,495	100%	6,437,646,163
No. of Travel Agencies	Approx. 38		Approx. 38
No. of Foreign Tourists in Japan	6,789,658	100%	8,350,853
No. of Foreign Tourists in Hokkaido	675,350	10%	689,150

Source: Japan Tourism Agency (2010b).

According to ANTO, 198 incoming agencies are registered in all provinces across Austria (see Austrian National Tourist Office 2008). There are 259 travel agents in Hokkaido (see Hokkaido Government 2010d); however, the number of incoming agencies is unconfirmed by HTO and by the Japan National Tourist Organization (JNTO).[1] In their official website (http://www.jnto.go.jp), 26 incoming travel agencies (one has already discontinued) are listed as JNTO's supporting members (Japan National Tourism Organization 2010).

Summarizing, we can state that the capacity of the tourism industry is higher in Austria. Before planning and implementing strategies or policies to attract more international tourism, it is therefore necessary that Hokkaido invests to develop the industrial infrastructure for welcoming more foreign tourists.

Comparison of e-tourism infrastructure

Comparison of general content

Markets work well if communication flows smoothly between the supply and demand side, within each side and across market places. This is especially important for an experience good such as tourism, where the information need of the consumer is very intense. For the product suppliers, the website has become one of the most important and convenient means of marketing to introduce the content, uniqueness and differentiation of the product (see Buhalis 2003). To compare the competence of Hokkaido and Austria in e-tourism, let us examine the websites of these two regions.

We start our investigation by estimating the size of the internet content about the two regions via systematic queries using Google. Google is estimated to have indexed eight billion pages (see Wöber 2010) and, according to ComScore (2009), is used by 67.5 per cent of worldwide searches. Customers who have not yet decided on a travel destination are likely to use a set of keywords such as 'tourism', 'tourist', 'travel' or 'trip' combined with the name of a destination or country in their primary travel planning stage. We thus use the paired keywords 'Austria tourism or tourist or travel or trip', 'Vienna tourism or tourist or travel or trip', 'Hokkaido tourism or tourist or travel or trip' and 'Otaru tourism or tourist or travel or trip' to measure the content of a destination available in the market in ten different languages as demonstrated in Figures 7.4 and 7.5.

As can be seen from Table 7.6, the size of the content found for Austria and Vienna was six times that of Hokkaido and Otaru, even when accepting Otaru's exceptional results in German and Spanish.

As shown in Figure 7.6, most of the Austrian content found was in English, and the rest was well distributed among the other languages. Information on Vienna is equally available in multiple languages corresponding to her in-scope markets. On the other hand, tourism information on Hokkaido and Otaru is mostly available in Japanese. In comparison to Austria/Vienna, the volume of information in English and other non-Asian languages is extremely small. Therefore, one can state that Hokkaido is off the radar for international tourists planning their trip via the internet.

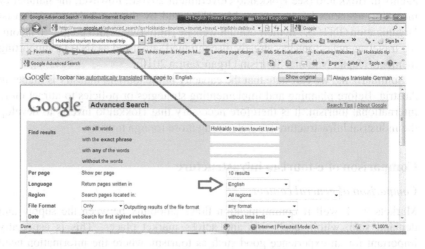

Figure 7.4 Screen shot of Google search setting.

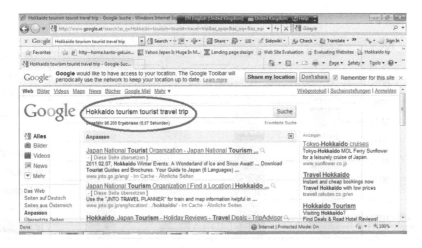

Figure 7.5 Screen shot of Google search results.

Table 7.6 URL results using paired keywords in each native language by Google search (as of 21 February 2011)

	Austria	Vienna	Contrast	Hokkaido	Otaru	Contrast
English	5,410,000	1,220,000	0.23	96,200	126,000	1.31
German	97,900	93,100	0.95	800	30,800	38.50
French	287,000	196,000	0.68	3,880	331	0.09
Italian	150,000	72,300	0.48	3,250	5,460	1.68
Spanish	800,000	230,000	0.29	11,600	66,700	5.75
Dutch	32,600	9,260	0.28	154	47	0.31
Russian	362,000	107,000	0.30	14,300	1,840	0.13
Japanese	275,000	264,000	0.96	753,000	331,000	0.44
Chinese	114,000	28,600	0.25	91,900	27,000	0.29
Korean	619,000	199,000	0.32	161,000	119,000	0.74
Average/Sum	8,147,500	2,419260	0.47	1,136,084	708,170	0.62[1]

Note:
1 Excluding abnormal results in German and Spanish.

A similar picture emerges when looking at hotel websites (see Table 7.7). The Viennese higher ratio of multilingual websites proves that Vienna has marked international competence in communication with the global market, whereas in Sapporo and Otaru approximately 60 per cent of hotels have websites in English and/or Chinese, Korean or Russian, in addition to Japanese. Summarizing, we can therefore state that there is a substantial gap between the degree of global reach between the touristic information systems currently used in Hokkaido and Austria.

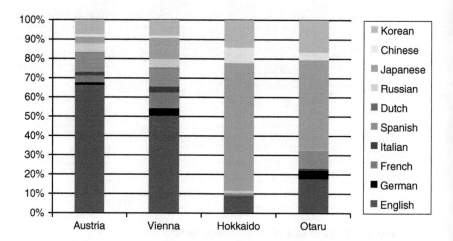

Figure 7.6 Language presence of online tourism information by destination by Google search (as of 21 February 2011).

Table 7.7 Website presence of accommodation in Vienna and Hokkaido (as of 21 February 2011)

Vienna	English/Multi	German only	No www.	Incorrect	Total
5–4 stars and	143	6	1	4*	154
Non-category	93%	4%	1%	3%	100%

Hokkaido	English/Multi	Japanese only	No www./Incorrect		Total
Sapporo					
Hotel	48	14	12		74
Japanese Inn	7	6	2		15
Pension YH	2	0	0		2
Total	57	20	14*		91
	63%	22%	15%		100%
Otaru					
Hotel	9	2	0		11
Japanese Inn	3	1	1		5
Pension YH	2	2	3		7
Total	14	5	4		23
	61%	22%	17%		100%

Note:
*Unavailable website, no website description or incorrect link on the HTO website.

Evaluation of destination websites

Methodology

It is advocated that the website become an important marketing tool in the tourism industry (see, e.g., Werther and Klein 1999). However, not all websites have been successful in e-marketing. If a website lacks easy access, usability and visibility it will not deliver the intended results. Websites with a usability problem cause users to feel pressured. This might cause potential customers to prematurely terminate their inquiry and leave the site with a negative image.

A natural gateway to the tourism content of a region is the official tourism website operated by the destination management organization. A tourism website has to meet the three requirements: effectiveness, efficiency and satisfaction. Only if all three requirements reach a certain minimum level of usability is official status given. The degree of satisfaction, however, depends on subjective values and personal perceptions, i.e. psychological and physical reactions when experiencing the user interface. Therefore, suitable methods are needed to assess the quality of a website reliably (see, e.g., Aaberge *et al.* 2004; Abdinnour-Helm and Chaparro 2007; Choi *et al.* 2007; Kaplanidou and Vogt 2004; Law *et al.* 2010; Manjome and Oikawa 2007).

Based on literature on website evaluation and in consideration of the characteristics of the tourism industry, a checklist was developed mainly based on Tapscott's design parameters of websites (Werther and Klein 1999, p. 288) and Douglas and Mills's modified Balance Scorecard (BSC) for website evaluations in the tourism and hospitality business (Douglas and Mills 2004, p. 279). It is comprised of five elements: (1) Objective, (2) User Friendliness, (3) Site Attractiveness, (4) Market Effectiveness and (5) Technical Features. The checklist developed has 82 items in total (see Appendix 7.1) and the rating scale excellent (5), sufficient (3), and unsatisfactory (1) was used to code the judgements.

In order to reduce the degree of subjectivity and to make the evaluation more comprehensive, a questionnaire to evaluate a user's level of satisfaction and perception was also designed (see Amento *et al.* 2000). As shown in Appendix 7.2, it consists of 21 questions based on the same criteria as the usability checklist. Each question allowed three answers, either yes, no or not sure. The questionnaire was sent by email to eight consumers with various demographic variables who usually travel abroad once a year or more. Before answering the questions, the participants were asked to first find the official destination websites of Austria and Hokkaido, i.e. http://www.austria.info/uk and http://en.visit-hokkaido.jp.

Results

Scores for each element in the checklist were calculated by totalling the scores of each subcategory. Overall scores were computed by adding each of the five elements. Figure 7.7 shows the fraction of the maximum number of scores achieved by the two websites. As can be seen from Figure 7.7, the ANTO website generally displayed excellent performance levels in all elements, and reached 82 per cent of the overall scores. The HTO website reached 62 per cent

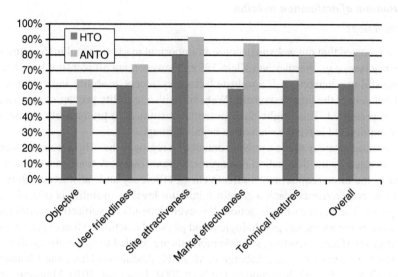

Figure 7.7 Performance levels according to the checklist.

and excelled in 'Site Attractiveness', with a high score of 80 per cent, while their performance in 'Objective' and 'Market Effectiveness' was significantly lower. Here, in particular, the categories Authority, Accuracy, Ease of Contact, Market Information, Consistency, Market Segments, Community Building, NetMechanic and Listing performed poorly, indicating potentials for improvement (see Appendix 7.1).

Replacing the positive answers 'yes' in the questionnaire with score 3 yields the overview over the survey results shown in Figure 7.8 (see Appendix 7.3). In general, these results are very similar to those of the checklist study except that the checklist evaluation for Hokkaido shows a significantly higher level of Site Attractiveness (77 per cent versus 41 per cent) and Market Effectiveness (86 per cent versus 30 per cent).

During the initial surfing of the HTO website, all respondents were inspired to plan their holidays in Hokkaido. The first impression of the HTO website was very positive. Six out of eight respondents (75 per cent) clearly understood that it was a tourism website, though seven out of eight respondents (87.5 per cent) had some difficulty in finding out who the web author was. However, half of the respondents did not know whether they would return to the HTO website to search for further information, or if they would recommend it to their friends. So, to sum up, in the end the respondents were not satisfied with the HTO website. What is behind this phenomenon? What kind of difficulties did they face? To answer these questions we combine the problem areas detected in the checklist evaluation with the negative answers in the survey to discuss the areas where the HTO website can improve using the ANTO website as a benchmark.

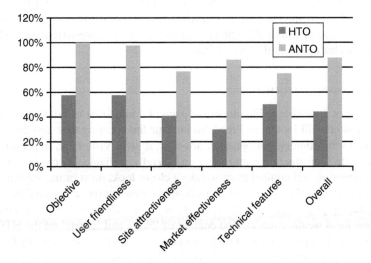

Figure 7.8 Performance levels according to survey.

Discussion

AUTHORITY AND EASE OF CONTACT

An 'About us' information page is not present on the HTO website, it is reachable only on the B2B travel agent site. On the B2C site, the contact address, phone number, and fax of HTO are placed prominently at the footer of each page, but there is no email address or 'contact us', so the users cannot easily contact HTO. Although the ANTO website also has no 'about us', it does have a 'contact' index on the menu of the header, introducing not only the head office in Vienna, but also all overseas offices with contact details. This information is also shown in the 'Terms and Conditions' in the footer. It is therefore much easier for users to find contact information online for ANTO than for HTO.

Most of the pages on the ANTO website have a small column for visitor care, which provides a phone number, email address and request forms for online brochures and newsletter subscriptions. The email address of HTO is not published on the B2C site. It seems that the HTO would rather avoid direct inquiries from consumers. Under the 'Contact us' on B2B site, the contact information of HTO and the Hokkaido-Sapporo Tourist Information Centre is introduced, but only the address, phone number and fax number are provided, with no hours of operation or location map.

FAQ is a list of questions which the HTO is commonly asked. However, there is no table of listed questions; users have to scroll until they find a similar question and its answer. If users cannot find a similar question, they are invited to enquire using the contact form at the end. This searching process is time consuming and finding the inquiry form takes too long.

The URL, http://en.visit-hokkaido.jp, contains a mixture of 'en' (English) plus the dash (–). Thus, while the URL of the ANTO website was memorable to most of the survey's respondents, half of them (four out of eight) answered that the URL of the HTO website was hard to remember.

ACCURACY AND MARKET INFORMATION

The top page of a website is like the cover page of a magazine or book: it is the first thing visitors will look at and read. To indicate the updating time and date of contents is not mandatory, but optional, however, it gives visitors an impression that the website's information is up-to-date and therefore reliable. In order to catch a visitor's attention and compel them to take a closer look, most of the attractive destination websites place the latest news from the destination or seasonal highlights on the top page together with time-related information, such as a calendar or the latest local weather report. The content of 'News and Events' on the HTO top page has not been updated attentively, while that of ANTO systematically lists seasonal highlights, which are regularly replaced and updated. For instance, the Sapporo Snow Festival, one of the largest winter events in Japan, was not listed on the top page before the event (7–13 February 2011). It is therefore not surprising that six out of eight respondents of the survey (75 per cent) had doubts about whether the contents on the HTO website were up-to-date. They found it easy to locate information on accommodation but were not satisfied with the information on events and attractions.

All respondents answered that on the HTO website, products and services were not only badly listed, but the information given was not thorough. Possibly, the grouping of the product services was perceived as overcrowded. Also there seems to be a lack of proper classification, and Hokkaido's main attributes are improperly presented in the navigation bar. Five out of eight respondents (62.5 per cent) replied that the text was neither clear nor easy to read, and almost everybody answered that the information received from search inquiries was not clear, relevant or appropriate.

The ANTO and VTB websites use a lot of image photos where tourists are enjoying the moment, but, in contrast, most of the photos on the Hokkaido website are scenic and static.

The website of HTO uses Google analytics as the ANTO site does. However, the search function within the HTO website seems to have a problem, as all respondents answered that the search function was slow to assist and to provide correct information.

For inexperienced website visitors who have no idea which keywords are effective, the ANTO website constantly lists 86 top keywords for activities in Austria in the right-hand upper column. These are popular city names and important attributes of Austria, such as Alps, culture, music, nature, ski and hiking. Furthermore types of travel, such as city breaks and packages for families and children, are available. In addition, for those who would like more details about certain places, 'Provinces and Regions' provides brief information on respective regions

In Japanese site   In other foreign languages sites

Figure 7.9 Marketing logos on the HTO website.

and links to regional tourist office websites. These add value to the ANTO website and increase its usability level.

CONSISTENCY

Layout refers to the basic framework of the website, and its design is determined by the usage of colours, images and fonts on the pages. Consistency in layout and design is a basic rule for a website to make it easy for visitors to navigate. When the main elements remain the same, visitors do not feel any uncertainty. Failing to be consistent will make them confused and leave the site. The ANTO website achieves a perfect performance in consistent layout and design. The pages always have the same look in any language and in any situation. Overall, HTO's website displays a common layout and design for each respective language, though some pages have useless blank space due to less content. The official logo of the HTO and the marketing corporate logo cannot be identified clearly. In the header, 'Hokkaido Official Tourism Website' is displayed on all pages accompanied with a smaller subtitle 'visit HOKKAIDO'. However, the Japanese site has a totally different logo and design (see Figure 7.9). Therefore if visitors who do not understand Japanese take a glance at this, they must be confused about whether it is the same official travel site or not. In such a case a consumer is likely to judge the site's credentials negatively, and will be induced to quickly leave it.

MARKET SEGMENTS

Marketing is the process of understanding the needs and demands of customers, identifying distinct target markets and developing marketing offers, which deliver key benefits and values to the target customers to satisfy their needs. The offer is a combination of product service, information and experiences. The destination brand carries many associations of the place, which creates an image of it in the consumer's mind. A destination that wants to attract more visitors must carefully study trends, identify the authentic attributes of the place and define the target segments. In order to achieve this goal, a DMO strives to build positive authentic images of the place and then match supply to demand (see, e.g., Briggs 2001; Grunn and Var 2002; Kotler *et al.* 2003).

The B2C website of HTO is available in five different languages: Japanese, English, Chinese (Mandarin and Cantonese), and Korean. There are 13 different languages on the VTB B2C website: English, German, Italian, French, Spanish, Russian, Hungarian, Polish, Romanian, Czech, Japanese, Arabic and Chinese. The ANTO B2C website is available in 27 languages for 33 countries. It is interesting to note that the ANTO B2C site is produced for each respective potential market area, not only for each language. For instance, ANTO runs three different English websites for three different market areas: USA/Canada, UK/Ireland and Australia. ANTO understands that consumers' interests and behaviours are different according to regional culture and lifestyle.

ANTO identified five fascinating attributes of holidays in Austria from their tourism resources: (1) Culture, (2) Nature, (3) Cuisine, (4) Well-being and (5) Hospitality (Österreich Werbung 2008). These are renamed with understandable words and put together in the folder 'Planning' at the top menu. It is also interesting that all main menus have a subtitle, which is visible only by touching the menu icon. For instance, the icon 'Planning' returns 'find your perfect holiday'. The ANTO website employs a hierarchical menu system, which allows the web author to deliver information to the market depending on the level of site visitor's interest. It also makes it easier for visitors to find out what they really want to know among the enormous content. Site visitors gravitate to their core interests without feeling stress.

By contrast, there are 53 submenus and 9 main menus on the HTO website. This makes it look overcrowded compared to the ANTO and VTB site. The structure of the HTO website does not follow a hierarchical system. This website is basically a single-page description of the subject, there is no further second or third hierarchical submenu. Some pages have external links or PDF files for further information. Therefore, website visitors need to visit each submenu and scroll down to the end of the page in their search to see whether there is any information available about their topic of interest. This is burdensome and time consuming. The essential information on Hokkaido sinks deeper in a given submenu page. For instance, information on 'Passport and Visa' and 'Entering the country/Customs house' is at the very bottom of the submenu 'before you leave' under the top menu 'Access', which is beyond the user's intuition. On the page 'Access', overseas airlines providing direct service flights to Hokkaido are listed. Actually, this is information on how to get to Hokkaido from neighbouring countries, but nothing else. Essential travel information and accessibility options to and within the destination are better relocated and described in easy words as ANTO and VTB do. The positioning of the main menu and its submenus on the HTO website should go through a significant overhaul to improve usability.

HTO needs to base the design of the destination website on the marketing strategy, because different market segments can be addressed online very efficiently. The website can focus on specific target groups for Hokkaido tourism. HTO's website focuses on leisure tourists and travel agents only, but fails to subdivide leisure tourists into travel purposes or group sizes. For example, one can show how much ski lovers can enjoy Hokkaido's natural attributes, how enjoyable, friendly and flexible Hokkaido is for young couples, families with children, budget travellers, special interest groups such as disabled persons, and business travellers or congresses/conventions. None of these can be found on the HTO website, as opposed to the ANTO offering.

COMMUNITY BUILDING

Websites are not only used to increase the awareness of products but also to maintain a close relationship with the consumer side and collect consumers' feedback and profiles (see Xiang and Gretzel 2010). Hokkaido has missed such opportunities, while the ANTO website utilizes Facebook, Twitter, TripAdvisor and blogs. It also invites website visitors to sign up for the newsletter at any moment. On the HTO website, there is only a link to Facebook. However, Facebook's placement in the centre of the top page makes the webpage look rather strange. A destination website should not primarily compel visitors to take a closer look at Facebook during their initial visit. Better approaches for building a community network need to be implemented, as Hokkaido does not have a significant presence in the social media.

NETMECHANIC AND SEARCH ENGINE LISTING

To evaluate the technical features of the two websites, a program by NetMechanic was used on 24 February 2011. The program reports a star rating for various features (NetMechanic 2011). ANTO's website loading time was 6.93 seconds, with a 4-star grade, while HTO's loading time was 151.25 seconds with 1-star grade. One reason for this deficiency is that HTO's website has 58 large images and heavy graphics, with a storage size of 509,928 bytes and a page size of 524KB. By contrast, ANTO's site only has 1,441 bytes and 10KB. Browser compatibility reported 16 problems with a 1-star grade for HTO, while ANTO had 10 problems, with a 2-star grade.

Visible listing on search engines is indispensable if one wishes to do well in the market. In the same manner as the previous search engine investigation, several pairs of keywords in multiple combinations with destination name and 'travel, tourist, info and site' were used in major search engines to find the websites of HTO and ANTO. As shown in Table 7.8, the ANTO site was listed at the top of the listing on Google, Yahoo, and MSN, while the HTO site was quite difficult to find within the first listing pages on Yahoo. It was not retrieved on MSN at all, but it did have the top listing on Google. Thus, search engine optimization is a significant technical challenge for Hokkaido.

Conclusions

Hokkaido has the potential to become an international player in tourism (a global growth industry) especially from emerging countries. One important asset for reaching this goal is an attractive offer in e-tourism. This research was undertaken

Table 7.8 Search engine listing results by keywords search of HTO and ANTO (as of 24 February 2011)

Search Engine/Keywords	HTO	ANTO
Google		
Official travel site	1st	1st
Official tourism site	1st	1st
Travel site	5th	1st
Travel info	1st	1st
Tourist info	1st	1st
Yahoo		
Official travel site	—	1st
Official tourism site	7th	1st
Travel site	—	1st
Travel info	3rd	1st
Tourist info	1st	1st
MSN bing		
Official travel site	—	1st
Official tourism site	—	2nd
Travel site	—	1st
Travel info	—	2nd
Tourist info	—	1st
Final evaluation scores	2	5

to investigate the correlation between the scale of e-tourism as measured by the amount of web content present, and the quality of the DMO website and tourism growth in Hokkaido when compared to Austria. More observations and detailed analyses are needed to verify the results found for this relationship due to the limitations of the small sample size used for the questionnaire. However, the eight respondents reflected the sample of typical consumers and the reliability of their answers was at an acceptable level.

This study confirms the growing importance of e-tourism management, identifying some weaknesses where Hokkaido can improve its performance versus Austria, and showing the extent of the challenge that Hokkaido currently faces. Change will happen in Hokkaido in the near future if these factors are engaged with dynamic and comprehensive marketing. The way to strengthen global competence of Hokkaido tourism is fairly complex. However, the Hokkaido government and the Hokkaido Tourism Organization are the only organizations that can demonstrate long-term vision and commitment, maximize the efficiency and effectiveness of the destination, capitalize market opportunities, formulate value chains and maximize consumer benefits.

Appendix 7.1 Checklist scorecards of website evaluation

	HTO		ANTO	
1. Objective (45)	21	46.7%	29	64.4%
Authority:				
Who developed the site?	HTO		ANTO	
Is it different from the webmaster?	HTO		ANTO	
'About us' is available?	2		2	
Can we contact the author or webmaster?	2		5	
What is the URL domain (gv, or, edu, ac, com, info, net......)?	.jp		.info	
Do their credentials allow them to speak about the subject with authority?	3		3	
5 × 3 Total 15	7	46.7%	10	66.7%
Accuracy:				
When was the website produced?	–		–	
Frequency of updating information. When updated recently? How often updated?	–		–	
5 × 2 Total 10	0	0%	0	0%
Purpose:				
The purpose of the site (what for, to whom) is clear.	5		5	
Easy to understand what the site is for by taking a glance of top page.	3		5	
Users can expect to find the value of travel, and what they can do at the destination on top page.	3		4	
The website inspires consumers to book holidays at the destination?	3		5	
5 × 4 Total 20	14	70.0%	19	95.0%
2. User friendliness (50)	30	60.0%	37	74.0%
Web mobility (ease of use):				
HOME button on all pages	5		3	
Site map or index availability	1		3	
Multi-language availability And how many languages?	3		5	
Search function	3		3	
Clear and easy navigation on each page	5		4	
5 × 5 Total 25	17	68.0%	18	72.0%
Ease of contact:				
Direct email	1		4	
Address, Tel, Fax	5		4	
Call centre	1		5	
FAQ	3		1	
URL is easy to remember	3		5	
5 × 5 Total 25	13	52.0%	19	76.0%

Continued

	HTO		ANTO	
3. Site attractiveness (60)	48	80.0%	55	91.7%
Web interface:				
Text is clear and easy to read	3		5	
Pages are clean and organized	4		5	
Page design is attractive and simple (effective use of web page space)	3		5	
Scrolling pages are not too long	3		5	
Limited horizontal scrolling in design	5		5	
Limited vertical scrolling in design	5		5	
Background is subdued	5		4	
Advertisements or flash animations do not distract user's attention away from content	5		4	
Pictures and images are impressive and of good quality	4		5	
5 × 9 Total 45	37	82.2%	43	95.6%
Visual entertainments:				
Virtual entertainment	4		5	
Testimonials, awards	2		4	
Photo gallery	5		3	
5 × 3 Total 15	11	73.3%	12	80.0%
4. Market effectiveness (130)	76	58.5%	114	87.7%
Market information:				
Current and timely information? Trend- and season-related?	2		5	
Information on hotels, restaurants, events, shopping is covered?	4		3	
News release	1		3	
5 × 3 Total 15	7	46.7%	11	73%
Consistency:				
Logo reflected on all pages	2		5	
The website displays originality in common design	4		5	
Corporate design in any page, in any language	2		5	
5 × 3 Total 15	8	53.3%	15	100.0%
Market segments:				
Leisure	1		1	
Business				
Family, children			1	
Couple			1	
Special interests groups (disability, meetings)			2	
B2B (tourism industry)	1		1	
Press, journalists			1	
1 × 8 Total 8	2	25.0%	7	87.5%

	HTO		ANTO	
Destination attributes:				
Culture			1	
Nature	1		1	
Art			1	
Recreation	1		1	
Sports	1		1	
Food	1		1	
People			1	
Product sources are classified into appropriate groups	3		5	
Is it possible to compare (service, price, etc) within the group?	4		4	
Are the headline indexes representing main attributes of the destination?	4		4	
Are these relevant to help user's research?				
Is there a bias in the presentation of info?	3		5	
(5×4) Total 27	18	66.7%	25	92.6%
Advertisements:				
The website provides accurate information with limited advertisements.	5		5	
Are the advertisements related to the tourism and supplementary to the web?	3		5	
5 × 2 Total 10	8	80.0%	10	100.0%
Trip planner:				
General travel information (Visa, currency, etc)	4		3	
Local weather information	4		2	
Help, Search function	3		5	
Map	3		5	
Transportation mode and schedule	3		5	
Event calendar	3		4	
Hotel, accommodation	3		4	
Availability of online booking	1		5	
Availability of digital brochures	5		4	
5 × 9 Total 45	29	64.4%	37	82.2%
Community building:				
Newsletter subscription	1		4	
Facebook, Twitter, TripAdvisor, etc.	3		5	
5 × 2 Total 10	4	40.0%	9	90.0%

Continued

Appendix 7.1 Continued

	HTO		ANTO	
5. Technical features (50)	32	64.0%	40	80.0%
NetMechanic and Listing:				
HTML	4		5	
Loading time	1		4	
Compatible browser	1		2	
Correct word spelling, grammar?	3		3	
Are the links (if any) functional?	5		5	
Priority listing in major search engines	2		5	
5 × 6 Total 30	16	53.3%	24	80.0%
Legal compliance:				
The Copyright is shown clearly	5		5	
Site contents usage policy	3		5	
Privacy policy	5		5	
Security	3		1	
5 × 4 Total 20	16	80.0%	16	80.0%
Grand Total (335)	207	61.8%	275	82.1%

Appendix 7.2 Questionnaire results

		Hokkaido		Austria	
A1	Is the purpose of the website clear? Is it easy to understand who and what it's for at the first glance at the home page?				
Yes		6	75.0%	8	100.0%
No		0	0.0%	0	0.0%
Not sure		2	25.0%	0	0.0%
	CONTROL	**8**	**100%**	**8**	**100%**
A2	Do you expect good value from the trip and from your experience of the destination?	H		A	
Yes		4	50.0%	8	100.0%
No		0	0.0%	0	0.0%
Not sure		4	50.0%	0	0.0%
	CONTROL	**8**	**100%**	**8**	**100%**
A3	Are you inspired to take a holiday in the destination after surfing the website for a short time?	H		A	
Yes		8	100.0%	8	100.0%
No		0	0.0%	0	0.0%
Not sure		0	0.0%	0	0.0%
	CONTROL	**8**	**100%**	**8**	**100%**

A4	Will you come back to this site or recommend it to your friends?	H		A	
Yes		4	50.0%	8	100.0%
No		0	0.0%	0	0.0%
Not sure		4	50.0%	0	0.0%
	CONTROL	**8**	**100%**	**8**	**100%**
A5	Could you find who developed this site, who are they?	H		A	
Yes		1	12.5%	8	100.0%
No		2	25.0%	0	0.0%
Not sure		5	62.5%	0	0.0%
	CONTROL	**8**	**100%**	**8**	**100%**
B1	Navigation bar was present on every page and helpful and well-organized?	Hokkaido		Austria	
Yes		7	87.5%	8	100.0%
No		0	0.0%	0	0.0%
Not sure		1	12.5%	0	0.0%
	CONTROL	**8**	**100%**	**8**	**100%**
B2	Do the format, design and layout complement your use of the site?	H		A	
Yes		5	62.5%	8	100.0%
No		0	0.0%	0	0.0%
Not sure		3	37.5%	0	0.0%
	CONTROL	**8**	**100%**	**8**	**100%**
B3	Overall user friendly site?	H		A	
Yes		7	87.5%	8	100.0%
No		0	0.0%	0	0.0%
Not sure		1	12.5%	0	0.0%
	CONTROL	**8**	**100%**	**8**	**100%**
B4	Search function in the website assisted quick and correct information?	H		A	
Yes		0	0.0%	7	87.5%
No		8	100.0%	1	12.5%
Not sure		0	0.0%	0	0.0%
	CONTROL	**8**	**100%**	**8**	**100%**
B5	The URL is easy to remember?	H		A	
Yes		4	50.0%	8	100.0%
No		4	50.0%	0	0.0%
Not sure		0	0.0%	0	0.0%
	CONTROL	**8**	**100%**	**8**	**100%**
C1	Is the text clear and easy to read?	Hokkaido		Austria	
Yes		1	12.5%	7	87.5%
No		5	62.5%	0	0.0%
Not sure		2	25.0%	1	12.5%
	CONTROL	**8**	**100%**	**8**	**100%**
C2	Is the page clean, organized and uncluttered?	H		A	
Yes		3	37.5%	8	100.0%
No		0	0.0%	0	0.0%
Not sure		5	62.5%	0	0.0%
	CONTROL	**8**	**100%**	**8**	**100%**

Continued

C3	*Are you informed of the price level by the given information?*	*H*			*A*	
Yes		0	0.0%	1	12.5%
No		6	75.0%	2	25.0%
Not sure		2	25.0%	5	62.5%
	CONTROL	**8**	**100%**	**8**	**100%**
C4	*Is the given information clear, relevant and appropriate to your research questions?*	*H*			*A*	
Yes		0	0.0%	6	75.0%
No		3	37.5%	0	0.0%
Not sure		5	62.5%	2	25.0%
	CONTROL	**8**	**100%**	**8**	**100%**
C5	*Which content is the most interesting for your research?*	*H*			*A*	
About Hokkaido		3	37.5%		
Activities		5	62.5%		
Travel Planner		0	0.0%		
Access		0			
Events		0			
Discover				1	12.5%
Planning				6	75.0%
Search and Book				0	0.0%
Essentials				1	12.5%
	CONTROL	**8**	**100%**	**8**	**100%**
C6	*Did the site motivate you to travel there alone and/or in a small group?*	*H*			*A*	
Yes		0	0.0%	5	62.5%
No		2	25.0%	0	0.0%
Not sure		6	75.0%	3	37.5%
	CONTROL	**8**	**100%**	**8**	**100%**
C7	*Use of colours improves visual appearance and impression?*	*H*			*A*	
Yes		7	87.5%	7	87.5%
No		0	0.0%	0	0.0%
Not sure		1	12.5%	1	12.5%
	CONTROL	**8**	**100%**	**8**	**100%**
C8	*Graphics (photos, images) are appropriate and supplementary to text?*	*H*			*A*	
Yes		7	87.5%	7	87.5%
No		0	0.0%	0	0.0%
Not sure		1	12.5%	1	12.5%
	CONTROL	**8**	**100%**	**8**	**100%**
C9	*Did graphics (photos, images) motivate you to travel there?*	*H*			*A*	
Yes		8	100.0%	8	100.0%
No		0	0.0%	0	0.0%
Not sure		0	0.0%	0	0.0%
	CONTROL	**8**	**100%**	**8**	**100%**

			Portion		Portion	
D1	*Every page looks similar and displays originality?*					
Yes			5	62.5%	8	100.0%
No			0	0.0%	0	0.0%
Not sure			3	37.5%	0	0.0%
		CONTROL	**8**	**100%**	**8**	**100%**
D2	*Up to date travel information?*		Portion		Portion	
Yes			2	25.0%	6	75.0%
No			0	0.0%	0	0.0%
Not sure			6	75.0%	2	25.0%
		CONTROL	**8**	**100%**	**8**	**100%**
D3	*Could you find any package information?*		Portion		Portion	
Yes			0	0.0%	7	87.5%
No			8	100.0%	0	0.0%
Not sure			0	0.0%	1	12.5%
		CONTROL	**8**	**100%**	**8**	**100%**
D4	*Could you find events?*		Portion		Portion	
Yes			0	0.0%	8	100.0%
No			0	0.0%	0	0.0%
Not sure			8	100.0%	0	0.0%
		CONTROL	**8**	**100%**	**8**	**100%**
D5	*Could you find accommodation?*		Portion		Portion	
Yes			8	100.0%	8	100.0%
No			0	0.0%	0	0.0%
Not sure			0	0.0%	0	0.0%
		CONTROL	**8**	**100%**	**8**	**100%**
D6	*Could you find interesting attractions?*		Portion		Portion	
Yes			4	50.0%	5	62.5%
No			0	0.0%	0	0.0%
Not sure			4	50.0%	3	37.5%
		CONTROL	**8**	**100%**	**8**	**100%**
D7	*Products and services are listed well and thoroughly?*		Portion		Portion	
Yes			0	0.0%	8	100.0%
No			4	50.0%	0	0.0%
Not sure			4	50.0%	0	0.0%
		CONTROL	**8**	**100%**	**8**	**100%**
D8	*Very informative content of destination features?*		Portion		Portion	
Yes			0	0.0%	5	62.5%
No			3	37.5%	0	0.0%
Not sure			5	62.5%	3	37.5%
		CONTROL	**8**	**100%**	**8**	**100%**
E1	*Could you find the website easily in the search process?*		*H*		*A*	
Yes			4	50.0%	6	75.0%
No			4	50.0%	2	25.0%
Not sure			0	0.0%	0	0.0%
		CONTROL	**8**	**100%**	**8**	**100%**

Continued

Appendix 7.2 Continued

F1	Gender		Portion	
Male			5	62.5%
Female			3	37.5%
		CONTROL	8	100%
F2	Age		Portion	
20–30			2	25.0%
31–40			1	12.5%
41–50			3	37.5%
Over 51			2	25.0%
		CONTROL	8	100%
F3	Marital Status		Portion	
Married			5	62.5%
Single			3	37.5%
		CONTROL	8	100%
F4	Have you ever been to Japan?		Portion	
Yes			6	75.0%
No			2	25.0%
		CONTROL	8	100%
F5	Have you ever been to Austria?		Portion	
Yes			7	87.5%
No			1	12.5%
		CONTROL	8	100%

Appendix 7.3 Performance level of questionnaire results

Elements (full scores)	No. of questions	HTO	Value%	ANTO	Value%
Objective (120)	5	69	58%	120	100%
User friendliness (120)	5	69	58%	117	98%
Site attractiveness (192)	8	78	41%	147	77%
Market effectiveness (192)	8	57	30%	165	86%
Technical features (24)	1	12	50%	18	75%
Overall (648)	27	285	44%	567	88%

Note: No = 1 point; Not sure = 2 points; Yes = 3 points; $N = 8$.

Appendix 7.4 Questionnaire results by sample

No.	A-Objective					B-User Friendliness					C-Site Attractiveness								
	A1	A2	A3	A4	A5	B1	B2	B3	B4	B5	C1	C2	C3	C4	C5	C6	C7	C8	C9
Hokkaido																			
1	3	3	3	3	2	3	3	3	1	1	1	2	1	1	Activities	1	3	3	3
2	3	2	3	3	2	3	3	3	1	1	1	2	2	1	Activities	1	3	3	3
3	3	2	3	2	2	2	2	2	1	1	1	3	1	2	About	2	3	3	3
4	3	2	3	2	3	3	3	3	1	3	1	3	1	1	Activities	2	3	3	3
5	3	3	3	3	2	3	3	3	1	3	2	2	1	2	About	2	3	3	3
6	3	2	3	2	2	3	2	3	1	3	1	2	1	2	Activities	2	3	3	3
7	2	3	3	3	1	3	3	3	1	3	2	3	2	2	Activities	2	2	3	3
8	2	3	3	3	3	3	2	3	1	1	3	2	2	2	About	2	2	3	3
Average	2.75	2.5	3	2.5	1.9	2.875	2.63	2.875	1	2	1.5	2.4	1.25	1.6		1.8	2.9	2.88	3

No.	D-Market Effectiveness								E-Technical	F-General Demography			
	D1	D2	D3	D4	D5	D6	D7	D8	E1	F1	F2	F3	F4
Hokkaido													
1	2	2	1	2	3	2	2	2	1	F	41–50	Single	3
2	3	3	1	2	3	3	1	2	1	F	Over 51	Married	1
3	2	2	1	2	3	3	2	2	3	F	Over 51	Married	3
4	3	2	1	2	3	3	1	1	3	M	20–30	Single	1
5	3	2	1	2	3	3	1	1	3	F	20–30	Single	3
6	3	2	1	2	3	2	1	1	1	M	41–50	Single	3
7	2	2	1	2	3	2	2	2	1	F	31–40	Single	3
8	3	3	1	2	3	2	2	2	3	M	41–50	Married	3
Average	2.6	2.25	1	2	3	2.5	1.5	1.625	2				

Continued

Appendix 7.4 Continued

No.	A-Objective					B-User Friendliness					C-Site Attractiveness								
	A1	A2	A3	A4	A5	B1	B2	B3	B4	B5	C1	C2	C3	C4	C5	C6	C7	C8	C9
Austria																			
1	3	3	3	3	3	3	3	3	3	3	3	3	2	2	Planning	3	3	3	3
2	3	3	3	3	3	3	3	3	3	3	3	3	2	2	Planning	2	3	3	3
3	3	3	3	3	3	3	3	3	3	3	3	3	2	3	Planning	2	3	3	3
4	3	3	3	3	3	3	3	3	3	3	3	3	2	3	Essentials	3	3	3	3
5	3	3	3	3	3	3	3	3	3	3	3	3	1	3	Planning	3	3	3	3
6	3	3	3	3	3	3	3	3	3	3	3	3	1	3	Planning	2	3	3	3
7	3	3	3	3	3	3	3	3	3	3	3	3	2	3	Planning	3	2	3	3
8	3	3	3	3	3	3	3	3	1	3	2	3	3	3	Discover	yes	2	2	3
Average	3	2.75	3	3	3	3	3	3	2.75	3	2.9	3	1.88	2.8		2.6	2.9	2.88	3

No.	D-Market Effectiveness								E-Technical	F-General Demography			
	D1	D2	D3	D4	D5	D6	D7	D8	E1	F1	F2	F3	F4
1	3	2	3	3	3	2	3	2	3	F	41–50	Single	1
2	3	3	3	3	3	3	3	3	1	F	Over 51	Married	3
3	3	2	2	3	3	2	3	2	3	F	Over 51	Married	3
4	3	3	3	3	3	3	3	3	3	M	20–30	Single	3
5	3	3	3	3	3	3	3	3	3	F	20–30	Single	3
6	3	3	3	3	3	2	3	2	3	M	41–50	Single	3
7	3	3	3	3	3	3	3	3	3	F	31–40	Single	3
8	3	3	3	3	3	3	3	3	1	M	41–50	Married	3
Average	3	2.75	2.9	3	3	2.63	3	2.625	2.5				

Note: 1 = No; 2 = Not Sure; 3 = Yes; N = 8.

Note

1 JNTO is an independent administrative organization under the Japan Tourism Agency (JTA) to promote inbound travellers to Japan. It is engaged in a diverse range of inbound tourism promotions overseas, marketing and promotion of international conventions and support for foreign tourists through Tourist Information Centres.

References

Aaberge, T., Grøtte, I. P., Haugen, O., Skogseid, I. and Ølnes, S. (2004) 'Evaluation of tourism web sites: A theoretical framework'. In Frew, A. J. (ed.) *Information and Communication Technologies in Tourism 2004*, Vienna: Springer-Verlag, pp. 305–16.

Abdinnour-Helm, S. and Chaparro, B. S. (2007) 'A balanced usability checklist approach to evaluate Palestinian hotel websites, *Electronic Journal of Information Systems in Developing Countries*, 31(2): 1–12.

Amento, B., Terveen, L. and Hill, W. (2000) 'Does "authority" mean quality? Predicting expert quality ratings of Web documents', 23rd Annual International ACM SIGIR Conference on Research and Development in Information Retrieval, New York: ACM Press, pp. 296–303.

Austrian National Tourist Office (2008) Austrian Incoming Agencies, http://www.austriatourism.com/xxl/_site/uk/_area/477930/_subArea/479916/incomerbueros.html. Retrieved on 19 December 2010.

Briggs, S. (2001) *Successful Tourism Marketing: A Practical Handbook*, 2nd edition, London: Kogan Page Limited.

Buhalis, Dimitrios (2003): *eTourism: Information Technology for Strategic Tourism Management,* England: Prentice Hall.

Choi, S., Lehto, X. Y. and Morrison, A. M. (2007) 'Destination image representation on the web: Content analysis of Macau travel related websites', *Tourism Management*, (28) 1: 118–29.

ComScore (2009) Press release: Global search market draws more than 100 billion searches per month, http://www.comscore.com/Press_Events/Press_Releases/2009/8/Global_Search_Market_Draws_More_than_100_Billion_Searches_per_Month. Retrieved on 21 January 2011.

Doolin, B., Burgess, L. and Cooper, J. (2002) 'Evaluating the use of the Web for tourism marketing: A case study from New Zealand', *Tourism Management*, 23(5): 557–61.

Douglas, A. and Mills, J. E. (2004) 'Staying afloat in the tropics: Applying a structural equation model approach to evaluating National Tourism Organization websites in the Caribbean'. In Mills, J. E. and Law, R. (eds), *Handbook of Consumer Behavior, Tourism and the Internet*, New York: Haworth Hospital Press, pp. 269–93.

Grunn, C. A. and Var, T. (2002) *Tourism Planning: Basics, Concepts, Cases*, 4th edition, New York: Routledge, pp. 33–73.

Hokkaido Chuo Bus (2010) Company profile, http://www.chuo-bus.co.jp/company/outline/. Retrieved on 19 December 2010.

Hokkaido Government (2010a) Hokkaido Tourism Statistics FY2009, http://www.pref.hokkaido.lg.jp/NR/rdonlyres/E0E57BA9-A008-457C-847C-9B9297381C86/0/honnpenn220804.pdf. Retrieved on 27 November 2010.

Hokkaido Government (2010b) Tourism statistics report, http://www.pref.hokkaido.lg.jp/kz/kkd/irikomi.htm. Retrieved on 21 April 2010.

Hokkaido Government (2010c) Tourism Statistics Report 2009, http://www.pref.hokkaido.lg.jp/file.jsp?id=84633. Retrieved on 27 November 2010.

Hokkaido Government (2010d) Current Status of Hokkaido Tourism, http://www.pref.hokkaido.lg.jp/NR/rdonlyres/D29CDDAB-AA3A-4460-9547-83D043493D55/0/gennkyou221109.pdf. Retrieved on 22 November 2010.

Japan National Tourism Organization (2010) JNTO Partners. Travel agencies, http://www.jnto.go.jp/partners/eng/travel_agencies.html. Retrieved on 21 December 2010.

Japan Railways Hokkaido (2010) Company profile, http://www.jrhokkaido.co.jp/corporate/company/com_2.html. Retrieved on 19 December 2010.

Japan Tourism Agency (2010a) Accommodation survey 2009, http://www.mlit.go.jp/common/000120208.pdf. Retrieved on 27 November 2010.

Japan Tourism Agency (2010b) Press release: Japanese top travel agencies sales turnover FY2009, http://www.mlit.go.jp/kankocho/news06_000067.html. Retrieved on 21 December 2010.

Kaplanidou, K. and Vogt, C. (2004) Destination Marketing Organization (DMO) websites: Evaluation and design: What you need to know, Travel Michigan, http://www.travelmichigannews.org/mtr/pdf/White_paper-Web_site_evaluation.pdf. Retrieved on 13 December 2010.

Kotler, P., Bowen, J. and Makens, J. (2003) *Marketing for Hospitality and Tourism, Third Edition*, Trans. Sho Hirabayashi, Japan: Pearson Education Japan.

Law, R., Qi, S. and Buhalis, D. (2010) 'Progress in tourism management: A review of website evaluation in tourism research', *Tourism Management*, 31(3): 297–313.

Manjome, A and Oikawa M. (2007) 'Simple usability evaluation method for sightseeing information website', Hokkaido Industrial Research Institute Report, Vol. 306, pp. 109–16.

NetMechanic (2011) Products: HTML Toolbox free sample, http://www.netmechanic.com/products/HTML_Toolbox_FreeSample.shtml. Retrieved on 24 February 2011.

ÖBB-Postbus (2010) The Company, http://www.postbus.at/en/The_Company/index.jsp. Retrieved on 19 December 2010.

Österreich Werbung (2008) *Das Markenhandbuch für den Österreichischen Tourismus*, Austria.

Statistics Austria (2010) Accommodation capacity. Accommodation establishments and bednights by Länder 2001 to 2009. Accommodation establishments and bed places by Austrian Länder and type of accommodation and changes compared to the reference period November 2008 to October 2009, winter season 2008/09 and summer season 2009 (in percentage), http://www.statistik.at/web_en/statistics/tourism/accommodation/accommodation_capacity/index.html. Retrieved on 18 December 2010.

Werther, H. and Klein, S. (1999) *Information Technology and Tourism: A Challenging Relationship*, Vienna: Springer-Verlag.

Wikipedia (2010): Österreichische Bundesbahnen, http://de.wikipedia.org/wiki/%C3%96-sterreichische_Bundesbahnen. Retrieved on 20 December 2010.

Wöber, K. W. (2010) Searching for tourism destinations and products on the internet, Session 7, MODUL University, Vienna, 13 July 2010, p. 4.

Xiang, Z. and Gretzel, U. (2010) 'Role of social media in online travel information search', *Tourism Management*, 31(2): 179–88.

8 Analysis of the traffic lines of tourists that visited Kamikawa district in Hokkaido based on data from the Kamui Mintara Stamp Rally*

Nozomi Kichiji

Introduction

Over recent years, the Japanese government has promoted measures to improve the development of tourism statistics. As a result, researchers now have easy access to information about tourism in Japan, such as surveys of visitor trends at well-known tourist attractions.[1] However, it remains difficult to gather information on tourist traffic lines inside these venues because it costs too much time to check them. Therefore, no data are available for analyzing tourist traffic lines, and it is unlikely that the Japanese government will develop such a database in the near future, owing to its high cost. However, the analysis of tourist traffic lines is essential for developing the tourism sector in Japan.

In light of this absence of national data, this chapter presents data gathered on tourist traffic lines in Kamikawa Central district (KCD). I obtained these data by tracking stamps on an application form used by participants in the Kamui Mintara Stamp Rally (KMSR). I also collected personal data, including gender, age, residence, accommodation type, and length of stay through a questionnaire that participants answered in order to be eligible for free gifts offered by the KMSR commission. Using these data, I can analyze tourist traffic lines in KCD as well as lengths of tourist stays. Since the number of samples from the KMSR is sufficient, the state of tourism in KCD is reflected in the results of the presented analysis.

This study thus aims to provide valuable information to managers and local government officers that work in the tourism sector in order to assist in designing a suitable strategy for promoting tourism. This chapter introduces the visualization and network analysis of tourist traffic lines, and its results suggest that we must formulate tourism promotional strategy from a trans-regional perspective.

The remainder of this chapter is organized as follows. The second section outlines the state of tourism in Hokkaido and Kamikawa district; the third section introduces KMSR; the fourth section describes the characteristics of tourists that visited KCD; the fifth section analyzes correlation among well-known tourist

---

*This chapter was largely revised and edited based on (Kichiji, 2011). However, this chapter contains an analysis of the stamp rally in 2011.

attractions; the sixth section shows visualization of tourist traffic lines; and the seventh section describes network analyses of tourist traffic lines. In the eighth section, we conclude the chapter.

The state of tourism in Hokkaido and Kamikawa district

Hokkaido prefecture is a leading tourist resort in Japan. Indeed, its tourism sector is the second largest in the country in terms of the number of nights stayed. Various tours via Sapporo, the capital of Hokkaido, are popular, and tourists that visit Hokkaido typically travel to several cities and stay for a number of days. Specifically, this chapter examines tourism in Kamikawa district, which is located in the middle of Hokkaido. Kamikawa district is controlled by the Kamikawa branch of the Hokkaido prefecture office. The population of Kamikawa district is approximately 520,000 and it comprises approximately 9.5 percent of the total population of Hokkaido prefecture. Asahikawa (with a population of approximately 350,000) is the largest city in Kamikawa, and it is based in Kamikawa district. The group made up of Asahikawa, Higashikawa, Higashikagura, Biei, Touma, Takasu, Pippu, Aibetsu, and Kamikawa comprises KCD. The population of this group is approximately 420,000. A number of renowned tourist attractions are located within the district, such as Asahiyama Zoo and the permanent pedestrian precinct in Kaimono Koen (in Asahikawa), the beautiful hills in Biei, and Souunkyo in the Mount Daisetsu National Park in Kamikawa town.

Figure 8.1 shows the number of tourists[2] that visited Kamikawa district and KCD between fiscal years 2008 and 2012 (April to March). In 2008–9, the number of tourists to Kamikawa district (KCD) decreased by 4.7 percent (7.6 percent) year-on-year, owing to the influence of the US-led financial collapse and soaring oil prices. In 2009–10, these numbers increased by 1.3 percent and decreased by 4.7 percent, year-on-year respectively. The reasons for the rise in the number of tourists that visited Kamikawa district were the television drama that was set in Furano, and the discount effect of the toll on the main expressway. The decline in the number of tourists that visited KCD was attributable to multiple factors. For example, a new influenza epidemic (which resulted in certain events being cancelled), the depression following the US-led financial collapse, and the unusual weather during the summer of that year. In 2010–11, the decrease in the number of tourists to Kamikawa district slowed. In the first half of 2011–12, the number of tourists recovered sharply to the level of 2008–9; however, in the second half, the Great East Japan Earthquake greatly decreased tourist numbers again. In summary, the number of tourists that visited KCD decreased from 2008–9 to 2011–12, not because of structural reasons, but because of the harmful effect of the business cycle and natural disasters.

Next, the structural problems for tourism in KCD are discussed. Figure 8.2 shows the proportion of day trips and overnight trips in KCD. This figure confirms that the percentage of day trips to overnight trips in Hokkaido is approximately 70 percent[3] higher than that in KCD. This result suggests that the ratio of day-trippers that visit KCD is higher than the ratio of those that visit Hokkaido.

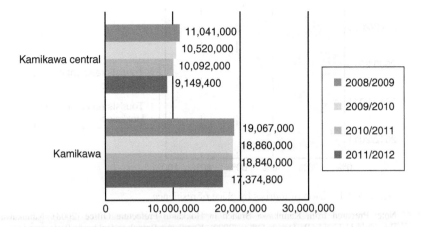

Figure 8.1 Number of tourists in Kamikawa district and KCD.

Note: Prepared by Kamikawa Branch in Hokkaido Prefecture Office (2008), Kamikawa Branch in Hokkaido Prefecture Office (2009), Kamikawa Branch in Hokkaido Prefecture Office (2010), Kamikawa Branch in Hokkaido Prefecture Office (2011).

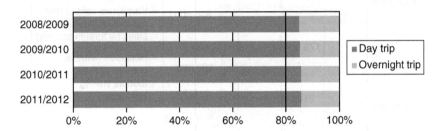

Figure 8.2 Percentage of day trips to overnight trips in KCD.

Note: Prepared by Kamikawa Branch in Hokkaido Prefecture Office (2008), Kamikawa Branch in Hokkaido Prefecture Office (2009), Kamikawa Branch in Hokkaido Prefecture Office (2010), Kamikawa Branch in Hokkaido Prefecture Office (2011).

Figure 8.3 shows the division of tourists that visited Kamikawa district by place of residence. The number of tourists from Hokkaido (Hokkaido tourists hereafter) is almost equal to the number of tourists from outside Hokkaido (non-Hokkaido tourists hereafter). In Hokkaido as a whole, the ratio is 9:1, so this result illustrates that the ratio of non-Hokkaido tourists that visit KCD is very high. However, in 2011–2012, this high ratio declined because of the effect of the Great East Japan Earthquake.

Figure 8.4 shows the number of overnight stays by country of origin for each district. It demonstrates that approximately 30 percent of foreign tourists that visited Hokkaido visited KCD. In 2009–10, the number of foreign tourists that visited KCD decreased faster year-on-year than that for Hokkaido as a whole, following

144   *N. Kichiji*

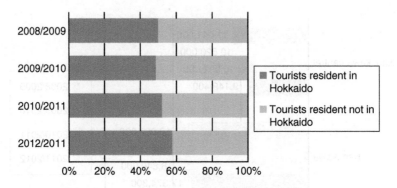

Figure 8.3 Division of tourists by place of residence.

Note: Prepared from Kamikawa Branch in Hokkaido Prefecture Office (2008), Kamikawa Branch in Hokkaido Prefecture Office (2009), Kamikawa Branch in Hokkaido Prefecture Office (2010), Kamikawa Branch in Hokkaido Prefecture Office (2011).

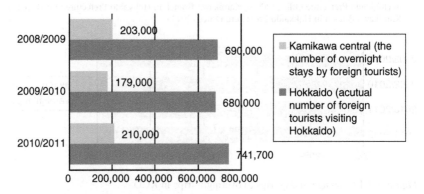

Figure 8.4 Number of overnight stays by country of origin, by district.

Note: Prepared from Kamikawa Branch in Hokkaido Prefecture Office (2008), Kamikawa Branch in Hokkaido Prefecture Office (2009), Kamikawa Branch in Hokkaido Prefecture Office (2010), Hokkaido Prefecture Office (2008), Hokkaido Prefecture Office (2009), Hokkaido Prefecture Office (2010).

the US-led financial collapse. In 2010–11, the number of foreign tourists that visited Hokkaido and KCD increased until March 2011 because of high travel demand from Asian travelers, but it decreased sharply thereafter. In terms of foreign tourists in the region, most came from Taiwan, followed by Hong Kong, China, and Korea. The number of tourists from Taiwan and Hong Kong has decreased in recent years, but the number from China is increasing rapidly. This upward trend is expected to continue in the medium term at least.

Figure 8.5 shows that the ratio of tourists that visited North Hokkaido (including KCD) to all Hokkaido in 2010 was 17.2 percent and that the ratio of overnight

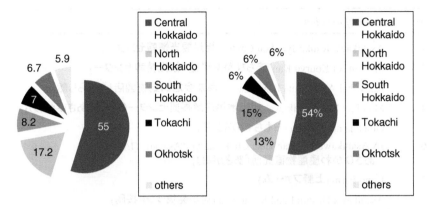

Figure 8.5 Number of tourists that visit Hokkaido and overnight stays in Hokkaido by district.

Note: Prepared from Hokkaido Prefecture Office (2010).

stays in North Hokkaido to all Hokkaido was 13 percent. A significant problem with tourism in KCD is that the rate of overnight stays is lower than the rate of tourists that visited North Hokkaido, in spite of the higher proportion of non-Hokkaido tourists compared with those that visit South Hokkaido (including Hakodate, the third largest city in Hokkaido). A possible solution could be that the tourism sector in KCD aims to enhance the rate of overnight stays. Wide-ranging cooperation among both the city and the eight towns in KCD is essential to promoting tourism.

Introduction to the KMSR

In a stamp rally, an individual visits certain locations to have his/her book stamped with rubber stamps. Each location has a unique stamp. Although there are prizes to be won from "stamp rallying," some people just participate for fun. Locations include railway stations, service stations,[4] tourist attractions, and shops.

In 2006, the KMSR was started by the KMSR committee.[5] It was introduced (1) to attract more tourists to KCD, (2) to create a model project for promoting inter-regional tours (taking advantage of the tourists that visited Hokkaido), and (3) to promote food tourism. Participants mail postcards to the KMSR committee after they have collected three to six stamps and answered the questionnaire printed on the front of them. These postcards are then entered into a prize draw.

Table 8.1 lists the locations that provided stamps in 2010 and 2011. Participants stamp their books free of charge from numbers 1 to 20; 101 to 105; and 110 to 114. Otherwise, they can stamp their books only when they purchase goods or services in the designated stamp locations. Promoters expect to attract customers through this stamp collection initiative and send them to other locations; participants are

Table 8.1 List of locations participating in the KMSR in 2010 and 2011

No.	Name of location
1	Asahikawa Kanko Jyouhou Center (旭川観光情報センター)
2	Machinaka Kouryu Kan (まちなか交流館　観光情報センター)
3	Kouyukai Asahiyama Doubutsuen (厚友会旭山動物園店(あざらし館))
4	Michi no Eki Asahikawa (旭川地場産業振興センター(道の駅あさひかわ))
5	Omocha no Yoshida (おもちゃのヨシダ)
6	JA Asahikawa No usanbutsu Chokubaijyo "Asagao" (JA あさひかわ農産物直売所「あさがお」)
7	Ueno Farm (上野ファーム)
8	Asahikawa Hashin Land Sakuraoka (旭川発信ランド桜岡)
9	Chairs Gallery (コレクション館　チェアーズ・ギャラリー)
10	Soba Izakaya Wakura (蕎麦居酒屋　和蔵)
11	Asahikawa Yokocho Gtouza no Pon (旭川横町　餃子のぽん)
12	Higashikagura Shinrin Koen (ひがしかぐら森林公園(管理棟))
13	YuYu Pippu (良佳プラザ　遊湯ぴっぷ)
14	Community hall Kura (コミュニティホール　蔵ら)
15	Taisetsu Zan Souunkyo Kurodake Ropeway (大雪山層雲峡・黒岳ロープウェイ)
16	Ryusei Ginga no Taki Kyukeisyo "Takimintara" (流星・銀河の滝休憩舎「滝ミンタラ」)
17	Gurume Koubou Kamukamu (ぐるめ工房か夢かむ)
18	Michi no Eki Higashikawa "Michikusa Kan" (道の駅ひがしかわ「道草館」)
19	Taisetsu Zan Asahidake Ropeway (大雪山旭岳ロープウェイ)
20	Michi no Eki Biei "Okanokura" (道の駅びえい「丘のくら」)
21	Tezukuri Nyuseihin Kurimari Noumu (手づくり乳製品クリーマリー農夢)
22	Asahiyama Doubutsuen Higashimon restaurant Mogumogu terrace (旭山動物園東門レストランモグモグテラス)
23	Wanomi (和のみ)
24	Asahikawa Ramen Mura (あさひかわラーメン村)
25	Kateiryouri Kasube (家庭料理　かすべ)
26	Tezukuri Toufuryouri no Mise "Densyoukan" (手作り豆腐料理の店「伝承館」)
27	Pizza house cocoperi (ピザハウスココペリ)
28	Kourinbou (光林坊)
29	Variety Kitchen Kamifusen Pippu branch (ばらえていきっちん紙風船　比布店)
30	Miso Ramen no Yoshino Kamikawa branch (みそラーメンのよし乃上川店)
31	Kiyoshi Syokudou (きよし食堂)

Table 8.1 Continued

No.	Name of location
32	Ramen no Tetsujin Shibayama (ラーメンの鉄人　しばやま)
33	Asahi Syokudou (あさひ食堂)
34	Teuchi Soba Hibiya Hanabusa (手打ちそば　日比谷　英（はなぶさ）)
35	Ekimae Antenna Shop (駅前アンテナショップ)
36	Goma Soba Tsuruki (ごまそば鶴)
37	Zerebu no Oka Restaurant (ぜるぶの丘レストラン)
38	Teuch Pasta Senmonten "Dagurasfa" (手打ちパスタ専門店　だふらすふぁー。)
39	Farm Restaurant Chiyoda (ファームレストラン千代田)
40	Roterudo Kitakurabu Honten (ロテル・ド・北倶楽部 本店)
41	The San Kuroudo (The Sun 蔵人)
42	Tsuboya Souhonten Nanakamado Kan (壺屋総本店　なゝ花窓館)
43	Roterudo Kitakurabu Chuwa (ロテル・ド・北倶楽部 忠和店)
44	Hokkaido Hatsu Hokkaido no Kanrintouya Kitakari (旭川発　北海道のかりんとう屋　北かり)
45	Hokkaido Hatsu Hokkaido no Kanrintouya Kitakari ya (旭川発　北海道のかりんとう屋　北かり屋)
46	Ice Koubou Tamura Farm Clover (アイス工房　田村ファーム)
47	Tanbo no Chiisana Purinya San "Pippurin" (田んぼの中の小さなプリン屋さん「ぴっぷりん」)
48	Kyouwa no Sato no Mochikoubou Aifukufuku (協和の里のもち工房　愛ふくふく)
49	Himeya Seipan Kashiho (ひめや製パン菓子舗)
50	Ice cream Koubou Bereru Taisetsukougen Asamogi Shijyou (アイスクリーム工房ベレル　大雪高原　朝もぎ市場)
51	Poire Tengetsuan (ポアールゝ月庵)
52	Taisetsu Jibeer Kan (大雪地ビール館)
53	Takasago Meiji Syuzou (高砂明治酒蔵)
54	Jizakegura Taisetsu no Kura (地酒蔵　大雪乃蔵)
55	Otokoyama Sakazukuri Siryoukan (男山酒造り資料館)
56	Asahiyama Doubutsuen Higashimon Baiten Tailn Tail (旭山動物園東門売店「テイルン・テイル」)
57	Boku Yuuki Kubo Nouen Chokubaisyo (ぼく勇気　久保農園直売所)
58	Kitano Mori Garden (北の森ガーデン)
59	Hirata Toufu Ten (平田とうふ店)
60	JA Biei Biei Senka (JA びえい　美瑛選果)
61	Iyashi no Kukan Gallery & Zatsuka Jiyuugaoka (癒やしの空間～ギャラリー＆雑貨時遊が丘)

Continued

Table 8.1 Continued

No.	Name of location
62	Miura Ayako Kinen Bungakukan (三浦綾子記念文学館)
63	Hokkaido Dentou Bijyutsu Kougei Mura Yuukaraori Kougeikan (北海道伝統美術工芸村 優佳良織工芸館)
64	Craft Brown Box "Arashiyama Tougei no Sato" (クラフトブラウンボックス 嵐山陶芸の里)
65	Hokuchin Kinenkan (陸上自衛隊第 2 師団 北鎮記念館)
66	Craft Kan (クラフト館)
67	Seikai no Konchukan Papillon Château (世界の昆虫館 パピヨンシャトー)
68	Hokkaido Ice Pavilion (北海道アイスパビリオン)
69	Takushinkan (前田真三フォトギャラリー「拓真館」)
70	Seibi no Mori Bijyutsukan (西美の杜美術館)
71	Morinoyu Hanakagura (森のゆ花神楽)
72	Kyouwa Onsen (協和温泉)
73	Souunkaku Grand Hotel (層雲閣グランドホテル)
74	Hotel Taisetsu (ホテル大雪)
75	Souukyou Kankou Hotel (層雲峡観光ホテル)
76	Souunkyou Chouyoutei (層雲峡朝陽亭)
77	Souunkyou Onsen Chouyou Resort Hotel (層雲峡温泉朝陽リゾートホテル)
78	Hotel Souun (ホテル層雲)
79	Mount View Hotel (マウントビューホテル)
80	Yumoto Ginsenkaku (湯元銀泉閣)
81	Tenninkaku (天人閣)
82	Tenninkyou Park Hotel (天人峡パークホテル)
83	Onyado Shikishima Sou (御やど しきしま荘)
84	Tenninkyou Grand Hotel (天人峡グランドホテル)
85	Grando Hotel Taisetsu (グランドホテル大雪)
86	Asahidake Manseikaku Hotel Bearmonte (旭岳万世閣ホテルベアモンテ)
87	Yumoto Yukomanso (湯元 湧駒荘)
88	La Vista Taisetsusan (ラビスタ大雪山)
89	Lodge Nutapukaushipe (ロッジ ヌタプカウシペ)
90	Shirogane Shiki no Mori Hotel Park Hills (白金四季の森 ホテルパークヒルズ)
91	Asahikawa Grand Hotel (旭川グランドホテル)
92	Loisir Hotel Asahikawa (ロワジールホテル旭川)
93	Shirogane Terminal Hotel (旭川ターミナルホテル)

Continued

Table 8.1 Continued

No.	Name of location
94	Hotel Resol Asahikaswa (ホテルリソル旭川)
95	Hotel Crescent Asahikawa (ホテルクレッセント旭川)
96	Fujita Kankou Washington Hotel Asahikawa (藤田観光ワシントンホテル旭川)
97	Asahikwa Washington Hotel (旭川ワシントンホテル)
98	Hotel Leopalace Asahikawa (ホテルレオパレス旭川)
99	Asahikawa Toyo Hotel (旭川トーヨーホテル)
100	Wafu Ryokan Sensyoen (和風旅館　扇松園)
101	Souunkyou Hanamonogatari (層雲峡花ものがたり)
102	Higashikawa Dontokoi Matsuri (東川どんとこい祭り)
103	Higashikawa Hana Matsuri (ひがしかぐら花まつり)
104	Takasu Nekka Festa 2010 (たかす熱夏フェスタ)
105	Asahikawa Kitano Megumi Tabe Marché (旭川「北の恵み　食べマルシェ」)
106	Muuminmura Chyokubai Café Muu (夢民村　直売カフェMuu)
107	Umeya Honten (梅屋　本店)
108	Kitano Megumi Tabe Marché in Seibu Department Store in Asahikawa (北の恵み食べマルシェ in 西武旭川店)
109	Biei Insyouha Yusaino no Niwa (美瑛印象派　油彩の庭)
110	Taisetsu Nousanbutsu Chokubaisyo (たいせつ農産物直売所)
111	Three F (スリーエフ)
112	Asahikawa Airport Information Center (旭川空港総合案内)
113	Michi no Eki "Tohma" Bussankan (道の駅とうま物産館)
114	JA Taisetsu Tanbo Art (JAたいせつ田んぼアート)

not eligible for free gifts unless they collect a minimum of three stamps. The list of locations with stamps in 2010 does not entirely match that in 2011. From number 106 onwards, new locations that were registered in the KMSR in 2011 are represented, whereas numbers 22, 25, 28, 31, 32, 45, 51, 61, 72, 80, 85, 88, and 102 were not registered in 2011.

The KMSR committee carried out a questionnaire survey (see Figure 8.6) to collect personal data on age, gender, address, and so on, in order to analyze the trends of tourists participating in the rally.

The following are the translated questions from the questionnaire in Figure 8.6. (1) Do you know the logo?; (2) What was your means of transport?; (3) How did you find out about the KMSR?; (4) How often do you participate in stamp rallies?; (5) What kinds of groups do you belong to?; (6) How many of the following seven tourist attractions have you visited?; (7) What is the length of your stay?;

(8) What is the name of the place of your overnight stay?; (9) What is your means of transport outside Hokkaido?; (10) Which airport or ferry did you use?; and (11) How did you arrange this trip?

There are two important areas of data for analyzing tourist trends in KCD in 2009. The first concerns how many tourist attractions a participant has visited out of the seven well-known attractions mentioned earlier. These data can be used to analyze the correlations between these seven attractions. The second is the data derived from the use of a unique stamp at each location, which can be used to carry out network analyses of the traffic lines of tourists that visited KCD. These network analyses are explained below.

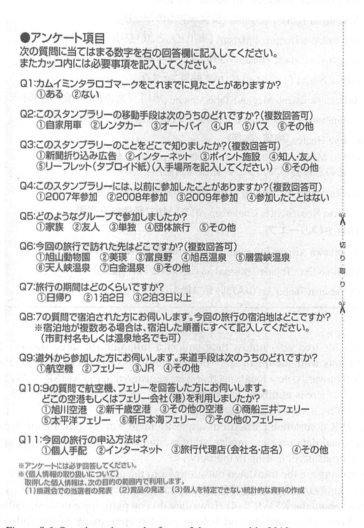

Figure 8.6 Questionnaire on the front of the postcard in 2010.

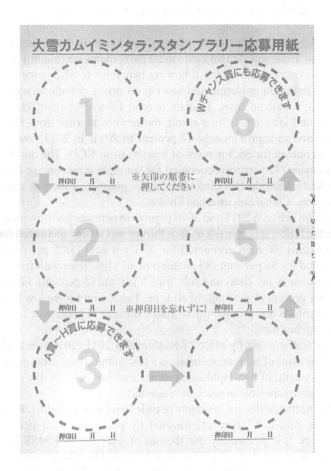

Figure 8.7 Reverse side of the postcard in 2010.

Table 8.2 Changes in the number of participants

Year	2006	2007	2008	2009	2010	2011
No. of participants	584	2,376	5,652	4,062	4,891	5,907

Note: Prepared from Daisetsu Kamui Mintara Stamp Rally Committee (2008, 2009, 2010, 2011).

Characteristics of tourists that visited KCD

The KMSR was held for the sixth time in 2011. Table 8.2 shows that the number of participants increased gradually between 2006 and 2008, but decreased in 2009 because of the US-led financial collapse. From 2010 to 2011, it increased year-on-year because of the economic recovery in Japan. Further, the KMSR in 2011–12 was not affected by the Great East Japan Earthquake because of the season in which it is held.

Table 8.3 shows KMSR participants by place of residence. In 2007, the proportion of participants from outside Hokkaido to all participants was slightly less than 60 percent. This decreased over the following two years to 31.2 percent in 2009 because of an influenza epidemic and soaring oil prices, which prevented tourists from making long-haul trips. Tourists instead favored cheaper, closer, and shorter trips in and after 2009. As a result, the ratio of tourists from KCD to all tourists increased to approximately 47 percent in 2011. In 2011, tourists from Asahikawa accounted for 86.5 percent of tourists from KCD. The number of tourists from Sapporo (42 percent) accounted for the highest percentage from Hokkaido except KCD. Outside Hokkaido, the largest number of tourists came from Tokyo, Kanagawa, Chiba, Saitama, and Osaka.

Comparisons of data between 2011 and 2010 (figures in parentheses throughout this section) show the following. Tourists in their thirties and sixties accounted for 68 percent (68 per cent). Women accounted for 57.1 per cent (58.5 per cent). Family trips accounted for 86 per cent (85 percent) of all trips. Trips with friends accounted for 7 per cent (8 per cent) and solo trips 5 percent (5 percent). Group tours accounted for 1 percent (1 per cent) of all trips. The reason for the low ratio of group tours to all trips is that group tourists[6] find it difficult to participate in the rally because of group bus travel.

Figure 8.8 shows traffic mode by place of residence in 2011 (2010). In total, 90.9 percent (92.2 percent) of all tourists used cars (including rental cars), while 10.0 percent (13.0 per cent) of non-Hokkaido tourists used buses. Thus, the main traffic mode is the car, irrespective of place of residence.

Figure 8.9 shows traffic modes for residents outside Hokkaido in 2011 (2010). Altogether, 75.8 per cent (74.7 percent) traveled by plane and 21.3 percent (20.8 percent) by ferry. It is noteworthy that the rate of ferry use by KMSR participants is higher than the average rate of ferry use in Hokkaido.[7] Since 2010, the KMSR committee has asked tourists which ferry they used (see Figure 8.10).

Figure 8.10 shows airport and ferry use by KMSR participants in 2011. Many participants from outside Hokkaido used Asahikawa airport and/or Shinchitose airport. More used Asahikawa airport than Shinchitose airport. Non-Hokkaido tourists who visited KCD typically arrived at Asahikawa airport first and then went on tours around the district. The data also show that non-Hokkaido tourists used more sea routes from Maizuru on the Sea of Japan than Sendai or Ooarai on the Pacific Ocean. This result suggests that many of the tourists who arrived by ferry used private cars and went on tours around Hokkaido. This kind of trip is likely to increase following the introduction of the discount on expressway tolls.

Figure 8.11 shows the length of overnight stays by place of residence in 2011. In 2011, questionnaire item 7 was modified to ask respondents to fill out their exact number of overnight stays. In addition, day trips by tourists that visited KCD in 2011 (compared to the figures for 2010 in parentheses) accounted for 52.6 percent (49.4 percent) of all trips, while overnight trips accounted for 47.4 percent (50.6 percent). Day trips by tourists from KCD accounted for 88.5 percent

Table 8.3 Changes in participants by place of residence

	2007	Component ratio	2008	Component ratio	2009	Component ratio	2010	Component ratio	2011	Component ratio
KCD	456	20.0%	1,776	31.4%	1,830	45.1%	2,181	44.6%	2,768	46.9%
Hokkaido	491	21.5%	1,614	28.6%	949	23.4%	1,268	25.9%	1,423	24.1%
Outside Hokkaido	1,337	58.5%	2,262	40.0%	1,266	31.2%	1,441	29.5%	1,711	29.0%
Unidentified	0	0.0%	0	0.0%	17	0.4%	1	0.0%	5	0.1%
Total	2,284	100.0%	5,652	100.0%	4,062	100.0%	4,891	100.0%	5,907	100%

Note: Prepared from Daisetsu Kamui Mintara Stamp Rally Committee (2008, 2009, 2010, 2011).

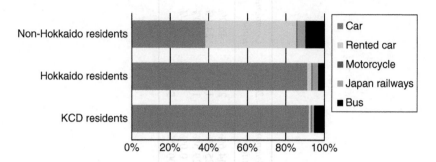

Figure 8.8 Traffic mode by place of residence in 2011.

Note: Prepared from the questionnaire.

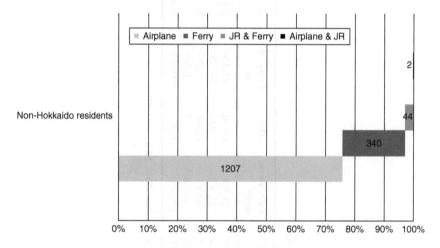

Figure 8.9 Traffic mode by non-Hokkaido residents.

Note: Prepared from the questionnaire.

(86.1 percent) of all their trips, while 91.2 percent (91.1 percent) of non-Hokkaido tourists stayed more than two nights. The ratio of day trips to overnight trips by Hokkaido tourists was approximately 55.0 percent (61.3 percent). Thus, the rate of overnight stays increased slightly year-on-year.

Table 8.4 shows the average length of touring trips around the KMSR by place of residence in 2010 and 2011. Since 2010, the KMSR committee has added a date and time field to the stamp to gather accurate trip information. As a result, I can obtain time-series data for the KMSR. The average length of touring during the KMSR was approximately 18 days. However, I do not rely on these numerical data, since the standard deviations are larger than the averages. Thus, the median or mode values better reflect the length of touring. The longest average length of touring was approximately one month by KCD tourists, while that by

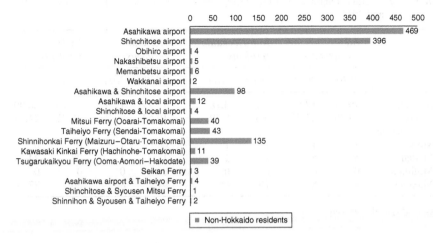

Figure 8.10 Airport and ferry use by KMSR participants in 2011.

Note: Prepared from the questionnaire.

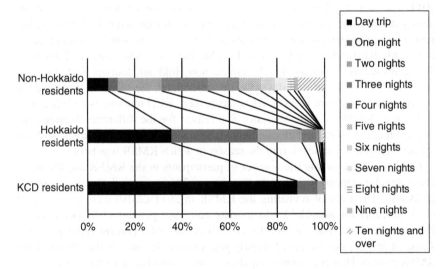

Figure 8.11 Length of overnight stays by place of residence in 2011.

Note: Prepared from the questionnaire.

Hokkaido tourists was approximately 11 days. The average length of touring outside Hokkaido was approximately four days. Further, typical non-Hokkaido tourists stayed overnight or for two nights. By contrast, typical KCD tourists toured around this area for one month (see bold values in Table 8.4). It is note-worthy that the mode of the length of touring by Hokkaido tourists increased from

Table 8.4 Average length of touring during the KMSR by place of residence in 2010 and 2011

	All participants		Non-Hokkaido residents		Hokkaido residents		KCD residents	
	2010	2011	2010	2011	2010	2011	2010	2011
Average	19.07	17.67	4.16	**3.78**	11.27	11.99	33.19	**28.99**
Standard Deviation	24.39	22.75	9.83	8.39	19.54	20.24	25.72	24.11
Mode	1	1	1	1	0	**1**	0	0
Median	5	5	1	**2**	1	1	28	**24**
Minimum	0	0	0	0	0	0	0	0
Maximum	91	87	79	85	91	86	86	87

Note: Prepared from stamp data.

zero days to one day. The result matches the decline in the rate of day trips shown in Figure 8.11.

Table 8.5 shows the average length of touring in Hokkaido during KMSR in 2011. The aim of Table 8.5 is to grasp the accurate trip actual situation by comparing the average length of trips in Hokkaido with the average length during KMSR. The mode of the length of touring in Hokkaido for non-Hokkaido tourists is 3 (4; Median) and during KMSR is 1 (2; Median) (see bold values in Table 8.5). The result seems to indicate that the typical non-Hokkaido tourists visited several cities and stayed for several days. On the other hand, the mode of the length of touring in Hokkaido for Hokkaido tourists (except KCD tourists) is 1 (1; Median) and during KMSR is 1 (1; Median). The reason for the difference between the average length (11.99) and mode (median) seems that Hokkaido tourists made an overnight trip many times during the season in which KMSR was held.

Figure 8.12 shows that the number of participants in the KMSR and the number of regular (repeat) tourists was very low in 2011, especially by those outside Hokkaido. The rates of revisiting the KMSR in 2011 (2010) were 13.6 percent (12.2 percent) for non-Hokkaido tourists and 19.9 percent (19.5 percent) for Hokkaido tourists. The rate for KCD tourists was 38.0 percent (36.1 perecnt). Thus, all revisit rates increased slightly year-on-year because of the efforts of the KMSR project. However, improving these figures must become one of the aims of the tourism strategy.

Correlation among well-known tourist attractions

To confirm, the seven well-known attractions mentioned by the questionnaire are Asahiyama Zoo, Biei, Furano, Asahidake, Souunkyo, Tenninkyou, and Shirogane.

Tables 8.6, 8.7 and 8.8 show correlations between the seven well-known tourist attractions for 2009–2011. The bold numbers indicate relatively high positive correlations. For example, Asahiyama Zoo is correlated with Biei, which means that

Table 8.5 Average length of touring in Hokkaido in 2011

	All participants		Non-Hokkaido residents		Hokkaido residents		KCD residents	
	During KMSR	During Hokkaido touring	During KMSR	During Hokkaido touring	During KMSR	During Hokkaido touring	During KMSR	During Hokkaido touring
Average	17.67	2.36	3.78	6.54	11.99	1.27	28.99	0.3
Standard Deviation	22.75	7.34	8.39	12.09	20.24	2.04	24.11	2.60
Mode	1	0	**1**	**3**	1	1	0	0
Median	5	1	**2**	**4**	1	1	24	0

Note: Prepared from the questionnaire.

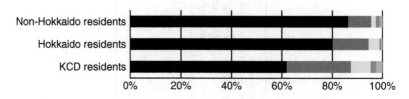

	KCD residents	Hokkaido residents	Non-Hokkaido residents
■ 1st	1712	1140	1481
■ 2nd	708	206	158
3rd	218	61	31
■ 4th	58	8	25
■ 5th	69	8	19

Figure 8.12 Number of KMSR participants by place of residence in 2011.

Note: Prepared from the questionnaire.

Table 8.6 Correlations[8] between the seven well-known tourist attractions in 2009

	Asahiyama Zoo	Biei	Furano	Asahidake	Souunkyo	Tenninkyou	Shirogane
Asahiyama Zoo	1	**0.13065**	**0.24494**	0.05622	0.04208	0.00331	0.06990
Biei		1	**0.52067**	0.06583	−0.06008	−0.00036	**0.22093**
Furano			1	0.09306	0.02502	0.03737	**0.1568**
Asahidake				1	0.00929	**0.21681**	0.09259
Souunkyo					1	0.01741	−0.04942
Tenninkyou						1	0.07452
Shirogane							1

Note: Prepared from the questionnaire.

tourists that visit Asahiyama Zoo are likely to visit Biei. Moreover, tourists that visit Biei are particularly likely to visit Furano and Shirogane. By contrast, tourists that visit Souunkyo are unlikely to visit any of the other six attractions, perhaps because of its isolated location. The correlations are thus shown to be affected by the geographical location of each attraction. The annual changes in significant correlations were also obtained using chi-square tests.

In addition, these tables show that tourists changed their patterns of behavior between 2009 and 2011. For instance, the correlation coefficient between Asahiyama Zoo and Biei decreased between 2009 and 2010 at a statistically significant level ($p < 0.01$).[12] This result shows that tourists that visited Biei in

Table 8.7 Correlations between the seven well-known tourist attractions in 2010

	Asahiyama Zoo	Biei	Furano	Asahidake	Souunkyo	Tenninkyou	Shirogane
Asahiyama Zoo	1	0.05533	**0.17883**	−0.04432	0.01725	−0.01318	−0.00059
Biei		1	**0.43043**	0.04251	−0.04448	0.01601	**0.16413**
Furano			1	0.04729	0.06083	0.03421	**0.12918**
Asahidake				1	0.07197	**0.17339**	**0.12024**[9]
Souunkyo					1	0.08897	0.01494
Tenninkyou						1	**0.10075**[10]
Shirogane							1

Note: Prepared from the questionnaire.

Table 8.8 Correlations between the seven well-known tourist attractions in 2011

	Asahiyama Zoo	Biei	Furano	Asahidake	Souunkyo	Tenninkyou	Shirogane
Asahiyama Zoo	1	**0.12216**	**0.19853**	0.07283	0.06396	0.03083	**0.11370**
Biei		1	**0.55199**	**0.12554**	−0.0038	0.05350	**0.23848**
Furano			1	0.1655	0.09001	**0.10554**	**0.20365**
Asahidake				1	0.09075	**0.21987**	0.06822
Souunkyo					1	0.06700	0.02997
Tenninkyou						1	**0.08052**[11]
Shirogane							1

Note: Prepared from the questionnaire.

2010 did not visit Asahiyama Zoo more than usual. However, the correlation between Asahiyama Zoo and Biei in 2011 recovered to the 2009 level. Additionally, the correlation coefficient[13] between Asahiyama Zoo and Shirogane increased rapidly between 2009 and 2010, although further analysis is necessary to understand why. Moreover, in 2011, the correlation coefficients[14] between Asahidake and three attractions (Biei, Furano, and Shirogane) increased sharply, whereas those[15] between Shirogane and Asahidake decreased because of the effect of a flood in August 2011 that severed the road from Biei to Shirogane and Asahidake.

Figure 8.13 shows the transition map of traffic lines in Kamikawa district from 2009 to 2011. The solid curved lines show the traffic lines, while the thickness of the line expresses the strength of the correlation. The solid outer lines show the areas of high correlation. In these solid outer lines, a tourist that visits an attraction can easily reach another attraction. By contrast, the broken outer lines show isolated attractions such as Souunkyo. Tourists that visit Souunkyo are likely to also visit Kitami or Abashiri in East Hokkaido for geographical reasons. Further, if they stay at another of the six attractions, the number of overnight stays in this

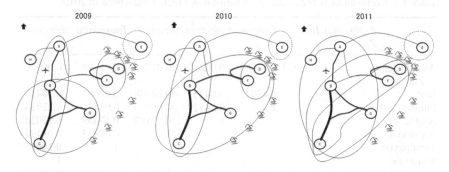

Figure 8.13 Transition map of traffic lines in Kamikawa district from 2009 to 2011.

Note: A: Asahiyama Zoo; B: Biei; C: Furano; D: Asahidake; E: Souunkyo; F: Tenninkyou; G: Shirogane; H: Service station in Asahikawa.

area must increase. This problem of geographical remoteness must be tackled to encourage day-trippers.

Visualization of tourist traffic lines

There are two methods of creating network graphs in order to visualize tourist traffic lines. One method is using the data from the answers to item 8 in the questionnaire, to create network graphs of tourist traffic lines around Hokkaido. The second method is using the data from the stamps and regarding the locations or places of overnight stays as nodes and traffic lines as links.

Figure 8.14 presents the network graph of the traffic lines of tourists that visited Hokkaido. This figure shows that tourists traveled throughout Hokkaido. However, it is difficult to understand the relation among nodes at a glance. Therefore, Figure 8.15 demonstrates the important relations between nodes after the links have been reduced using K-cores. This figure clearly shows that the traffic lines include the seven investigated tourist attractions. In particular, those from Sapporo to Asahikawa, Souunkyo, Asahidake, and Furano are prominent in Kamikawa district. In general, the findings agree with the results presented in Tables 8.6, 8.7, and 8.8.

Notably, Tomamu, Obihiro, Otofuke, Akanko, Abashiri, and Kushiro are shown to be closely linked with Kamikawa district. Figure 8.15 also shows the various tours via Sapporo.

Figure 8.16 shows the network graph of the traffic lines of KMSR participants in 2010 created using KMSR data. Because this network is so complicated that relations between nodes cannot be understood at a glance, Figure 8.17 and Figure 8.18 (showing an enlarged network graph of tourist traffic lines for KMSR participants in 2011) were created by removing the links with a weight of less than 80 people. These figures show that many tourists passed through three service stations: Asahikawa, "Okanokura" in Biei, and "Michikusakan" in Higashikawa

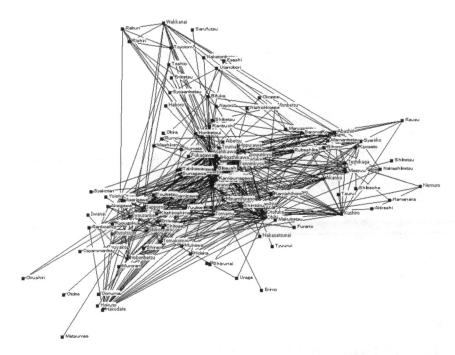

Figure 8.14 Network graph of the traffic lines of tourists that visited Hokkaido in 2011 based on KMSR data.

Note: Prepared from the questionnaire.

(Figure 8.17). The magnitude of the link from A to B indicates the number of tourists moving from A to B. This demonstrates that the magnitudes of the links from the service station in Asahikawa to that in Okanokura, from Okanokura to Michikusakan, and from Asahikawa to Michikusakan are very large. This network graph thus clearly shows that the network hubs are these three service stations. In Figure 8.18, the service station "Tohma" was newly registered with the KMSR in 2011, and thus we should not consider this to be a change in traffic lines.

Both these figures show that tourists traveling by car tend to "drop in" at service stations. In particular, KMSR participants drop in at these "free" locations. However, visiting locations that demand an entrance fee is important for enhancing total economic activity in an area. In this regard, the cake shop "The Sun Kuroudo," ice cream stand "Clover," and souvenir shops "Hirata Tohfu" and "Biei Senka" are important. Data on traffic lines are thus crucial for managers and local government officers when designing tourism strategies.

Network analyses of tourist traffic lines

This section investigates the characteristics of the network of tourist traffic paths in KCD using network analysis by year and place of residence. As described earlier,

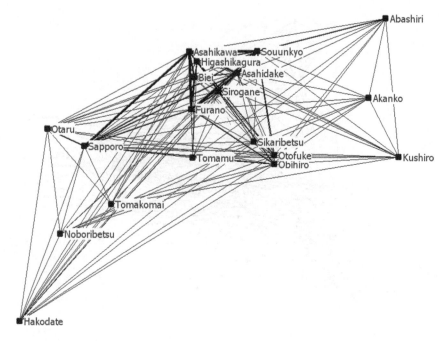

Figure 8.15 Enlarged graph of Figure 8.14 in 2011.[16]

Note: Prepared from the questionnaire.

I regard locations as nodes and traffic lines as links. Tables 8.9 and 8.10 indicate the number of nodes, average node degree (i.e. average number of links connected to this node), density of the network,[18] clustering coefficient,[19] and average path length[20] by year and place of residence, respectively. For comparison purposes, I have included the clustering coefficient and average line length of a random graph of the same size and average degree in these two tables.

Table 8.9 shows that average node degree and network density increased incrementally each year. A link is generated by a tourist moving from location "A" to location "B" and vice versa. Hence, a location that has a high node degree means many tourists traveled through it, while a high density value means that tourist traffic lines are dispersive rather than skewed. Dispersive traffic lines are better than concentrated traffic lines because more locations would benefit from the KMSR. Therefore, a high average node degree and high density are better for economic activity. The results presented in Table 8.10 show that the economic benefit of the KMSR is rising.

Both the clustering coefficient and the average line length are large compared with those in the random graph. This finding suggests that these networks are not characteristic of "small-world" networks (Watts and Strogatz, 1998). The large clustering coefficient means that the six attractions are closely related to each

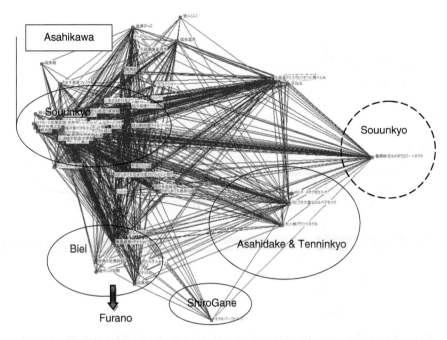

Figure 8.16 Network graph of tourist traffic lines for KMSR participants in 2010.

Note: Prepared using stamp data.

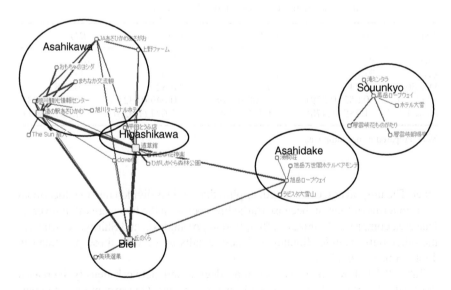

Figure 8.17 Enlarged network graph of tourist traffic lines for KMSR participants in 2010.[17]

Note: Prepared using stamp data.

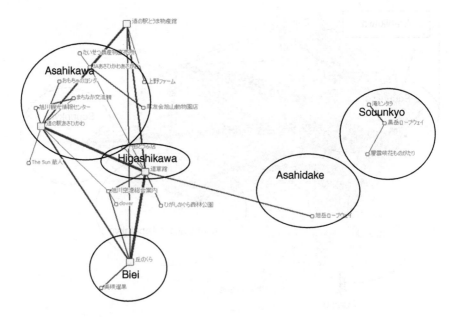

Figure 8.18 Enlarged network graph of tourist traffic lines for KMSR participants in 2011.
Note: Prepared using stamp data.

Table 8.9 General characteristics of KMSR networks by year

Year	2008	2009	2010	2011
Size	95	113	105	101
$\langle k \rangle$	21.8	30.32	33.68	33.78
Density	0.24	0.276	0.323	0.338
$C(C_{rand})$	0.652 (0.229)	0.608 (0.268)	0.649 (0.32)	0.693 (0.33)
$l(l_{rand})$	1.785 (1.478)	1.751(1.386)	1.677 (1.323)	1.667 (1.311)

Note: Prepared using stamp data.

other. The large average line length implies that KCD is divided into two locational areas in terms of tourism because traffic lines between the two were often severed. One area comprises Asahikawa, Biei, Furano, Asahidake, and Shirogane, whereas the other only includes Souunkyo. These results agree with those presented in Tables 8.6, 8.7, and 8.8.

Table 8.10 shows that average node degree and network density increased drastically by place of residence with two exceptions. One exception is the network density of non-Hokkaido tourists in 2009 because of the US-led financial collapse and influenza epidemic. Another exception is the average node degree of Hokkaido tourists except for those from KCD in 2011, for which further analysis

Table 8.10 General characteristics of KMSR networks by place of residence

Year	2008	2009[21]	2010	2011
Residence	KCD			
Size	92	111	104	97
$\langle k \rangle$[22]	12.2	19.59	23.55	22.32
Density	0.134	0.178	0.235	0.214
$C(C_{rand})$	0.579	0.586	0.65	0.613
	(0.133)	(0.181)	(0.243)	(0.215)
$l(l_{rand})$	2.032	1.916	1.769	1.832
	(1.819)	(1.574)	(1.448)	(1.495)
Residence	Hokkaido			
Size	92	107	102	100
$\langle k \rangle$	9.2	13.39	16.13	15.7
Density	0.101	0.122	0.155	0.157
$C(C_{rand})$	0.612	0.579	0.554	0.592
	(0.1)	(0.125)	(0.158)	(0.157)
$l(l_{rand})$	2.149	2.074	1.938	2.006
	(2.038)	(1.801)	(1.663)	(1.672)
Residence	Outside Hokkaido			
Size	92	104	100	99
$\langle k \rangle$	12.72	14.79	17.41	18.08
Density	0.14	0.135	0.167	0.1808
$C(C_{rand})$	0.622	0.51	0.603	0.618
	(0.138)	(0.142)	(0.174)	(0.183)
$l(l_{rand})$	1.945	2.027	1.915	1.902
	(1.778)	(1.724)	(1.611)	(1.587)

Note: Prepared using stamp data.

is necessary. However, the economic benefit of the KMSR for all residents is rising. Moreover, Table 8.10 shows that the average node degree and network density of non-Hokkaido tourists are both higher than those for Hokkaido tourists, except for KCD. These results show that non-Hokkaido tourists tend to visit spas and overnight accommodation more often compared with Hokkaido tourists because of the lengths of their tours (see Table 8.5).

The advantage of using network analyses to examine tourist traffic lines is in understanding the structure of tourism by numerical means. In the case of analyzing large networks, conventional network analysis is necessary, since visualization is difficult. In this chapter, the visualizations presented in this section are supported by statistical data on these networks.

Concluding remarks

The traffic lines of tourists that visited KCD were investigated using a questionnaire, visualizations, and network analyses. The main findings are summarized below. Tourists favored cheaper, closer, and shorter trips in and after 2009. As a result, the ratio of tourists from KCD to all tourists increased to approximately 47 percent in 2011. Family trips accounted for approximately 85 percent of all trips, while the main traffic mode was the car (including rental cars) irrespective of place of residence during the KMSR. Three-quarters of non-Hokkaido tourists traveled by plane and approximately 20 percent by ferry. It is noteworthy that the rate of ferry use by KMSR participants is higher than the average rate of ferry use in Hokkaido (7.8 percent in 2010). Interestingly, non-Hokkaido tourists used more sea routes from Maizuru on the Sea of Japan than Sendai or Ooarai on the Pacific Ocean.

Tourists from Hokkaido, as well as those from outside Hokkaido, typically stayed overnight during the KMSR. Tourists from KCD traveled around this district for one month, visiting several cities and staying in each for a few days. By contrast, Hokkaido tourists made overnight trips many times during the season in which the KMSR was held.

The number of regular (repeat) tourists was very low, especially by those outside Hokkaido. The rates of revisiting the KMSR in 2011 (2010) were 13.6 percent (12.2 percent) for non-Hokkaido tourists and 19.9 percent (19.5 percent) for Hokkaido tourists. The rate for KCD tourists was 38.0 percent (36.1 percent). Thus, all revisit rates increased slightly year-on-year because of the efforts of the KMSR project. However, improving these figures must become one of the aims of the tourism strategy.

I investigated the correlations between seven well-known tourist attractions using the questionnaire. These attractions were Asahiyama Zoo, Biei, Furano, Asahidake, Souunkyo, Tenninkyou, and Shirogane. We found that Souunkyo is isolated from the other six attractions because of its geographical position. This result shows the need for wide-ranging cooperation between Souunkyo and the other areas in KCD in order to promote region-wide tourism.

I next used network analysis to visualize tourist traffic lines and found that the investigated seven well-known attractions are important for tourism in Kamikawa district. Additionally, Sapporo, Abashiri, Tomamu, Obihiro, Otofuke, Akanko, and Kushiro are important for tourism in KCD, while four service stations in Kamikawa district are crucial hubs for Kamikawa tours and/or participants of the KMSR. As a tourism strategy, visiting locations that demand an entrance fee is important for enhancing total economic activity in the area, since service stations are free to enter.

Finally, I investigated the characteristics of the network of tourist traffic lines in KCD using network analysis by year and place of residence. High average node degree and high density were found to be better for economic activity. Moreover, the large clustering coefficient suggested that the six attractions are closely related to each other. The large average line length implied that KCD is divided into two locational areas in terms of tourism because traffic lines between the two are often severed.

This study has several limitations. First, it cannot fully deal with foreign tourists that visit this area or group bus travel using data on the KMSR. Greater effort should thus be made to study the trends of foreign and group bus tourists. Never-theless, I conclude that visualization and network analysis are both necessary to understand tourist traffic lines. The information acquired from the presented net-work analysis might provide guidance to managers and local government officers when designing tourism strategies.

Acknowledgments

We express our appreciation to the Kamikawa Branch Office in Hokkaido prefec-ture and the KMSR committee for their support and cooperation in this research. This work was supported by the Center of Education and Research for Topological Science and Technology at Hokkaido University.

Notes

1 Hokkaido Keizai Bu Kanko Kyoku (2010).
2 Kamikawa Branch in Hokkaido Prefecture Office (2008), Kamikawa Branch in Hokkaido Prefecture Office (2009), Kamikawa Branch in Hokkaido Prefecture Office (2010), Hokkaido Prefecture Office (2011).
3 Hokkaido Prefecture Office (2008), Hokkaido Prefecture Office (2009), Hokkaido Prefecture Office (2010), Hokkaido Prefecture Office (2011).
4 Service station is the same as "Michi no Eki" in this chapter. However, not all service stations are called "Michi no Eki" in Japan. "Michi no Eki" is a government-designated public rest area found along roads and highways in Japan. They provide 24-hour access to the following services: Parking; Restrooms; and Facilities for sharing information. As of March 2012, there are 987 Roadside Stations across Japan, including 92 in Hokkaido.
5 The committee comprised the Kamikawa branch in the Hokkaido office, Asahikawa city office, Higashikagura town office, Biei, Touma, Takasu, Pippu, Aibetsu, and Kamikawa.
6 It should be noted that the effect of group tourists is likely to be underestimated in the KMSR data because the ratio of tourists using cars (including rental cars) is very high compared to those using buses. This is especially applicable to Souunkyo, which many group tourists visit.
7 This was 7.8 percent in 2011 Hokkaido Prefecture Office (2008), Hokkaido Prefecture Office (2009), Hokkaido Prefecture Office (2010).
8 There are subtle differences in the correlation coefficients between this chapter and those presented by (Kichiji, 2010) because the data on Asahiyama Zoo and Biei had defects, which I subsequently fixed (see Table 8.6)
9 There were no significant differences between these two correlations.
10 There were no significant differences between these two correlations.
11 There were no significant differences between these two correlations.
12 $r_{2009} = 0.13065$, $r_{2010} = 0.05533$, $n_{2009} = 4005$, $n_{2010} = 4892$, Z-value $= 3.57$.
13 Tests were two-sided and Z-value $p < 0.01$. The correlation coefficient was statistically significant.
14 Tests were two-sided and Z-value $p < 0.01$. The correlation coefficients were statisti-cally significant.
15 Tests were two-sided and Z-value $p < 0.01$. The correlation coefficient was statistically significant.
16 K-cores in graph theory were introduced by Seidman (1983) and Bollobas (1984) as a method of (destructively) simplifying graph topology to aid analysis and visualization.
17 The method of K-cores attaches a high value to vertex connectivity. However, I stress the weights of links for visualizations in Figures 8.17 and 8.18.

18 Density is simply the ratio of the number of adjacencies that are present divided by the number of pairs, namely the proportion of all possible dyadic connections actually present.
19 The clustering coefficient measures the level of cohesiveness around any given node. It is expressed as the fraction of connected neighbors, $c_i = 2e/[k_i(k_i - 1)]$ where e_i is the number of links between the neighbors of node i and $k_i(k_i - 1)$ is the maximum number of possible interconnections among the neighbors of the node. C in Table 8.9 indicates the average value of the clustering coefficient.
20 For non-directional, unweighted graphs, the number of edges in a path that connects vertices i and j is called the length of the path. A geodesic path (or the shortest path) between vertices i and j is one of the paths that connects these vertices with minimum length (many geodesic paths may exist between two vertices); the length of the geodesic path is the geodesic distance d_{ij} between vertices i and j.
21 There are subtle differences in the correlation coefficients and average path lengths between this chapter and those presented by (Kichiji, 2010) because the data on Asahiyama Zoo and Biei had defects, which I subsequently fixed (see Table 11).
22 $\langle k \rangle$ represents the average degree of all nodes.

References

Bollobas, B (1984) "The evolution of sparse graphs in Graph theory and combinatorics," in *Proceedings of the Cambridge Combinatorial Conference in honor of Paul Erdos,* Academic Press, pp. 35–57.
Daisetsu Kamui Mintara Stamp Rally Committee (2008) *Statistical data on Daisetsu Kamui Mintara Stamp Rally in 2008.*
Daisetsu Kamui Mintara Stamp Rally Committee (2009) *Statistical data on Daisetsu Kamui Mintara Stamp Rally in 2009.*
Daisetsu Kamui Mintara Stamp Rally Committee (2010) *Statistical data on Daisetsu Kamui Mintara Stamp Rally in 2010.*
Daisetsu Kamui Mintara Stamp Rally Committee (2011) *Statistical data on Daisetsu Kamui Mintara Stamp Rally in 2011.*
Hokkaido Keizai Bu Kanko Kyoku (2010) *Kanko Titen Doukou Chousa* (A survey of trends in well-known tourism sites).
Hokkaido Prefecture Office (2008) *Hokkaido Kankou Irikomi Kyakusu Chousa Houkokusyo* (A survey of tourists visiting Hokkaido in 2008).
Hokkaido Prefecture Office (2009) *Hokkaido Kankou Irikomi Kyakusu Chousa Houkokusyo* (A survey of tourists visiting Hokkaido in 2009).
Hokkaido Prefecture Office (2010) *Hokkaido Kankou Irikomi Kyakusu Chousa Houkokusyo* (A survey of tourists visiting Hokkaido in 2010).
Hokkaido Prefecture Office (2011) *Hokkaido Kankou Irikomi Kyakusu Chousa Houkokusyo* (A survey of tourists visiting Hokkaido in 2011).
Kamikawa Branch in Hokkaido Prefecture Office (2008) *Kamikawa Shichou Kannai Kankou Irikomi Kyakusu* (A survey of the number of tourists visiting Kamikawa district in 2008).
Kamikawa Branch in Hokkaido Prefecture Office (2009) *Kamikawa Shichou Kannai Kankou Irikomi Kyakusu* (A survey of the number of tourists visiting Kamikawa district in 2009).
Kamikawa Branch in Hokkaido Prefecture Office (2010) *Kamikawa Shichou Kannai Kankou Irikomi Kyakusu* (A survey of the number of tourists visiting Kamikawa district in 2010).
Kamikawa Branch in Hokkaido Prefecture Office (2011) *Kamikawa Kannai Kankou Irikomi Kyakusu Chousa Houkokusyo* (A survey of the number of tourists visiting Kamikawa district in 2011).

Kichiji, N. (2010) "Kamikawa Chubu Kankoukyaku no Dousen Bunseki I" (Network analysis of the traffic line of the tourists visiting Kamikawa Central district in Hokkaido, Japan I (in Japanese)), *Shinka Keizaigaku Ronsyu*, 15: 514–2.

Kichiji, N. (2011) "Network analysis of the traffic lines of the tourists visiting Kamikawa Central District in Hokkaido, Japan-based on the data from the 'Kamui Mintara' Stamp Rally," *Economic Journal of Hokkaido University*, 40: 89–112.

Seidman, S.B. (1983) "Network structure and minimum degree," *Social Networks*, 5(3): 269–87.

Watts D.J. and S.H. Strogatz (1998) "Collective dynamics of small-world networks," *Nature*, 393: 440–42.

9 Analysis concerning perception of the farm village landscape

A case study of two farm villages in Hokkaido

Tomochika Toguchi

Introduction

Awareness of importance and consideration of landscape in Japan has existed since ancient times, but its modern history began in the early twentieth century when the City Planning and Zoning Act was enacted in 1919. A heightened consciousness and consideration of the value of the landscape have risen in recent years. At the beginning of the twentieth century, Japan was one of the small, late-start countries on the edge of the Far East. It was a stage of development for the country when rapid modernization and economical development were valued most. Under the slogan "wealthy nation and strong army" Japan tried to catch up with the levels of development, wealth and military strength of other countries in Europe. The purpose of the City Planning and Zoning Act at that time was to ensure functional urban development, not preservation of landscape.

After World War II, the Western model of functional urban development was actively introduced to land that had become vast burnt ruins. The city design that is modeled after Western urban design (where the streets are laid out in a grid pattern, at right angles) can be observed in Nagoya city, where the headquarters of the world-famous Toyota automobile company is located, and in the central city of Sapporo in Hokkaido in the north of Japan. Hokkaido is the northern-most late-start province in Japan, and it is the place where functional urban development can be observed more noticeably than in other regions of the country. In Hokkaido, colonization by new settlers, and development of towns and cities, started late in the mid nineteenth century, and advanced more rapidly from the beginning of the twentieth century. Moreover, it is a place where the pioneer's migration process introduced a township system similar to that of the United States in order to promote land development.

Hokkaido is the biggest prefecture in Japan. It accounts for 22 percent of the land mass, and mainly plays the role of food production and agricultural base. Although Japan is located along the "Pacific Ring of Fire", a seismically active volcanic zone, with many geographical features of a mountain terrain, Hokkaido is an island with wide continental-type plains and granary areas similar to those found in Europe and the United States.

When traveling in Hokkaido, one can see (as the car travels across the land) that there are many suburban-type large-scale stores in the farming areas. These appear to be mushrooming, as in the United States, though Hokkaido is supposed to be a place where functional urban development is promoted. However, increased awareness and concerns about matching and functioning landscapes in recent years are being enforced with the enactment of the Three Laws of the Green Landscape. Still, there are no uniform standards of landscape maintenance yet, and how such operations will be implemented in each of the municipalities is not certain.

The aim of this chapter is to analyze the assessment of the rural landscape by awareness, observation, and perception by individual people in order to utilize the results for the development of generic areas of Hokkaido. Covering the entire area of Hokkaido, the Contingent Valuation Method (CVM) has established these observational techniques, in order to understand the target landscape and propose concrete maintenance actions needed for advancing the rural development project.

Method of analysis

The Contingent Valuation Method (CVM) is the main method of analysis of landscape assessment. Economic conversion by Willingness to Pay (WTP) is a very effective method, and has been used in many previous studies in Japan. However, the analysis in this chapter was done on a micro-perspective level and aimed to understand the objectives of landscape analysis by combining a questionnaire with a photo survey.

A landscape can be assessed from a variety of perspectives and depending on how we look at those, and how we take into consideration the main object, the assessment of the landscape changes. In this chapter, the analysis was limited to the view which a person moving in a car would have from the main road of the object site, and what he or she would evaluate looking from the fixed aspect of the view which is being studied.

A sample of the questionnaire form used in the analysis is shown in Figure 9.1.

The questionnaire is a set of five-part, simple questions about the landscape, clarifying an individual's perception. Its aim is to point out what is seen (and where) in the photograph and describe the individual's emotional perception of the picture. The questionnaire gives priority to the perception of the landscape on a very micro and individual level and also to the extraction of the contents of the landscape composition. We targeted two areas that represent characteristic rural landscapes in Hokkaido. Eleven items were evaluated in Naganuma-cho and five items were evaluated in Kutchan-cho villages.[1]

Students were used as testees; they were asked questions while the photographs used in the questionnaire were projected onto the screen. The reason for choosing students is that individual impressions vary greatly if there are changes in the color, display form, and size of photos during the questionnaire. In order to secure a constant number of the sample necessary for analysis, and perform the

Check your impression of the following picture.

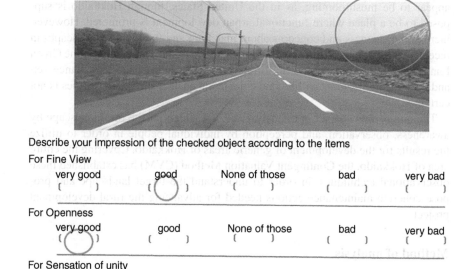

Describe your impression of the checked object according to the items

For Fine View

very good	good	None of those	bad	very bad
( )	( )	( )	( )	( )

For Openness

very good	good	None of those	bad	very bad
( )	( )	( )	( )	( )

For Sensation of unity

very good	good	None of those	bad	very bad
( )	( )	( )	( )	( )

Figure 9.1 Example of a questionnaire.

questionnaire in the same place and under the same conditions, the use of students as testees is general practice in existing landscape research in Japan.

The results of this survey were analyzed by principal component analysis (PCA), to determine how targets are derived from the perception of a rural landscape.[2] We explain the differences in the results section. In the village of Naganuma-cho, 11 items were prepared for the questionnaire, to provide a detailed mental assessment of the subjects, but the perception gave an infinite variety of answers (Table 9.1). Therefore, only five items were prepared from Kutchan village to provide focus and make the questionnaire more compact.

The object of analysis

The objects of the study, two villages chosen for the survey, represent strong, characteristic features of Hokkaido. One of them, Naganuma-cho, is located near a big city, Sapporo, which is a suburban agriculture area that produces rice, this being the major crop in Japan. Another area, Kutchan, produces one of the major crops of Hokkaido – potatoes. To show the Naganuma area's characteristic rural landscape, its beauty, the characteristic paddy fields and the areas where local people live, the landscapes prepared for tourism and the administrative part of the town, we decided to take photographs of a straight farming road. This was

Table 9.1 The results of PCA in Naganuma-cho

No.	First PCA	Contribution ratio	Second PCA	Contribution ratio	Cumulative contribution ratio
1	Beautiful	32.15%	Feeling of oppression	14.86%	47.01%
2	Beautiful	32.31%	Feeling of oppression	13.27%	45.58%
3	Cooped up feeling	29.76%	Feeling of oppression	15.14%	44.91%
4	Cooped up feeling	29.69%	Feeling of oppression	12.69%	42.38%
5	Feeling of oppression	30.53%	Rare scene	15.66%	46.19%
6	Openness	34.68%	Continuity	13.79%	48.47%
7	Fine	25.82%	Continuity	15.60%	41.42%
8	Calmness	29.84%	Rare scene	13.39%	43.23%
9	Cooped up feeling	30.18%	Feeling of oppression	14.32%	44.50%
10	Openness	34.27%	Feeling of oppression	14.32%	44.50%
11	Openness	37.39%	Rare scene	12.30%	50.12%
12	Beautiful	38.00%	Calmness	12.18%	50.18%
13	Feeling of oppression	41.63%	Rare scene	12.30%	53.93%
14	Beautiful	41.44%	Rare scene	13.51%	54.95%
15	Sense of scale	42.81%	Beautiful	12.64%	55.45%
16	Beautiful	39.03%	Continuity	14.18%	53.21%
17	Openness	37.83%	Farm identity feeling	13.49%	51.32%
18	Beautiful	40.08%	Rare scene	12.13%	52.21%
19	Fine	39.12%	Feeling of oppression	14.65%	53.81%
20	Familiarity	37.95%	Continuity	14.40%	52.35%
21	Feeling of oppression	34.38%	Disagreeable	12.29%	46.64%
22	Feeling of oppression	32.34%	No calmness	14.30%	46.64%
23	Openness	37.74%	Rare scene	13.01%	50.75%
24	Fine	33.38%	Rare scene	14.67%	48.05%
25	Sensation of unity	35.82%	Continuity	12.67%	48.49%
26	Feeling of oppression	35.89%	No familiarity	14.85%	50.74%
27	Calmness	33.07%	Rare scene	14.59%	47.66%
28	Openness	33.92%	Feeling of oppression	14.18%	48.10%
29	Beautiful	38.52%	Feeling of oppression	12.36%	50.88%
30	Beautiful	39.73%	Sensation of unity	12.49%	52.22%

representative of a place that satisfies the conditions, where the rice fields and people's living space are adjacent, and agricultural land improvement works have been done and have been maintained evenly. The setting position of the targeted area in the Naganuma analysis is described in Figures 9.2 and 9.3.

The length of the farming road used in the questionnaire was 6.8 km for each survey, and the images were taken under the conditions assumed appropriate for how a person driving a car would view the scenery. We assumed the viewing range to be at 1 m in height, with an angle of elevation of 5 degrees, and a viewing angle of 60 degrees from the car window. Both sides of the route in the object region were rice fields, and the pictures were taken in September after the harvest.

The questionnaire survey of the scenery in Naganuma was given to 155 students who study eco-management and environmental economics at a university in the city of Sapporo. The form of the questionnaire has a five-part layout as is shown in Figure 9.1, and it shows which object on the screen was related to the questions that were selected. The principal component analysis (PCA) over every single view of the landscape was presented by the survey, combined with a mental

Figure 9.2 The farming routes analyzed and the Naganuma-cho map.

Source: Google map (http://maps.google.co.jp/).

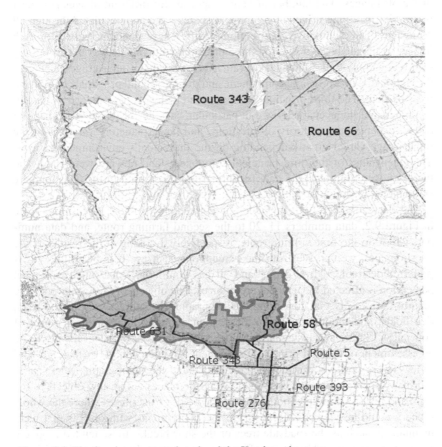

Figure 9.3 The farming route analyzed and the Kutchan-cho map.

perception of each image. The explanatory variables of each image in the principal component analysis are expressed as follows (11 items):[3]

$$\text{Data 1–30 } Z_i = \sum_n (a_{mn}x_1 + a_{mn}x_2 + \cdots + a_{mn}x_{11}) \qquad (9.1)$$

where $i = 30$.

The formula above indicates the overall impression of the presented photo in the questionnaire: y is the dependent variable, X represents the questions of the questionnaire (explanatory variable), a is the constant term, i is the number of photos that were presented, m is the explanatory variable on a case by data number, and n is the number of samples.

For the results of 11 items with 11 explanatory variables, in order to analyze the images one by one, α was classified separately. The analysis was done in each of the 30 images. The number of valid responses for different images per sheet was different, so the principal component scores were not calculated through all 30 images. The cumulative contribution of different respondents varied for each image, so the analysis of the first three principal components was useful in only over 65 percent of all 30 images overall. The eigenvalue is an average 38 percent throughout the first principal component, and, for the second principal component, is 27 percent. The third principal component's eigenvalue was judged as insufficient, because items characterized in particular, such as "beautiful" or "image of calm", occupied the majority of questions, and the explanatory variables of the same image varied greatly depending on the individual's environmental views. The eigenvalues of the third principal components and onward were small and therefore were omitted. The data for three rural roads used in the questionnaire assessment are shown in Table 9.1.

The data numbers 1–10 in Table 9.1 correspond to the third farming route in Figure 9.2, data numbers 11–20 to the second farming route, and data numbers 21–30 to the first farming route, respectively. Looking at the results of the questionnaire, we can see from the perceptions such as "It is beautiful," "It is preferred/desirable," "It is calm," and "It has familiarity," that much emotional perception is affected by personal preferences. The objects of these answers were mainly the objects that run along the geographical features, such as the road, rice fields, and mountains. In the perception of many images, the feelings of "openness," "little space/stagnation/oppression," and "View" seem mainly to be an assessment of the first principal component. The perception of "feelings" and "View" were positive affirmative perceptions, and the photographs where these affirmative perceptions had been made were the places with a few objects to the right and left (for example, both sides of the road) or the places where the whole scenery could be viewed. Moreover, in the photographs with objects that were maintained, such as the roadside trees or the snowbreaks, these tended to give a positive impression and lead to an affirmative perception. It is guessed that objects, such as roadside trees or snowbreaks, reinforce the feeling of maintained "View" and this forms the perception of the scenery as that of a "Scenic Vista," so it leads to an affirmative perception.

The features of the photos that had positive assessments were the viewpoint direction, when looking forward and both sides of the road were open along the view direction. On the contrary, the negative perceptions of "Little/no space" and "Sense of oppression" were perceived when there was a tendency to have unfinished objects of accommodation or forest in the photos, or where many road signs and signboards existed. Particularly negative perceptions were obtained in the scenery pictures where many objects existed on the right and left, on both sides of the road, and in the direction of the viewing aspect.

Because the target object of the questionnaire was a farming route and the pictures were taken in a straight line along the road, where features such as mountains are hardly seen, the object gained affirmative positive perceptions like "Sense of relief," "Sense of scale" or negative perceptions, such as "Cooped-up feeling," and

"Sense of oppression" depending on either visibility of the horizon and the direction of the viewing aspect, or on whether certain objects existed on the right and left-hand sides of the road.

In other words, rural areas differ from urban areas in that the composition objects of the landscape are far fewer, and it is thought that artificial objects in the landscape are perceived as being more emphasized. Moreover, "Cooped-up/oppression/little or no space" feelings are perceived, and these tend to lower the assessment of a rural landscape.

Kutchan village was another object of the analysis. Kutchan is a farming area where potatoes, which are the staple crop of Hokkaido, are produced. In recent years it has become a worldwide leisure spot, which has good quality mountain resorts, and it is visited by many skiers, mainly from Australia. A similar survey questionnaire to the one above was done, by using the photographs taken of the main road in Kutchan-cho. The photographs used are shown in Figure 9.3. In 2011, landscape maintenance works were scheduled in Kutchan, and the height limitations to buildings ordinance were enforced in 2010.

The analysis using the questionnaire was carried out for the specification of the landscape ordinance in the district of Kutchan-cho. The testees were, again, students, and 213 valid responses were obtained. The perception items were squeezed into five items based on the analyses of Naganuma-cho. Figure 9.3 shows the designated area of the landscape ordinance specification district.

The method of analysis similarly used PCA and was expressed as follows:

$$\text{Data } 1\text{--}20 \ z_i = \sum_n (a_{mn}x_1 + a_{mn}x_2 + \cdots + a_{mn}x_5) \qquad (9.2)$$

where $i = 20$.

The formula above indicates the overall impression of the photograph presented in the questionnaire: y is the dependent variable, X represents the questions of the questionnaire (explanatory variable), a is the constant term, i is the number of photographs that were presented, m is the explanatory variable on a case by data number, and n is the number of samples.

Unlike the survey from Naganuma-cho, emotional perceptions such as "It is beautiful" and "It is desirable" were squeezed to items like "Fine view" and "Sense of oppression," and the number of the perception items was reduced, so the gathered information accumulation/contribution ratio has risen considerably. It is understood from the results in Table 9.2 that perceptions concerning the view, such as "Openness" and "Fine view," were obtained from many of the photographs. The Kutchan-cho views similarly obtained positive perceptions such as "Sense of relief" and "Fine View" when the viewing objects were few on the ground in Tables 9.3 and 9.4.

Kutchan is enclosed by mountains and there are few flat rice fields, in contrast to Naganuma. However, affirmative perceptions of "Openness" and "Beautiful" were obtained in Kutchan as well as in Naganuma, when a few objects were depicted in its rural landscape photographs. Negative perceptions of a "Sense

Table 9.2 The target object of the questionnaire in Naganuma-cho

No.	Road	Farmland and grassland	House	Telegraph pole	Signboard
1	22.86%	29.28%	10.00%	–	–
2	17.46%	18.25%	5.56%	24.60%	–
3	8.80%	12.00%	12.80%	17.60%	–
4	9.09%	6.61%	19.83%	20.66%	12.40%
5	12.90%	12.10%	–	14.52%	9.68%
6	10.08%	7.56%	–	–	11.76%
7	10.00%	15.00%	0.83%	12.50%	9.17%
8	6.61%	8.26%	0.83%	19.00%	1.65%
9	6.14%	–	17.54%	17.54%	15.79%
10	13.45%	20.17%	2.52%	18.49%	–
11	16.38%	8.62%	5.17%	13.79%	1.72%
12	8.40%	6.72%	2.52%	11.76%	8.40%
13	5.69%	13.01%	12.20%	8.94%	–
14	8.80%	12.80%	11.20%	9.60%	4.80%
15	12.07%	14.66%	–	5.17%	0.86%
16	12.07%	1.72%	3.45%	6.90%	–
17	9.40%	11.11%	4.27%	19.66%	11.97%
18	0.83%	15.00%	14.17%	0.83%	2.50%
19	–	4.17%	14.17%	0.83%	5.00%
20	15.20%	18.40%	0.80%	10.40%	–
21	6.50%	–	17.89%	27.64%	21.95%
22	12.50%	11.61%	7.14%	15.18%	6.25%
23	13.93%	18.03%	–	16.39%	–
24	8.06%	20.16%	–	16.94%	8.06%
25	13.93%	3.28%	7.38%	9.02%	18.03%
26	11.20%	–	21.55%	24.14%	13.79%
27	8.47%	15.25%	12.71%	11.86%	3.39%
28	14.17%	10.00%	0.83%	7.50%	6.67%
29	12.60%	12.61%	2.52%	9.24%	5.04%
30	13.45%	8.40%	5.88%	12.61%	22.69%

of oppression" were obtained in areas where the administrative facilities and the commercial establishments were concentrated. Similarly to that of Naganuma, the perception objects in Kutchan were also the "Mountains," "Road," and "Fields" items. From the study it is well understood that "View" strongly influences the landscape perception in the farming areas in Hokkaido.

Summary

In recent years, work on landscape maintenance is increasing in the rural areas of Hokkaido, and many discussions are held on the concrete measures for this.

In this chapter we try to understand the issue of perception of the landscape by performing an analysis of rural landscapes. In the analysis of two study areas, where the continental features of Hokkaido are characteristically presented,

Table 9.3 The results of PCA in Kutchan-cho

No.	First PCA	Contribution ratio	Second PCA	Contribution ratio	Cumulative contribution ratio
1	Sensation of unity	68.48%	Feeling of oppression	26.29%	94.77%
2	Fine view	94.89%	Rare scene	2.79%	97.69%
3	Openness	88.15%	Rare scene	9.97%	98.12%
4	Openness	89.72%	Rare scene	7.98%	97.69%
5	Openness	83.73%	Rare scene	14.24%	97.97%
6	Sensation of unity	91.32%	Rare scene	6.51%	97.83%
7	Openness	77.76%	Sensation of unity	19.44%	97.20%
8	Sensation of unity	88.56%	Rare scene	9.36%	97.92%
9	Sensation of unity	65.84%	Feeling of Oppression	23.72%	89.55%
10	Openness	93.46%	Rare scene	5.48%	98.94%
11	Fine view	93.95%	Rare scene	4.86%	98.81%
12	Fine view	75.45%	Feeling of Oppression	20.82%	96.27%
13	Sensation of unity	81.73%	Feeling of Oppression	16.45%	98.18%
14	Openness	76.06%	Feeling of Oppression	21.71%	97.77%
15	Sensation of unity	95.76%	Usual scene	3.49%	99.25%
16	Sensation of unity	79.61%	Feeling of oppression	17.82%	97.43%
17	Feeling of oppression	93.93%	Fine view	4.88%	98.81%
18	Fine view	86.76%	Openness	11.25%	98.01%
19	Fine view	94.60%	Feeling of oppression	3.98%	98.58%
20	Fine view	90.39%	Feeling of oppression	6.64%	97.03%

similar results and similar perceptions of the objects were obtained in spite of the different geographical features and conditions of the key objects.

In the rural areas, where the objects that obstruct the view are few compared to the urban settings, both in the rice-producing district and in the potato-farming area, the item "View" strongly influenced testees' perception of the landscape. The perception objects were those objects that run along geographical features, such as "Mountains," "Road," "Fields," and "Rice fields" (see Table 9.4). Negative perceptions were obtained in the photographs where the objects were too few, or in the photographs with many artificial objects. Such negative assessments were obtained mostly in the areas with administrative facilities and commercial

Table 9.4 The target object of the questionnaire in Kutchan-cho

No.	Mount	Road	Farmland and grassland	Lined with trees	House	Telegraph pole	Signboard
1	85.02%	9.18%	26.09%	–	32.37%	73.43%	9.66%
2	–	35.27%	34.78%	–	64.25%	84.06%	59.42%
3	35.27%	52.66%	–	–	48.79%	56.04%	12.08%
4	6.76%	53.14%	–	–	31.88%	76.33%	73.91%
5	6.76%	53.14%	11.11%	84.54%	31.88%	76.33%	73.91%
6	–	60.39%	2.90%	–	–	13.04%	1.45%
7	52.66%	34.78%	–	0.48%	26.57%	86.96%	64.25%
8	–	75.36%	–	–	–	6.76%	–
9	0.48%	42.03%	63.29%	–	59.42%	88.41%	60.87%
10	79.71%	34.78%	–	57.97%	–	8.70%	17.87%
11	57%	28.99%	–	3.86%	39.61%	60.39%	36.71%
12	50.24%	47.34%	0.48%	–	38.65%	75.36%	54.59%
13	76.33%	33.82%	15.94%	–	–	8.70%	18.36%
14	69.57%	34.30%	62.32%	0.97%	59.90%	69.57%	17.87%
15	58.94%	51.21%	–	–	–	1.93%	–
16	14.19%	30.92%	–	0.48%	33.33%	88.41%	77.29%
17	78.26%	20.29%	3.86%	–	44.93%	59.90%	20.77%
18	66.18%	34.30%	–	–	41.06%	86.96%	43.96%
19	3.86%	63.29%	–	–	38.65%	72.95%	56.04%
20	2.42%	30.62%	–	–	70.05%	77.29%	41.06%
21	–	74.40%	–	77.78%	–	–	–

establishments, while, in the places rich with nature, an affirmative perception was more likely to be obtained. Negative or positive values of the perception of rural landscapes are supposed to indicate a relationship between human economic activities and its trade-offs.

Although landscape views in the rural areas of Japan have started to be evaluated relatively late (in recent years) and some landscape maintenance work is being done, the treatment and handling of the landscape tends to be subjective, so the maintenance objects tend to become complex too. From the results of the questionnaire, it was understood that "the view" is the key factor in the maintenance of the landscape, and the landscape maintenance that puts human economic activities in agreement with nature is most desired in Hokkaido.

Notes

1 According to a survey carried out at the town hall in Naganuma in 2007. Explanation of the differences of perception items. At the site of the Naganuma-cho study 11 items were prepared to see the detailed mental perception of the landscape, but personal preferences of the survey subjects were multifarious and the results of the PCA were too diverse to interpret. Therefore, at the second site of Kutchan-cho, the perception items were compacted to five.
2 Using the questionnaire items from the previous studies we wrote a landscape assessment questionnaire, referring to the perception criteria which were commonly used in those previous existing studies. The perception criteria were meant to be well suited to depicting the changing rural landscape.
3 The points are well annotated by Kato and Yoshida (2004) in detail, describing the movement of the eyes of a human subject viewing a landscape.

References

Appleyard, Donald (1964) *View From the Road*, Cambridge, MA: MIT Press.
Kato Yusuke and Yoshida Hironobu (2004) "An analysis of sequential landscape in the historic site of Oka Castle," *Journal of the Japanese Institute of Landscape Architecture*, 76(5): 637–42.
Kimura, Kurita, Saitho, Uemura, and Nagai (2003) "Characteristic for photographic image in stepped rice fields," Japan Society of Photogrammetry and Remote Sensing.
Nakamura, Yoshio (2005) "Socio-Cultural Basis for Generating Meaningful Landscape," *City Planning*, 54(1).
Okada Minoru, Kobayashi Akihiro, Akikawa Shoichiro, Uchiumi Shizu, and Honda Kazushige (2005) "Land use and landscape assessment of farmland in case of Biei Town, Hokkaido," Papers of the 23rd Scientific Research Meeting.
Tomidokoro Yasuko, Asakawa Shoichiro, and Matusushima Hajime (2005) "Perception and evaluation of wetland landscapes in Iburi Region, Hokkaido", Papers of the 23rd Scientific Research Meeting.

Part III

Medical management

10 Quality initiatives in healthcare

Lessons from the Japanese experience

Tomonori Hasegawa

Background

Quality and safety in healthcare have become major concerns in modernized societies over the past ten years. In 2001, the Institute of Medicine of the US National Academy of Sciences published the report "Crossing the Quality Chasm: A New Health System for the 21st Century" that emphasized the huge discrepancy between the expected quality of healthcare and the care actually provided. This report concluded that the healthcare system would need to change dramatically to assure the higher quality standards that society demanded[1] and initiated a worldwide movement towards quality, accountability, and safety in healthcare provision.

As in other East Asian countries, Japanese society is ageing rapidly. This rapid ageing is a unique experience in the history of human beings. It is estimated that South Korea and Chinese Taiwan will follow Japan by experiencing similar challenges in the next 20 to 30 years and that China will follow suit within 50 years.

Ageing changes a nation's disease structure. Evidence-based medicine (EBM) has thus been regarded as a method to introduce scientific thinking into healthcare. Most information for EBM is derived from clinical studies, such as randomized controlled trials, and clinical practice guidelines and critical paths based on EBM are representative methods to standardize and optimize clinical practice. These methodologies, however, assume the presence of a single-disease model, namely when an otherwise healthy person that has a single disease/injury is the target of medical intervention. Unfortunately, in an aged society, patients typically suffer from several chronic conditions simultaneously. To assure high-quality healthcare, a new methodology is thus clearly needed.

This chapter addresses these quality issues in healthcare with special attention to the influence of the ageing population. Because Japan, South Korea, and Chinese Taiwan share common cultural backgrounds, we review the healthcare issues in these countries in order to offer recommendations to the rest of the world.

Ageing

The salient feature of ageing in Japan is its high growth rate compared with other developed countries. In 1970, people aged 65 or over comprised 7 percent of the total population, but this proportion doubled to 14 percent by 1995. By comparison, this same share change took 115 years in France, 85 years in Sweden, and 47 years in the United Kingdom. Longer life expectancy, a low fertility rate, and immigration restrictions are all contributing factors to this rapid ageing, although the impact of the country's low fertility rate is the biggest determinant.

The ageing index, which measures the proportion of people aged 65 and over to those aged 15–64 years, indicates the burden of aged people on the working population. Figure 10.1 shows the global trend in the ageing index, with this index increasing notably in Asia, especially in East Asia. Among East Asian countries, Japan has the highest index. It is estimated that South Korea and Chinese Taiwan (data not shown) will catch up with Japan in the 2030s and China in the 2050s.

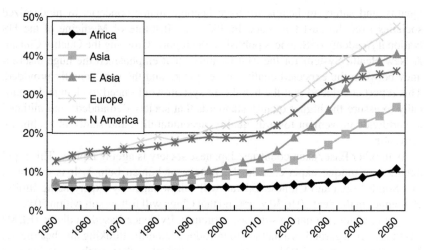

Figure 10.1 Trend of ageing index in the world.

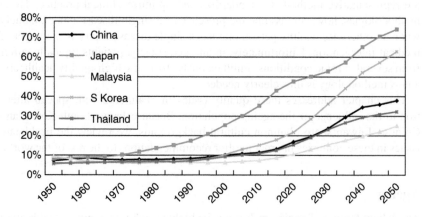

Figure 10.2 Trend of ageing index among East and Southeast Asian countries.

Change in disease structure

An aged society has a different disease structure from that of a younger society. For example, the incidence and prevalence of chronic and lifestyle-related diseases are relatively higher among elderly people. To prevent lifestyle-related diseases, changes in lifestyle such as establishing healthy behavior at a young age are essential. This highlights the ethical issue of forcing a change in an individual's behavior and stewardship based on a strong relationship between the individual and surrounding organizations such as governments and employers. The Health Promotion Act (2005) prescribes the role of central and local governments and companies in establishing healthy behavior and promotes smoking cessation. Based on this act, smoking is now prohibited in public facilities such as schools and hospitals.

Most elderly patients that visit healthcare organizations (HCOs) suffer from multiple chronic conditions (MCCs). Figure 10.3 presents three representative chronic conditions in elderly patients, namely diabetes mellitus, hyperlipemia, and hypertension, showing that more than 90 percent suffer from *more than one* of these conditions. Physicians report now rarely seeing patients that have only one of these three chronic conditions.

Influence of MCCs on healthcare

MCCs have a huge effect on healthcare, to the point of necessitating a change in the healthcare provision system. In 2000, Japan introduced a long-term care

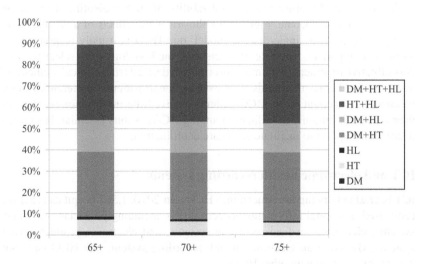

Figure 10.3 Comorbidities and complications among people aged 65 or over.

Source: Data from National Patient Survey 2008.

Note: DM: diabetes mellitus, HL: hyperlipemia, HT: hypertension.

Single condition model	Multiple condition model
• Acute disease, Trauma • Single disease • Treatment standing in a row • Treatment starts and ends within one healthcare facility • Evidence derived from RCTs	• Chronic disease • MCC, C&Cs • Treatment based on patients' preference, and time course taken into account • Coordination among healthcare facilities • RCT difficult to conduct

Figure 10.4 Change of disease paradigm.

(LTC) insurance system to cover dependent elderly people. By 2009, 4.7 million dependent elderly people (16.2 percent of the elderly population) used LTC services at a cost of 7.3 trillion yen. Care managers, a profession responsible for care coordination, were also introduced. Although care managers play an important role in planning and assigning LTC services, their activities are limited to LTC, and most elderly patients with MCCs that visit HCOs for acute conditions or worsening MCCs cannot use care coordination services. Further, continuous care from the acute to the chronic stage is not yet guaranteed.

Changes in patient conditions offer another challenge to adopting a scientific methodology. As discussed earlier, in modern medicine most scientific information is derived from clinical studies using EBM and technology assessments (TA); however, the applicability and generalizability of such "scientific information" are open to serious debate. Figure 10.4 illustrates the effects of a change in disease paradigm. In a single-disease model, one HCO is usually responsible for an individual patient. The role of a scientific methodology is to select the most cost-effective treatment, with most information derived from clinical studies such as randomized controlled trials. However, although patients' preferences should be taken into account, most MCC patients receive little information on choosing their treatment options. Coordination among HCOs is thus essential, but there is insufficient support to facilitate such care coordination.

ICT and electronic health recording systems

ICT is gradually being introduced into HCOs. In 2010, 1,567 hospitals (18.1 percent) used a hospital information system (HIS), including physician order entry systems, electronic medical recording systems, and electronic health recording systems. By using an electronic health recording system, one HCO can share patient information with other HCOs.

Our questionnaire results suggest that the proportion of hospitals that have paperless HIS increased from 31.1 percent in 2008 to 41.9 percent in 2010, while those that have electronic health recording systems increased from 7.2 percent in

2008 to 10.9 perecnt in 2010.[2] Hospitals that have highly integrated HISs showed higher levels of satisfaction and were more likely to answer that the purpose of the HISs was sharing information and quality improvement rather than improving effectiveness. A HIS can also contribute to effective healthcare. Our analysis, using the National Patient Survey and Hospital Survey, showed that for 13 of 15 representative operative procedures, hospitals that have HISs had shorter hospital stays after adjusting for gender and age.[3]

Nationwide patient registration offers a powerful tool to investigate the missing links between patient conditions and treatment results. Since randomized controlled trials and other clinical studies are difficult to conduct and their information difficult to generalize in this MCC era, the importance of this kind of national database has increased. In 2011, Japan's Ministry of Health, Labor and Welfare (MHLW) decided to allow researchers to use claims data, although a system for the appropriate use of national data and an analytical framework to contribute to evidence-based health policy and quality healthcare should also be developed.

Quality initiatives

Quality assurance began about 100 years ago, when Florence Nightingale (1820–1910) and Ernest Amory Codman (1869–1940) started to measure healthcare outcomes such as mortality and surgical site infection in Western countries.[4] In Japan, we can see the outcomes of each physician at Koishikawa Shogun's Hospital in the 1830s. With advances in healthcare, long-term outcome data, such as five- or 10-year survival rates, became necessary. However, because it took considerable effort to collect these data and because outcomes could not be fully controlled by HCOs, other tools to measure quality were investigated. Consequently, in the 1960s three viewpoints to evaluate healthcare quality were developed by Avedis Donabedian (1919–2000).[5] These three areas of healthcare (structure, process, and outcome) are still measured using clinical indicators (CIs).

Another representative tool to evaluate healthcare is a peer review. A peer review can be conducted at different levels, from the patient level to that of the whole healthcare system. The third-party accreditation of a HCO began in 1917 as a voluntary activity led by the US College of Surgeons.[6] In 1952, the Joint Commission was established, and this continues to be the leading organization in this field. When Medicare and Medicaid were introduced as the public health insurance system in the United States in 1965, hospitals needed to be accredited by the Joint Commission or other accreditation bodies in order to be reimbursed by Medicare and Medicaid. Further, in some developed countries, every HCO is now requested to submit data to healthcare authorities, while public reporting and pay-for-performance reimbursement systems are being introduced. Over the past ten years, accreditation has become popular in many developed countries and even mandatory in some. In modernized society, a quality assurance system is commonly seen as a crucial part of a healthcare system.

In Japan, the Japan Council for Quality Healthcare (JCQHC) was established in 1995 as a non-profit organization whose mission was to improve the quality and

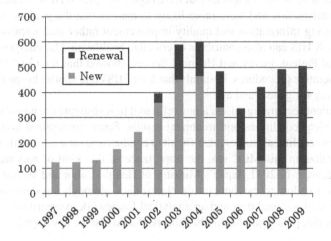

Figure 10.5 Number of hospitals accredited with the JCQHC.

safety of healthcare.[7] The MHLW and other HCOs, such as the Japan Medical Association, hospital associations, and the Japan Nursing Association cooperated to establish and manage the JCQHC. In 1997, it began hospital accreditation and by November 2012, 28.1 percent (2,414/8,580) of hospitals were accredited by the JCQHC. In Japan, accreditation remains voluntary and there are few incentives for hospitals to be accredited; however, accreditation is now mandatory in other Asian countries such as Chinese Taiwan, South Korea, and Singapore.

The activities of the JCQHC include (1) hospital accreditation, (2) a clearing house for clinical practice guidelines, (3) a nationwide incident/accident reporting system, and (4) a non-fault compensation system for cerebral palsy. Japan is one of several countries that have a nationwide incident/accident reporting system. From 2002, every university and national hospital has been obliged by law to report to the JCQHC medical accidents that incur significant damage to patients. The JCQHC publishes quarterly reports concerning these trends, as well as failure modes and possible preventive methods. Similarly, a non-fault compensation system is regarded as an effective method to strengthen the patient-healthcare staff relationship by supporting financially victims of medical accidents and facilitating the analysis of medical accidents and their prevention. The causes of medical accidents are often difficult to clarify, and it is difficult and time-consuming for patients to seek compensation. In 2009, only 25.3 percent of medical accident lawsuits paid compensation to patients (Data from the Supreme Court), while low and delayed compensation can add to the stress on medical accident victims. In 2009, the non-fault compensation system was introduced as a social experiment for cerebral palsy. Babies diagnosed with medium or severe levels of cerebral palsy are now compensated automatically, without needing to demonstrate the fault of healthcare staff.

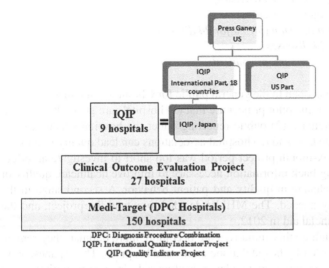

Figure 10.6 Three-tier structure of the clinical outcomes evaluation project by the AJHA.

The All Japan Hospital Association (AJHA) has led the quality initiative using CIs in Japan.[8] The AJHA, one of the largest hospital associations in Japan mainly composed of private hospitals, began its performance measurement project using CIs in 2004. This project has a three-tier structure (see Figure 10.6). The first component uses electronic reimbursement claims data (DPC/PDPS), while the second uses these claims data as well as patients' clinical data such as age, gender, and outcomes. The third has a different data structure altogether, and this is a part of the International Quality Indicator Project, an international project across 18 countries run by the Press Ganey Corporation in the United States.

In 2010, the MHLW decided to provide financial aid to three organizations engaged in performance measurement activities. It requested (1) the participation of ≥25 hospitals, (2) ≥10 CIs including patient satisfaction, and (3) the hospital name to be open to the public (with some CIs). After the AJHA modified the second tier to satisfy the MHLW's conditions, it was entitled to receive financial aid as well as the Japan Hospital Association and National Hospital Organization. A six-month pilot project was then conducted with 27 participating hospitals submitting 24,895 pieces of patient admissions data. The CIs used in this pilot project are shown below:

- *patient satisfaction 1: general satisfaction*
- *patient satisfaction 2: would you recommend to your family?*
- falls
- nosocomial infection
- restraint

- *length of stay (for major 24 diseases)*
- mortality (for major 24 diseases)
- *unscheduled re-admission (for major 24 diseases)*
- *cost (for major 24 diseases)*
- *antibiotics use for pneumonia patients.*

The hospital name is open to the general public for CIs shown in italics.

The lessons from this pilot project are that (1) hospitals are generally supportive of quality initiatives, (2) public reporting under the hospital's name can be
accepted with some CIs, and (3) hospital associations can lead quality initiatives.
Unfortunately, a six-month project period was too short to investigate an effective way of feeding back information necessary to improve healthcare quality or
to demonstrate a change in quality and patient behavior. A second stage in the
project was clearly needed. The MHLW decided to extend the project, and the
AJHA got the financial aid in 2012.

In Japan, although quality initiatives are becoming more popular, they remain
voluntary activities led by hospital associations and hospitals. The Japanese government seems to be reluctant to play a leading role in quality initiatives by
showing a roadmap and powerful and firm leadership in addition to an appropriate
policy package to improve healthcare quality.

Public reporting

Quality healthcare should offer transparency and accountability. In developed
countries, more and more healthcare information, especially that on healthcare
providers, is being made publicly available, such as the "Hospital Compare" system of the US Department of Health and Human Services and the UK's National
Health Service. In Japan, since the revision of the Medical Law in 2006, HCOs
have been requested to collect and submit patient information to the prefectural
government, which then publishes it via its website. The influence of this public reporting on patients' choices of HCOs and on healthcare quality is likely to
be investigated further in the future. The front page of the *"HIMAWARI"* (Tokyo
Metropolitan Medical Institution Information) is shown in Figure 10.7. People can
search for a HCO by place, specialty, and business hours. As for university teaching hospitals, people can find out the number of patients and operation volumes of
each hospital.

Lessons and challenges from the Japanese experience

Because Japan and other Southeast and East Asian countries are ageing rapidly,
they have a responsibility to convey information on their experiences to the rest
of the world. Modern societies pay more attention to safety and quality issues
in healthcare, but the effectiveness and usefulness of the traditional scientific
methodology used in EBM and TA are limited because of ageing and its impact on
disease structure. The introduction of ICT and nationwide patient registration will

Figure 10.7 "*HIMAWARI*" (Tokyo Metropolitan Medical Institution Information).

Source:http://www.himawari.metro.tokyo.jp/qq/qq13enmnlt.asp.

offer a new methodology to investigate missing links, as well as useful information for dealing with patients that suffer from MCCs.

Quality initiatives in Japan began as voluntary activities by hospitals and hospital associations, and there remains insufficient support from the Japanese government. The pilot project discussed herein suggests that most hospitals are supportive of increased transparency and accountability in healthcare and agree with the public reporting of clinical data using CIs. While quality initiatives have focused on acute inpatient care, few methods and CIs have been developed to measure the quality of LTC, outpatient care including home healthcare, and care coordination, which would play important roles in the care of elderly patients with MCCs. A quality assurance system for elderly care should also be developed as a priority.

Notes

1 Institute of Medicine, Committee on Quality of Health Care in America (1999) "Crossing the Quality Chasm – A New Health System for the 21st Century," Washington, DC: National Academy Press, p. 11.
2 Seto K., Matsumoto K., Kitazawa T., and Hasegawa T. (2011) "Introduction of Hospital Information System (HIS) in hospitals in Japan-results of questionnaire survey," 7th Joint Seminar on Biomedical Sciences, Hat Yai, Thailand, 2011, p. 10.
3 Matsumoto K., Seto K., and Hasegawa T. (2011) "Impact of introducing EMR on medical practice at Japanese hospitals," 7th Joint Seminar on Biomedical Sciences, Hat Yai, Thailand, 2011, p. 10.

4 Ernest Amory Codman (2000) *The End Result of a Life in Medicine*, New York: W B Saunders.
5 The Joint Commission History, http://www.jointcommission.org/assets/1/18/Joint_Commission_History_20111.PDF, last accessed on November 19, 2012.
6 Donabedian, A. (1966) "Evaluating the quality of medical care" *Milbank Mem Fund Q* 44(3): 166–206.
7 The Japan Council for Quality Health Care http://www.report.jcqhc.or.jp/index.php, last accessed on November 19, 2012.
8 The All Japan Hospital Association, http://www.ajha.or.jp/eng/, last accessed on November 19, 2012.

11 Analysis of hospital function for neuronal and circulatory diseases in secondary medical service areas in Hokkaido

Katsuhiko Ogasawara, Ryoya Asaoka,
Yuji Sase, Tomoki Ishikawa, and
Kenji Fujimori

Introduction

Community healthcare system and healthcare planning

An appropriate environment, where people living in a local area can consult physicians within the area and have appropriate and reliable medical services is a necessary element of any community. For people to have better medical services, the environment must be based on healthcare planning, so that not only clinical functions for various diseases, but also a wide variety of consecutive general medical services, from prevention and healthcare education to rehabilitation, are available.

According to the first revision of the Medical Service Law in 1985, all prefectural governments were required to formulate a "regional medical system plan." Furthermore, there was a geographical element to this plan, which necessitated the planning of required sickbeds and aims to arrange a healthcare delivery system for each medical service area. In addition, prefectural governments were required to draw up "healthcare planning," including policies based on the regional characteristics of every secondary medical service area since 1990. After the second revision of the Medical Service Law in 1994, there was a further revision in 1996. According to the third revision, the creation of community healthcare supporting hospitals and convalescent beds for long-term care was instituted in the secondary medical service areas.

Community healthcare supporting hospitals are those with more than 200 sickbeds, and they have network functions for securing the community healthcare system, such as healthcare delivery to referred patients, shared use of facilities and staff, emergency medical care functions and clinical training functions. Those hospitals have core functions in the secondary medical service areas.[1,2]

When the Medical Service Law was revised in 2007 for the fifth time, there was a switch from the quantity control of the number of sickbeds by total volume, to quality evaluation for community healthcare coordination and medical safety. This involved the formulation of plans that were easy to understand for people and patients living in rural areas, and evaluations based on numerical targets.[3] As for community healthcare cooperation, its object was the division of healthcare roles and the completion of health welfare and medical care services in the medical service area. In order to achieve this, it has become essential to construct the community healthcare cooperation system for the four diseases (cancer, stroke, acute cardiac infarction and diabetes) and the five medical services (emergency medicine, disasters medicine, medical care service in rural areas, perinatal care service and pediatric care service). It was decided that the medical plan, which addressed the medical functions required for the four diseases and five medical services, would develop hospitals with each of these specific functions, together with their numerical targets.[4]

Of the four diseases, speedy medical examination and treatment are essential for the acute diseases such as stroke and acute cardiac infarction. In Hokkaido, with its wide geographical area, it is particularly important to have the appropriate environment in order to provide enough medical services to patients in every medical service area, including not only urban and local, but also rural regions.

DPC system and MDC

The DPC (Diagnosis Procedure Combination) system has been used as a comprehensive evaluation and payment system for 82 hospitals that have had specific functions since 2003. The DPC system is a method of classifying patients, based on the homogeneity of the demand of medical resources, such as hospital days and cost of medical treatment, and clinical similarities. In 2008, the number of sickbeds of all the hospitals providing DPC data exceeded 500,000 and the geographical distribution covered almost all areas in Japan.[5] The structure of the DPC code is shown in Figure 11.1.

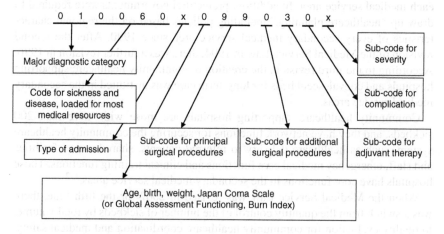

Figure 11.1 DPC code structure.

The MDC (Major Diagnosis Category) has 18 categories, which are divided by disease. For example, neuronal disease is classified as 01, respiratory disease as 04, and circulatory disease as 05.

Medical service areas

There are three kinds of medical service area: primary, secondary and tertiary. These are the geographical and administrative units for the efficient and proper assignment of health and medical resources and the systematization of a health and medical supply plan. They provide comprehensive medical services, from health management, prevention of disease and early detection, to diagnosis, treatment, and rehabilitation in order to respond to regional medical demands. The primary medical service area deals with ordinary health management based on municipalities, and it offers primary care for residents, such as diagnostics and the treatment of common diseases and slight injuries.

The secondary medical service area responds to general medical demands other than specialty requirements, and it aims to provide comparatively specialized medical care, which requires treatment in hospital. The location of secondary service areas takes into account geographical and social conditions, such as transportation systems. In Hokkaido, there are 21 secondary medical service areas (Figure 11.2).

The tertiary medical service provides advanced medical techniques and specialized medical treatment for diseases with a low frequency of occurrence. In principle the tertiary services are zoned based on prefecture, but there are six tertiary medical service areas in Hokkaido because it has such a wide geographical area.

Purpose of this study

The purpose of this study is to analyze the hospital function for neuronal disease (MDC code 01) and circulatory disease (MDC code 05) in Hokkaido secondary medical service areas, using indexes that are calculated by correcting for hospital days in DPC and numbers of patients.

Methods

Hospitals and data studied

In our study we considered 94 DPC hospitals (during 2003, 2004, 2006, 2008, and 2009) and DPC preparing hospitals (during 2006, 2008, and 2009) in the secondary medical service areas of Hokkaido. The three secondary medical service areas Nemuro, Kita-oshima-hiyama, and Minami-hiyama were excluded because they do not have DPC hospitals. The medical service areas where the number of DPC hospitals and DPC preparing hospitals constitute less than 50 percent of hospitals dealing with acute diseases were also excluded. The following data were

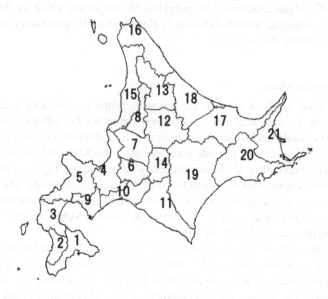

1: Minami-oshima	8: Kita-sorachi	15: Rumoi
2: Minami-hiyama	9: Nishi-iburi	16: Soya
3: Kita-oshima-hiyama	10: Higashi-iburi	17: Hokumo
4: Sapporo	11: Hidaka	18: Enmon
5: Shiribeshi	12: Kamikawa-chubu	19: Tokachi
6: Minami-sorachi	13: Kamikawa-hokubu	20: Kushiro
7: Naka-sorachi	14: Furano	21: Nemuro

Figure 11.2 Secondary medical service areas in Hokkaido.[6]

obtained from the DPC evaluation committee in 2010:

1 survey concerning discharged patients from July to December 2009;
2 ratio of number of patients based on MDC code by each hospital.

Formulation and visualization of indexes

In our study, three indexes (patient ratio, index of patient composition, and index of hospital days) were used to visualize the hospital functions in each of the secondary medical service areas.

In addition, the hospital functions in each of these areas were visualized by the chart shown in Figure 11.4. The size of the circle shows the patient ratio, and the *x*-axis and *y*-axis show the index of patient composition and the hospital day respectively. The explanation for each index is as follows.

Patient ratio

The patient ratio was calculated by comparing the number of patients with neuronal and cardiovascular diseases in the targeted hospitals, DPC hospital and DPC preparing hospital, of each medical service area with that of Hokkaido as a whole. A higher patient ratio shows the higher number of patients per population.

Index of patient composition

The index of patient composition is shown in Figure 11.3. The index of patient composition is defined to be the ratio of hospital days (a) calculated by the number of patients of each DPC in each hospital to the average hospital days of all the hospitals (b) after adjusting the average hospital days of each DPC to the standard value (average of all hospitals) and to show the severity of their patients:

$$\text{Index of patient composition} = a/b.$$

This means that the higher the index, the more seriously ill patients are treated. In each of the secondary medical service areas, the average value of the index of each hospital was considered to be the index of patient composition of that secondary medical service area.

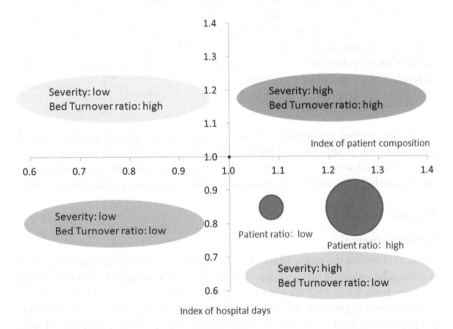

Figure 11.3 Concept of indicator for patient composition and length of stay in hospital.[7]

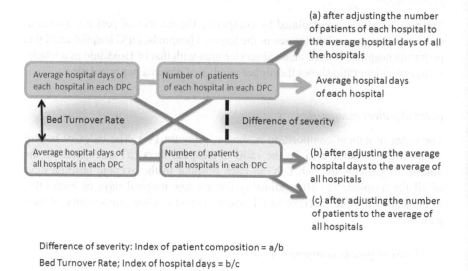

Difference of severity: Index of patient composition = a/b
Bed Turnover Rate; Index of hospital days = b/c

Figure 11.4 Interpretation of each index.

Index of hospital days

The index of hospital days is shown in Figure 11.5. The index of hospital days is defined to be the ratio of the average hospital days of all hospitals (*b*) to hospital days calculated from the average hospital days of each DPC in each hospital (*c*), after adjusting the number of patients of each DPC to the standard value (average value of all hospitals) to show the difference of hospital days, in other words, the difference of turnover rate of sickbeds:

$$\text{Index of hospital days} = b/c.$$

This means that the higher the index is, the fewer hospital days are involved. In other words, it indicates the high turnover rate of sickbeds. In each of the secondary medical service areas, the average value of the index of each hospital was considered to be the index of hospital days of that secondary medical service area.

Results

Neuronal disease

Table 11.1 shows the index value of neuronal and circulatory diseases in each of the secondary medical service areas. The selected and visualized results of neuronal diseases from Table 11.2 are shown by graph in Figure 11.5. As the medical service area with higher patient ratios, in other words, the higher number of patients per population, Kushiro, Nishi-iburi, Kamikawa-chubu, Minami-oshima, Tokachi, Kamikawa-hokubu, and Kita-sorachi medical service areas were selected. Kushiro

Table 11.1 The indicators calculated for MDC01 by secondary medical service area

	Patient rate	Indicator of patient composition	Indicator of length of stay in hospital
Minami-oshima	1.33	0.96	1.27
Sapporo	0.96	0.93	1.07
Shiribeshi	0.13	0.89	0.67
Minami-sorachi	0.43	1.21	0.77
Naka-sorachi	0.84	1.07	0.99
Kita-sorachi	1.20	0.79	0.60
Nishi-iburi	1.27	0.96	1.46
Higashi-iburi	0.88	1.1	1.19
Hidaka	0.27	0.79	0.97
Kamikawa-chubu	1.48	0.98	1.39
Kamikawa-hokubu	1.31	0.96	0.81
Furano	0.55	0.71	0.78
Rumoi	0.73	0.93	0.8
Soya	—	—	—
Hokumo	0.91	0.99	1.24
Enmon	0.53	0.90	0.83
Tokachi	1.2	0.89	1.23
Kushiro	1.71	1.06	0.83

Table 11.2 The indicators calculated for MDC05 by secondary medical service area

	Patient rate	Indicator of patient composition	Indicator of length of stay in hospital
Minami-oshima	1.12	1.09	1.00
Sapporo	1.19	1.06	1.10
Shiribeshi	0.28	1.04	0.77
Minami-sorachi	0.65	1.02	0.83
Naka-sorachi	1.41	1.07	1.09
Kita-sorachi	0.54	1.12	0.48
Nishi-iburi	1.24	1.19	0.95
Higashi-iburi	0.95	1.18	0.94
Hidaka	0.25	1.34	0.55
Kamikawa-chubu	1.05	1.31	0.83
Kamikawa-hokubu	1.36	1.05	0.87
Furano	0.38	1.19	0.49
Rumoi	0.27	1.3	0.72
Soya	0.52	0.93	0.95
Hokumo	0.55	1.10	1.03
Enmon	0.72	0.99	0.87
Tokachi	0.69	1.04	1.11
Kushiro	1.10	1.27	0.71

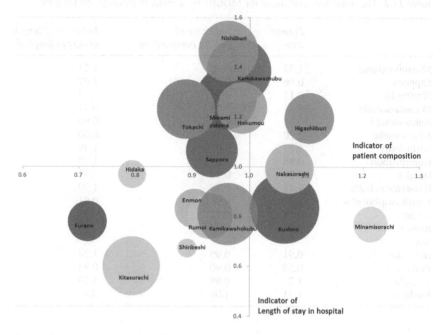

Figure 11.5 Bubble chart for each indicator of MDC01.

medical service area was classified as the medical service area with a comparatively higher index of patient composition and lower index of hospital days. Nishi-iburi, Kamikawa-chubu, Minami-oshima, and Tokachi medical service areas were classified as the medical service areas with an index of 1 or lower of patient composition and comparatively high index of hospital days. Kamikawa-hokubu medical service area was classified as the medical service areas with an index of 1 or lower of patient composition and with a low index of hospital days. Kita-sorachi medical service area had lower indexes both in patient composition and hospital days. On the other hand, as the medical service areas with a lower patient ratio, Minami-sorachi, Naka-sorachi, Higashi-iburi, Hokumo, Rumoi, Enmon, Furano, and Sapporo medical service areas were selected.

Minami-sorachi medical service area has a high index of patient composition, and in contrast, Furano medical service area has a lower index of patient composition. Hidaka and Shiribeshi medical service areas can be considered not to have appropriate indexes that show the hospital function within the service areas, as the number of DPC hospitals is less than 50 percent of all the hospitals which treat acute diseases.

Circulatory diseases

Figure 11.6 shows the visualized results of circulatory diseases. As the medical service areas with high patient ratios, Kamikawa-chubu, Kamikawa-hokubu,

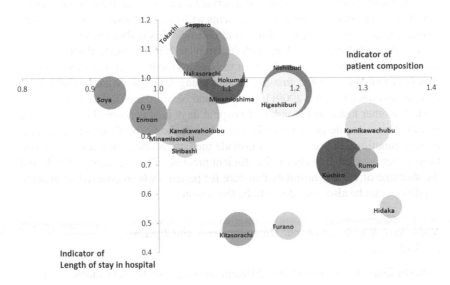

Figure 11.6 Bubble chart for each indicator of MDC05.

Kushiro, Nishi-iburi, Naka-sorachi, and Sapporo medical service areas were selected. The indexes of patient composition of these service areas were higher than 1 and in Kamikawa-chubu, Kushiro, and Nishi-iburi medical service areas, the indexes were high compared with other service areas. As for the indexes of hospital days, those of Naka-sorachi and Sapporo medical service area were a little higher, Nishi-iburi and Minami-oshima were near 1, Kamikawa-chubu and Kamikawa-hokubu were a little lower, and Kushiro were low. On the other hand, as the medical service areas with a low patient ratio, Rumoi, Higashi-iburi, Furano, Kita-sorachi, Enmon, and Soya medical service areas were selected. In these service areas, however, the indexes of patient composition were high. Furano and Kita-sorachi medical service areas showed a lower value of the index of hospital days than those of other service areas.

Discussion

Neuronal disease

Kushiro medical service area

In Kushiro medical service area, the patient rate was high, the index of patient composition was a little high, and the index of hospital days was low. Because of the high patient ratio, it can be considered that the number of patients per population is higher than those of other medical service areas. In addition, it can also be considered that the percentage of patients with serious disease is high because the index of patient composition is high.

From these results, Kushiro medical service area seems to have enough functions to provide medical care to lot of patients with neuronal disease and to provide physical treatment to patients with severe disease. This is thought to be because there is no acute hospital with enough functions in Nemuro medical service area, therefore the patients tend to move out to Kushiro medical service area. Another reason is that the airborne first-aid system using helicopters has actually been carried out (since October 2009) in Kushiro and Nemuro medical service areas.

On the other hand, as the index of hospital days is low, hospital days are long and the turnover rate of sickbeds is low. Though the hospitals in this area have enough functions and resources to provide medical services to a lot of patients, they do not have enough ability for efficient practice. The excess of sickbeds and the shortage of backup hospitals that care for patients who recovered from acute conditions can be also considered to be the reason.

Nishi-iburi, Kamikawa-chubu, Minami-oshima, and Tokachi medical service areas

In Nishi-iburi, Kamikawa-chubu, Minami-oshima, and Tokachi medical service areas, the patient ratio is high, the index of patient composition is near 1 (or a little lower) and the index of hospital days is high. In these areas the number of patients per population is high because the patient ratio is high. In Tokachi medical service area, the number of patients within the medical service area is high because there is not enough patient movement.

As the number of patients per population is high, it can be considered that these four medical service areas have enough functions to provide medical services to patients with neuronal disease. In addition, as the index of patient composition is near 1 and is not high, we cannot say simply that these medical service areas do not have enough functions to provide medical services to patients with severe disease. There is also a possibility that the index is low because these areas are dealing with hospitalized patients of various kinds of severity.

In these medical service areas, it would be necessary to make a distinction between clinics that accept patients with slight illness and acute hospitals that deal with severely ill patients. These medical service areas also have high turnover rate of sickbeds because not only is the index of hospital days high, but the patient rate is also high. In other words, it can be said that they have enough functions to provide medical services efficiently.

Kamikawa-hokubu medical service area

In Kamikawa-hokubu medical service area, the patient rate was high, the index of patient composition was near 1, and the index of hospital days was low. As this medical service area also has a high patient ratio, they have enough functions to provide medical services to many patients. The fact that index of patient composition was near 1, indicates the possibility that the medical service area does not have enough function to deal with severely ill patients, and that patients with slight illness are hospitalized as well. In addition, because the index of hospital days was low, the turnover rate of sickbeds was low. We consider this to be due to bad practical efficiency, an excess of sickbeds and a shortage of backup hospitals.

Kita-sorachi medical service area

In Kita-sorachi medical service area, both indexes of patient composition and hospital days were low. We think this area has enough functions to provide medical services because the patient ratio is high. However, as the index of patient composition is low, there is a possibility that it does not have enough functions to deal with severely ill patients. In addition, as this medical service area has a low index of hospital days, it has problems, such as bad practical efficiency, excess sickbeds and a shortage of backup hospitals.

Minami-sorachi, Naka-sorachi, Higashi-iburi, Hokumo, Rumoi, Enmon, Furano, and Sapporo medical service areas

Minami-sorachi, Naka-sorachi, Higashi-iburi, Hokumo, Rumoi, Enmon, Furano, and Sapporo medical service areas had low patient ratio. There is a possibility of outflow of patients in these service areas, and they have problems such as shortages of physicians, nurses, hospitals and sickbeds. However, it is impossible to say that Sapporo medical service area does not have enough medical functions. Therefore, it can be considered that the patient ratio of Sapporo medical service area was low because the ratio of young adults in the population is high. In these service areas with low patient ratios, Minami-sorachi medical service area has high index of patient composition.

We considered that the medical service area has enough specialty function to treat severe diseases in spite of the outflow of patients to other medical service areas. In the medical service areas with a low index of hospital days, though they have no function to make efficient medical practices because of the low turnover rate of sickbeds, the hospital days become longer to increase the turnover rate of sickbeds with fewer patients (because of the low patient ratio and small number of patients per population).

Circulatory diseases

Kamikawa-chubu, Kamikawa-hokubu, Kushiro, Nishi-iburi, Minami-oshima, Naka-sorachi, and Sapporo medical service areas

In Kamikawa-chubu, Kamikawa-hokubu, Kushiro, Nishi-iburi, Minami-oshima, Naka-sorachi, and Sapporo medical service areas, the patient ratio was high, the indexes of patient composition were higher than 1 in every service area and the indexes of hospital days were near 1.

Because of the high patient ratio and high index of patient composition, these medical service areas have enough function to provide medical services to a lot of patients and to take care of a lot of severely ill patients. Therefore, Kamikawa-chubu, Kushiro, and Nishi-iburi medical service areas have a higher index of patient composition than other service areas.

There is a possibility of inflow of patients from other service areas to these service areas. However, in Kushiro medical service area, it is apparent that the index of hospital days was very low. From the results for neuronal diseases, we found that Kushiro medical service area had a low index of hospital days and that it did not have enough function to provide efficient medical services. As the index of hospital days was also low for circulatory diseases, there is a possibility of excess sickbeds or shortness of backup hospitals in the whole medical service area.

Rumoi, Higashi-iburi, Furano, Kita-sorachi, Enmon, and Soya medical service areas

In Rumoi, Higashi-iburi, Furano, Kita-sorachi, Enmon, and Soya medical service areas, the patient ratios were low. We consider that there are outflows of patients to the neighboring six medical service areas because of insufficient functions, such as shortages of physicians, nurses, sickbeds and hospitals in the consideration of neuronal diseases. In Furano and Kita-sorachi medical service areas, the index of hospital days was about 0.5. This can be considered to be due to insufficient functions to provide efficient medical services and excess sickbeds (for the small number of patients per population).

Limitation of this study

Our study analyzed 94 target hospitals that were introducing and preparing a DPC system in Hokkaido. Not all of the hospitals dealing with acute disease in Hokkaido are DPC hospitals. Therefore, all the hospitals could not be covered. We suppose that we can obtain more accurate indexes when all the acute hospitals become DPC hospitals in future. In our study, we used the number of patients per population; however, we want to obtain the regional hospital functions in a more detailed way by presenting the number of sickbeds and physicians per population by the size of circles or using parameters divided by ages of patients. In addition, though we carried out the analysis by each secondary medical service area, we can further develop the study to look at advanced medical planning for four diseases and five medical services, using the same analysis for each hospital.

Conclusions

Our research visualizes the characteristics of each medical service, such as the ability to provide medical services to many patients or to deal with severely ill patients, by using graphs with three indexes; patient ratio, which represents the number of patients per population; the index of patient composition, which represents the severity of patients dealt with; and the index of hospital days, which represents the turnover rate of sickbeds. In consequence, we can obtain the following results;

- Neuronal diseases: Kushiro medical service area has a high patient rate and can deal with severe patients. Kita-sorachi medical service area has a low patient rate, but the provision for patient severity is also low and inefficient.
- Circulatory diseases: Kamikawa-chubu, Kushiro, and Nishi-iburi medical service areas can provide medical services to many patients and also can take care of many patients of a high severity level. Furano and Kita-sorachi medical service areas have low efficiency and a small number of patients per population.

In the future, we want to add other indexes and to obtain more accurate characteristics of each of the secondary medical service areas to develop more advanced medical planning.

Notes

1 Ittoku Okubo (2007) "Primary, secondary and tertiary revision of Medical Service Law – security of medical service area for citizens and study of Medical Service Law," *Libra*, 8(1): 57–64.
2 Koichi Otsubo (2009) "A brief review of some contributions to the literature on regional health planning in Japan," *Bulletin of Geo-environmental Science*, 11: 213–25.
3 See http://qq.kumanichi.com/medical/2007/08/2007-31.php.
4 See http://law.e-gov.go.jp/htmldata/S23/S23HO205.html.
5 *Introduction to DPC for the Clinician*, 2nd edition, Jihou, 2009.
6 See http://www.pref.hokkaido.lg.jp/hf/cis/.
7 *DPC Data Utilization Book*, 2nd edition, Jihou, 2008.

Part IV
Marketing strategy

Marketing strategy

12 Global marketing strategy of one of the world's leaders in printing technology, "Heidelberger Druckmaschinen"

A case study

Ralf T. Kreutzer

Introduction of Heidelberg and the research question

Heidelberg is not only one of the most beautiful cities in Germany. It is also the name of a globally successful technology-driven company, which has been a worldwide partner to the print media industry for more than 160 years by delivering high-tech printing machines: Heidelberger Druckmaschinen AG. Heidelberg combines precision mechanical engineering and integrated software development with a customer-centered marketing approach on a worldwide basis. It has a workforce of around 16,000 employees. Heidelberg's 250 support centers in 170 countries, and team of over 5,000 sales staff, 3,200 of which are service technicians, guarantees the most comprehensive sales and service network in the entire industry. Heidelberg generates 85 percent of its sales through its own sales channels and achieves around 87 percent of its sales abroad. In the last fiscal year (2010/11) it reached a turnover of 2.6 billion Euros (Nuneva, 2011c, pp. 5, 26f.; Schreier, 2012, p. 33). Heidelberg is the undisputed global market leader of sheet-fed printing machines production (N. A., 2010a, p. 13).

The total print production volume has a size of around 400 billion euros worldwide and amounted to 30 billion euros in Europe in 2012. The main areas of this industry are 40 percent for advertising (mailings, brochures), 35 percent for publishing (books, magazines, newspapers) and 25 percent for packaging (boxes, labels; Schreier, 2012, p. 33; *Horizont*, 2012, p. 4f.; Nuneva, 2011a; Heidelberg, 2010, p. 117).

The key performance indicators of Heidelberg can be found in Figure 12.1. It becomes apparent that Heidelberg was significantly hit by the financial crisis in the fiscal years 2008/09 and 2009/10. Without state loans of 850 million euros, the company couldn't have survived the global crisis (N. A., 2009b; N. A., 2011m, p. 18). However, the fiscal years 2010/11 and 2011/12 demonstrate that Heidelberg was on the right trajectory to achieve the turnaround, though the situation remained difficult.

A Heidelberg printing machine consists of an average of 150,000 components, which themselves have around 30,000 single parts each. The tolerances which

	2006–2007	2007–2008	2008–2009	2009–2010	2010–2011
Incoming orders	3,853	3,649	2,906	2,371	2,757
Turnover	3,803	3,670	2,999	2,306	2,629
EBITDA	491	391	51	−25	104
Profit/loss from ordinary business operations	362	268	−49	−130	4
In % of turnover	9.5	7.3	−1.6	−5.6	0.2
Special impacts	–	–	−179	−28	2
Financial result	−62	−69	−119	−127	−149
Annual net profit/loss	263	142	−249	−229	−129
In % of turnover	6.9	3.9	−8.3	−9.9	−4.9
Gearing (%)	38.9	33.7	85.6	120.0	28.4

Figure 12.1 Key performance indicators of Heidelberg – in million euros (N. A. 2011f, pp. 75, 78, 81).

have to be met are in the range of a thousandth of a millimeter, i.e. the sixtieth part of a hair. The weight of a Heidelberg printing machine ranges from 50 to 200 tons and the price starts at 100.000 euros, but can also be up to several million euros (Nuneva, 2011a; Heidelberg, 2008, pp. 8, 16).

Heidelberg's overall marketing approach has global, regional and local aspects, which operate simultaneously and are based on the *customer-oriented marketing strategy concept* (Becker, 2009, pp. 147–388; Kreutzer, 2010a pp. 158–88). The key points are summarized in Figure 12.2. The *market field strategy* defines the current focus of Heidelberg on printing machines (including pre- and post-press machines), consumables and technical and performance services (including financial services). The implementation of the *stimulation strategy* leads to a clear focus on the premium market.

Based on a comprehensive *market segmentation strategy*, Heidelberg defined 14 target groups with a clear focus on the market segments shown in the dark grey in Figure 12.3. Within the market area strategy, Heidelberg defined the world market as the target of the company (Nuneva, 2011c, pp. 20, 35).

The execution of Heidelberg's strategic marketing approach is based on a customer life cycle model, which is backed up with a variety of life cycle-oriented

Figure 12.2 Strategic market concept of Heidelberg – based on the customer-oriented strategy concept.

Market segments														
Digital services			General commercial			Specialists								
			Commercial Print											
Inplants & authorities	Prepress services	Digital printers	Quick printers	Small businesses	Industrial	Com web printers	Newspaper printers	Publishing houses	Packaging printers	Label printers	Direct mail printers	Other spec. Printers	Postpress specialists	

Figure 12.3 Segmentation of the direct target groups of Heidelberg (Nuneva, 2011c, p. 20).

communication instruments (see Figure 12.4; or additional dialog instruments in b2b brand building (Kreutzer, 2010a)).

The research objective of this case study is to investigate how Heidelberg was able to achieve its dominant market position, to survive the financial crisis and to manage the turnaround in an environment that continued to be very challenging.

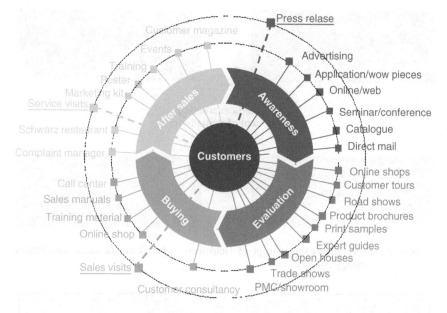

Figure 12.4 Customer life cycle model and communication instruments (Nuneva, 2011c, p. 21).

In addition to this, it evaluates which challenges Heidelberg has to master in the future to keep its position. This part is based on in-depth research using the SWOT analysis and Porter's Five Forces to identify the strengths and weaknesses of the company in its competitive environment and the opportunities and threats that lay ahead of it (see Figure 12.5). The development and discussion of Heidelberg's strategic approach is based on the key findings of this analysis.

SWOT analysis of Heidelberg

The implementation of the SWOT analysis can be combined with the Five Forces Concept (Porter, 2008, p. 26; Figure 12.6). The identification of the strengths and weaknesses of Heidelberg as the first step of the SWOT analysis could be recognized as the dominant outcome of the analysis of rivalry among existing competitors. The remaining areas of the Five Forces Concept are used to define the opportunities and threats of the whole industry within the second step of the SWOT analysis.

Identification of strengths and weaknesses of Heidelberg

The key targets of the SWOT analysis are the evaluation of the company's performance in relation to its main competitors and the evaluation of future market

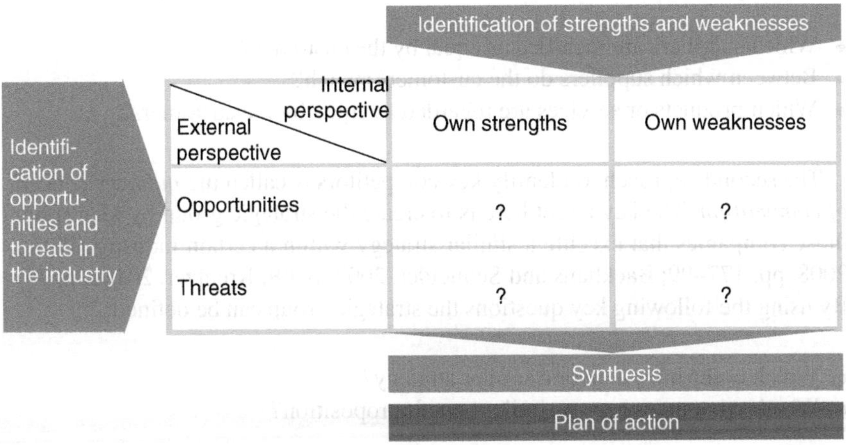

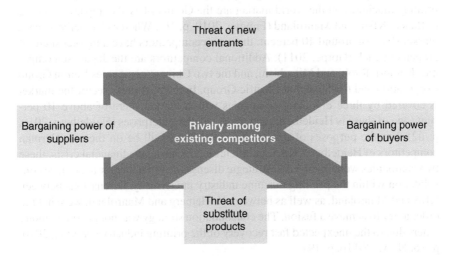

Figure 12.5 Outline of Heidelberg's strategic analysis.

Figure 12.6 Five Forces Concept (based on Porter, 2008, p. 26).

aspects. The outcome of this evaluation delivers the informational background for the synthesis of internal and external factors in order to define strategies (Kreutzer, 2010a, pp. 74–83; Pepels, 2006, pp. 523–29). The first part of the SWOT analysis focuses on the internal aspects in order to identify the strengths and weaknesses of the company. These have to be defined in comparison to the main competitors. In order to identify key competitors, two concepts can be used. The market concept of competition tries to identify the relevant alternatives from a customer's point of view. The target is to identify the customers' relevant set (Kreutzer, 2010a, p. 75).

By using the following key questions the relevant set can be defined:

- Which suppliers are regarded as equal by the customers?
- Between which suppliers do the customers switch?
- Which products or services are regarded as equal by the customers?

The second approach to identify key competitors is called the *industry concept of competition*. The key target here is to create the strategic group by identifying those companies that execute a similar strategy within a certain industry (Porter, 2008, pp. 177–99; Backhaus and Schneider, 2007, p. 68; Kreutzer, 2010a, p. 75). By using the following key questions the strategic group can be defined:

- Which companies deliver a similar strategy?
- Which companies have a similar benefit proposition?

Using the second approach, the following main competitors of Heidelberg were identified as part of the strategic group: The two main competitors in sheet-fed printing machines on the world market are the German-based companies Koenig & Bauer (KBA) and Manroland (Freytag, 2010, p. 16). Whereas Heidelberg has a market share of around 40 percent, these two competitors have a market share of 20 percent each (Gorpe, 2011). Additional competitors are the Japanese companies Komori, Ryobi and Mitsubishi, and the two Chinese companies Beiren Group Corporation and the Shanghai Electric Group. In the post-press sector the market is covered by three dominant companies with a market share of above 10 percent (one of these is Heidelberg) and many smaller enterprises (Heidelberg, 2010, p. 62). For the purposes of this analysis, the focus will be on the two German competitors of Heidelberg: KBA and Manroland. During the financial crisis, these two companies were involved in strategic discussions for a merger to achieve consolidation within the printing machine industry in Germany. Discussions between KBA and Manroland, as well as between Heidelberg and Manroland, were held in order to try to achieve a fusion. The consolidation strategy was not pursued among others due to the unexpected fast recovery of the printing industry (Freytag, 2010, p. 16; N. A., 2011b, p. 19).

In order to analyze Heidelberg's specific strengths and weaknesses, in comparison to its main competitors, the following strategic criteria were defined as the basis for the evaluation:

- strategic approach
- market position
- company and brand reputation
- production facilities and workforce
- product portfolio according to customers' needs
- interconnectedness with customers
- financial outlook 2011–12.

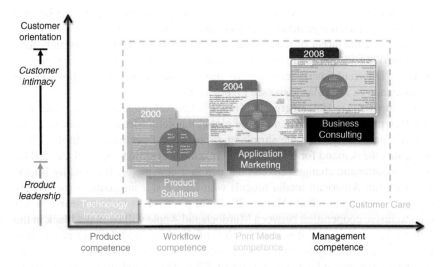

Figure 12.7 Strategic development of Heidelberg, 2000–08 (Heidelberg, 2011a).

Strategic approach

An analysis of the strategic approach of Heidelberg in Figure 12.7 shows the step-by-step development of strategic focus. Starting with a product competence approach and a clear focus on product leadership, Heidelberg switched (in 2000) to a *workflow competence approach* aiming at an increase in customer intimacy. To achieve this shift, Heidelberg acquired around 100 companies to cover the whole business chain (Nuneva, 2011a). Based on this shift of focus, Heidelberg was able to integrate itself more intensively in the workflow of its clients by covering pre-press, press and post-press steps as well as workflow management. The basis was the printing shop workflow, called *Prinect* – consisting of the words "print" and "connect" – which created an additional USP (unique selling point) (Heidelberg, 2008, pp. 25f.).

Heidelberg's strategic development was deepened in 2004 by implementing a print media competence approach, with additional support in the area of selling the printed products by Heidelberg's clients. This strategic move was reinforced in 2008 by the *management competence approach*, which provided customers with complete value chain support by Heidelberg (Porter, 2010, p. 167). These two steps increased customer orientation and boosted the level of customer intimacy at the same time. The signification changes were based on a *brand steering wheel*, which defines the key elements of the overall marketing approach. By doing so Heidelberg outpaced its competitors with the strategic approach and became the "best-in-breed" company to achieve a real USP (Porter, 1996, p. 64f.). A success factor of this cultural change from "product competence" to "management competence" was "to embrace" the employees during the entire process – for

people do not like change (Nuneva, 2011a). The challenge here was to moti-
vate "affected people" to become "involved people" – a key challenge in internal
marketing and in change management processes (Kreutzer, 2008).

To achieve the target of management competence, Heidelberg constantly uses
benchmarking in combination with a consistent and continuous improvement
process. Different instruments are in use for measuring and improving the
performance on a regular basis (see Figure 12.8).

In comparison to Heidelberg, KBA is still intensively engaged in the production
of rotary printing machines and is the global market leader in this sector, which
suffers significantly from the shrinking circulation of newspapers. In the US in
particular, the demand for rotary printing machines is close to zero (N. A., 2011c,
p. 14). A dramatic change here can be seen in a new project initiated by Rupert
Murdoch (an American media mogul) who launched a magazine – exclusively
designed for Apple's iPad (Mejias, 2011a, b, p. 35). It is not yet clear whether
this exclusive cooperation between Murdoch and Apple will be in the black in the
future – but in any case, it proves the shift of the changing relevance of different
communication channels from paper to screen, i.e. from offline to online. This
challenges the whole business concept of KBA. Manroland overcame its defensive strategic attitude by launching a cooperation with Dutch producer of digital
printing machines Océ (N. A., 2011d, p. 16). By taking this step, Manroland tried
to compensate for the shrinking demand for its core product: machines for rotary
offset printing.

Of the triad Heidelberg, KBA and Manroland, the latter was the first to become
engaged in digital printing by establishing strategic alliances. The cooperation
of Manroland covers the larger printing shops with digital printing facilities.
Heidelberg started a similar collaboration with the Japanese company Ricoh, targeting the segment of smaller digital printing machines. The task for Heidelberg

Consistent and continuous improvement process

Measuring tools	Instruments to improve performance
• Customer feedback	• Line-up
• Complaint management	• Information evenings
• Demo reports	• Improvement teams
• Employee satisfaction	• Topics specialists
• Employees' ideas	• Buddy/mentor
• Success measurement	• Employees' discussion

Figure 12.8 Benchmarking and continuous improvement process at Heidelberg (Nuvena,
    2011c, p. 29).

and Manroland is not the production of digital printing machines, but the completion of their own product range by selling machines produced by third parties (N. A., 2011d, p. 16; N. A., 2011l, p. 14). The last of the triad, KBA, initiated a cooperative relationship in this business field with Donnelley & Sons. As opposed to the approach of Heidelberg and Manroland, KBA will produce digital printing machines itself (N. A., 2011c, p. 16). The advantage for Heidelberg, in this context, is the full integration of digital printing machines within the Heidelberg software concept. Therefore the users of Heidelberg digital printing machines do not have to change the installed workflow systems (Gorpe, 2011), and Heidelberg is not using a mere OEM (original equipment manufacturer) approach for providing the market with digital printing machines.

Market position

Heidelberg has achieved a global market share of around 40 percent in the sheet-fed sector, and serves around 200,000 customers (with 400,000 installed printing machines) in 170 countries with its products and services. The export ratio is above 80 percent (Nuneva, 2011a). Family businesses (smaller in size) with up to 20 employees account for 80 percent of customers. The remaining 20 percent are large printing companies striving for excellence in productivity and quality (Heidelberg, 2008, p. 16). The combination of large, medium-sized and even small international customers offers a well-balanced customer portfolio.

Whilst KBA achieved an operational profit even during the financial crisis, Heidelberg needed to be massively supported by state funds in order to survive (Nuneva, 2011c, p. 34). Nevertheless KBA still faces a phase of transition and has to reduce its workforce and production capacities once more due to fundamental changes in demand (N. A., 2011i, p. 17; N. A., 2011k, p. 17). In 2010 and 2012, Manroland also had to reduce its workforce again after becoming bankrupt (N. A., 2010d, p. 54; Murphy, 2012, p. 21).

Company and brand reputation

Heidelberg focuses intensively on its company and brand reputation. Following a very dynamic phase of expansion by acquisition and internal growth, as well as the IPO (initial public offering) in 1997, Heidelberg's brand and product appearance was very heterogeneous (see Figure 12.9).

This situation was overcome by a comprehensive brand management process, which led to a very clear *corporate design concept* shown in Figure 12.10 (Nuneva, 2011c). The concept shows the relevance of brand building in the b2b sector (Baumgarth, 2010, pp. 37–62).

For many years Heidelberg suffered significantly from the copying of many of its marketing activities (e.g. image and advertising campaigns). To avoid a copy- and paste-mentality in the market, Heidelberg created the *Hei-Tech-concept* by making the switch from "HIGH TECH" to "HEI TECH" (see Figure 12.11). This offers Heidelberg the possibility to combine its achievements and business claims

Figure 12.9 Heterogeneous brand appearance in the past (Nuneva, 2011c, p. 14).

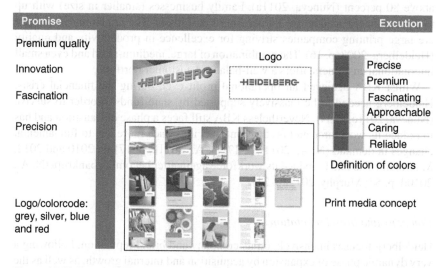

Figure 12.10 Brand architecture at Heidelberg – logo of Heidelberg, color code and print media concept (Nuneva, 2011c, p. 16).

with the proper name of Heidelberg. By doing so, it was able to penetrate the market in a way that is impossible to copy directly (Gorpe, 2011).

Heidelberg has defined the key trends and challenges in the market as follows (Heidelberg, 2011a):

> In order to achieve and maintain competitive advantage, companies in the print media industry need to act holistically and optimize their strengths

wherever possible. To best partnership and guide our customers through their challenges, we have to concentrate on answering the most relevant customer topics today:

Lean Manufacturing:

Be efficient with best results in the shortest time by using integrated production processes with the best tools available.

Ecological Printing:

Think economically and print ecologically by saving resources and reducing waste, emissions and energy consumption.

Differentiation through Print Applications:

Surprise your customers with applications offering more than they expect, adding value to their communication materials.

Web-to-Print:

Make sure you get repeat jobs by adding web-to-print to your portfolio.

Short Run Printing and Communication Management:

Stay successful in ultra short runs and choose the equipment that fits best for your communication and production needs.

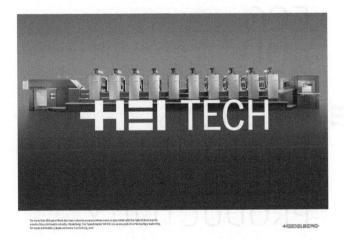

Figure 12.11 HEI-TECH branding strategy of Heidelberg (Heidelberg, 2011a).

Packaging Trends:

Look for sustainable materials in the value chain in the production of multi-function packages that save costs.

These key trends and challenges were transferred into solutions for Heidelberg, which are directly linked to the brand by using the *HEI-concept* (Figure 12.12). This *innovative branding* makes it impossible for competitors to move in the same direction – at least as far as the communication is concerned. By doing so Heidelberg is able to create a special kind of UAP (unique advertising proposition; see Kreutzer, 2010b, p. 135).

The overall communication approach of Heidelberg – based on the HEI-concept – is presented in Figure 12.13.

Production facilities and workforce

The large majority of the Heidelberg machines are only produced in Wiesloch-Walldorf (close to Heidelberg). Therefore the core competences in production, with all the relevant internal and external resources, are located there. In addition to Wiesloch-Walldorf, Heidelberg runs a production facility for smaller printing and folding machines in Qingpu, China. With its production site in China, Heidelberg has installed a strategic bridgehead to cover this huge market. The two Chinese competitors, Deirin and the Shanghai Electric Group, acquire smaller competitors on the world market to create a global network.

The backbone of Heidelberg's production is its highly qualified workforce, which has an above average education. Around 90 percent of the employees in the production area are skilled workers. Heidelberg has invested a lot in the ongoing training of its employees (Heidelberg, 2008, p. 8). Due to the economic crisis, the

Figure 12.12 Claiming of different achievements by Heidelberg (Heidelberg, 2011a).

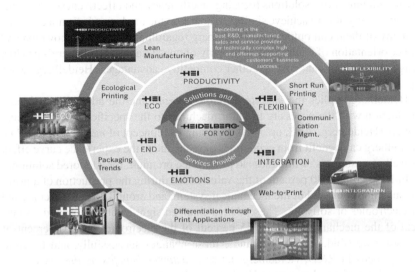

Figure 12.13 Heidelberg brand campaign – based on the HEI-concept (Heidelberg, 2011a).

company had to lay off more than 4,000 of the previously 20,000 skilled employees in order to stabilize the financial figures (N. A., 2009a, p. 16). Therefore good teams were changed and good practices and processes had to be redesigned. The reduction of the workforce potentially increases the risk of workforce shortages and, thereby, the company's dependence on the workforce. The dramatic cut of the workforce also affected Heidelberg's reputation as an employer. Thus, Heidelberg now focuses on the improvement of its employer branding too (Heidelberg, 2010, p. 120). With its cost saving program, "Heidelberg 2010," the company achieved a reduction of annual costs of around 400 million euros (ibid. p. 30).

KBA and Manroland also suffered from a brain drain. Due to the financial crisis, KBA had to dismiss 550 of its 7,000 employees and Manroland laid off 500 of its 7,500 employees (N. A., 2010b, p. 45; N. A., 2011c, p. 14) – both are still reducing their workforce in 2012 (N. A., 2012b, p. 16; N. A., 2012c, p. 14). Based on the specific production concept, Heidelberg is highly dependent on suppliers due to a vertical range of manufacture of about 40 percent; i.e. that 60 percent of the value of a product is delivered by third parties (Heidelberg, 2008, p. 6; Simon, 2007, p. 275). Therefore Heidelberg implemented a comprehensive *risk management system* in order to assure the reliability of its suppliers and quality of the suppliers' components. The economic crises also affected the suppliers and strengthened their risk of insolvency (Heidelberg, 2010, p. 120).

Product portfolio according to customers' needs

Heidelberg offers a large range of – interconnected – products and services in the focused market segment. It covers significant needs of its customers and provides them with innovative solutions focusing on efficiency and effectiveness. Competitors are hardly able to achieve similar standards in the market and it is not expected that any of them can outperform Heidelberg regarding its level of innovation and target-orientation of equipment and supply of consumables. Heidelberg's product range offers significant cost and other competitive advantages (Heidelberg, 2010, pp. 116, 118).

Heidelberg applies the *module principle* to combine the advantages of mass production with the necessity to tailor machines to the specific needs of its customers (Heidelberg, 2008, pp. 4, 6). By using the concept of *mass customization*, Heidelberg can benefit from economies of scale due to the experience curve effect as well as customers' willingness to pay a price premium for a tailored solution.

In 1980, around 80 percent of the value added during the production of a printing machine consisted of the mechanical system, and around 20 percent consisted of electronics or software. These shares changed significantly to around 45 percent of the mechanical system, 35 percent of the electronics and 20 percent of the software (ibid. p. 10). To handle these changes successfully, and to avoid wrong focus in R&D, Heidelberg defined *customer benefits as the key drivers* for any kind of development at Heidelberg. Therefore the company implemented an *open innovation concept* (Kreutzer, 2011a, pp. 208–10; Reichwald and Piller, 2006, pp. 97–135) and now involves lead customers in every step of development. Heidelberg also created a team of experts from R&D, product management, product control and production and service, to jointly define the direction of further developments. The results are fixed in a *technology roadmap*. All in all, around 8 percent of the workforce is directly or indirectly engaged in the development of new solutions (Heidelberg, 2010, p. 118; Heidelberg, 2008, p. 10; Nuneva, 2011c, p. 25).

The main competitors' resources appear too limited to compete with Heidelberg in this area. Based on a niche strategy, KBA has a less diversified product range and has been significantly hit by the change of demand. At the latest fair in China, KBA was able to sell 250 machines for printing packages and just one for printing newspapers – which is a significant change to its previous sale figures. The American newspaper industry does not invest in printing machines any more – and the Asian threshold countries do not start with a newspaper printing industry. These countries leapfrog this paper-based stage of development and instantly start with the online distribution of information. KBA is the world's largest producer of printing machines for newspapers – but this delivers only 20 percent of the company's turnover (N. A., 2011e, p. 20). The relevant market of KBA is expected to turn over only to 50 percent of the market volume before the crisis (N. A., 2011h, p. 17).

At Manroland, the dependency on printing machines for newspapers is even higher than at KBA. A collaboration between these two companies is regarded as a more or less necessary step to overcome the above-mentioned challenges (N. A., 2011e, p. 20). Such a step is considered necessary for staying in the market and is connected with a high level of fixed costs, and there are high exit barriers at the same time. It has to be considered that such a collaboration might be blocked by the Federal Cartel Office in Germany, or the World Trade Organization – due to the significant market shares of these two companies.

Service offers and interconnectedness with customers

The global economic crisis enforced the consolidation of the printing industry – that means of Heidelberg's customers. The remaining printing shops have to change from traditional handicraft businesses to modern industrial plants to meet the demands of their customers (Heidelberg, 2010, p. 61). To achieve the turnaround, printing plants need support from third parties – and Heidelberg is able to deliver what they need (Porter, 1996, p. 66f.; Simon, 2007, p. 179). Heidelberg offers comprehensive solutions (including services and consumables) for these customers, including web-to-print, lean manufacturing and ecological printing (Heidelberg, 2010, p. 118; ibid. p. 39). One key success factor of Heidelberg is therefore the *combination of equipment and services* – tailored to the needs of customers based on the concept of *customer centricity*. The range of services goes beyond traditional service dimensions like technical training and spare parts delivery, but also covers the category groups mentioned in Figure 12.14. Technical service is still a core competence, however, Heidelberg has integrated much further by providing additional services – so-called *performance services* for business and people development as well as for productivity and process optimization. With this width of services Heidelberg acts as a *success consultant* for its customers.

To achieve a high level of customer and service orientation Heidelberg defined *Ritz-Carlton* as its service level benchmark (for an analysis of the Ritz-Carlton service concept, see Kreutzer, 2008, pp. 68–73). The company tries to achieve a

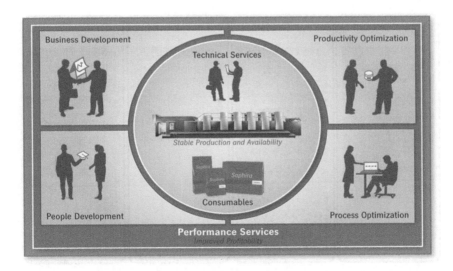

Figure 12.14 Service range of Heidelberg (Heidelberg, 2011a).

similar service standard in treating its customers like kings and queens – especially when they visit the production facilities of Heidelberg during customer tours. The overall concept of these customer tours is shown in Figure 12.15. An *integrated touch point management* is necessary to accomplish this outstanding treatment of its customers (Nuneva, 2011a, c, p. 21).

This service approach creates two very important side effects: *customer insights* and *additional profits*. Heidelberg need not rely exclusively on traditional market research alone to learn about the needs and requirements of its customers. By consulting customers in interconnected fields in the printing part of its business, Heidelberg learns about changes of need and requirement at a very early stage. Capturing and understanding these weak signals contributes substantially to Heidelberg's success. Based on cutomers' insights, Heidelberg can create a *learning relationship* with its customers (Peppers and Rogers, 2011, p. 1). This customer knowledge cannot be copied by competitors, and it therefore generates an important competitive advantage, which could stimulate the above-mentioned additional profits. In order to understand these implications of good customer relationships on profit, a focus on the counterpart of TCO (total cost of ownership) is necessary, and can be defined as TRO (total revenue of ownership). While TCO refers to the ownership of a machine, TRO is linked to the "ownership" of a customer relation and the value (customer value) connected with it (Kreutzer, 2009, pp. 35–47).

Based on information about needs and requirements gathered within the learning relationship, Heidelberg can provide its customers with tailored solutions. The broad range of services offered by Heidelberg also facilitates a bridging of the investment gap, by offering added value services and consumables to existing customers after they have invested in equipment (see Figure 12.16).

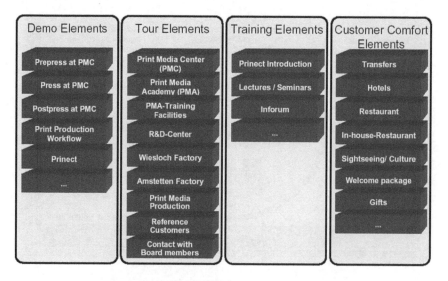

Figure 12.15 Elements of the customer tours (Nuneva, 2011c, p. 22).

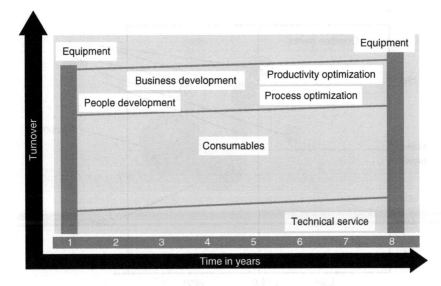

Figure 12.16 How to bridge the investment gap by additional service offers and consumables – schematic diagram.

An additional benefit of these value adding services is that Heidelberg can reduce the volatility of its business. The overall development of the printing industry is directly influenced by global economic growth. However, it has to be mentioned that the positive impact of a recovery is limited. While a boom in the past led directly to a strong demand for printing products, the situation has changed: Due to the shift of marketing budgets to online media, the direct impact of a recovery of the global economy on the printing sector is less positive and direct than before (Gorpe, 2011). Based on the introduction of the above-mentioned services, Heidelberg was able to achieve a more balanced portfolio of products and services (see Figure 12.17). An additional driver to enforce the level of interconnectedness between the company and its customers is the financial service offered. Heidelberg supports its customers to finance their investments (Heidelberg, 2010, p. 31). The interesting point about offering services, in addition to the core products, is that – despite working in just one industry – the different service offers face different growth rates in comparison to the core product.

Financial outlook

Manroland planned to achieve a turnaround and operate in the black within 2011, after an operational loss of 66 million euros in 2010. The turnover decreased from 1.11 billion to 0.942 billion euros. The size of the workforce (of 7,034) was significantly reduced in 2011. By doing so, an annual amount of 50 million euros was saved (N. A., 2011b; N. A., 2010b; N. A., 2011d). All these activities could not

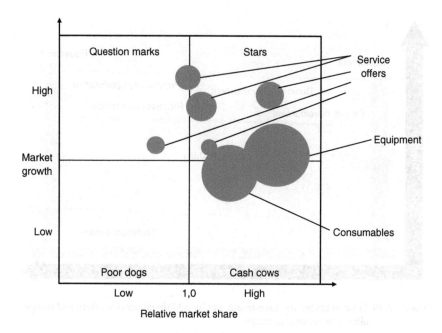

Figure 12.17 Product and service portfolio of Heidelberg – schematic diagram.

prevent Manroland from going bankrupt in 2011 (N. A., 2012a,). Triggered by this development, an additional 2,000 jobs were cut (Murphy, 2012). In the meantime Manroland was divided in two parts. The division "printing machines for newspapers" was acquired by the German conglomerate Possehl. Tony Langley acquired the sheet-fed division; this part of the company is now called Manroland Sheetfed (N. A., 2012b; Smolka, 2012; N. A., 2012c).

After three difficult years, Heidelberg is trying to achieve an operational profit in the fiscal year 2012/13. Incoming orders have increased due to a partial recovery of the market and the bankruptcy of Manroland. The top management sees a chance of gaining an additional turnover of 50 to 100 million euros in 2012 based on this development (Smolka, 2012). The drivers behind the general development are the booming threshold and emerging countries, which achieved a 45 percent share of Heidelberg's turnover. Meanwhile Heidelberg attains a higher turnover in China than in Germany. The cost reduction program of Heidelberg was very effective, but led to a reduction of 4,000 out of 20,000 employees before the crisis. In 2011, still, 1,000 employees have to work part-time (N. A., 2011h, p. 17). Nevertheless, Heidelberg has to face a deficit of 130 million euros for the fiscal year 2010/11. The result is financially burdened by high finance costs – not least for state loans. After the payback of all of these state loans, the fiscal year 2011/12 will be less strained by financial costs. Heidelberg is trying to achieve a net profit in 2012/13 (N. A., 2011f, p. 15; Hock, 2011).

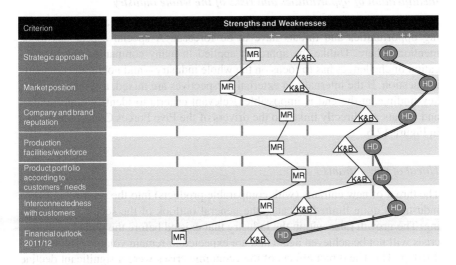

Figure 12.18 Strengths and weaknesses of Heidelberg in comparison to its competitors KBA and Manroland (MR).

Heidelberg itself defined its medium-term target of a turnover of 3 billion euros. Even so, its relevant market volume is expected to increase to only 80 per-cent of what it was before the crisis. Despite the digital revolution, the overall print production volume is expected to grow by 1 percent per year until 2015 (Gorpe, 2011). To diversify the business, Heidelberg launched a *make-to-order* product under the name *Heidelberg System Manufacturing* in 2010. Contracts have been signed with 20 companies from different industries (e.g. automotive and engineering). In the medium term, a three-digit turnover is expected (N. A., 2011h, p. 17).

KBA faced a decreased turnover of 1.18 billion euros in 2011, but achieved an operating profit in 2011. In addition, incoming orders increased by 20 percent to 1.5 billion euros in 2011. This development was also supported by the bankruptcy of Manroland (N. A., 2012b, p. 16). KBA was the only company of the German triad that achieved a profit during the global crisis. The overall workforce of KBA was also reduced by 25 percent; at the end of 2010, 6,400 people worked for this company, 550 less than the year before. The company is much less encumbered with debts than Heidelberg, as it was able to survive the crisis without state loans (N. A., 2011c, p. 14).

The identification of Heidelberg's strengths and weaknesses can be recognized as the dominant outcome of the analysis of the rivalry among existing competi-tors as part of the Five Forces Concept (see Figure 12.6). The overall findings of the first step of the SWOT analysis are summarized in Figure 12.18. The posi-tions of Heidelberg and its competitors are calculated via a sophisticated scoring model.

Identification of opportunities and risks of the whole industry

In addition to the identification of Heidelberg's strengths and weaknesses, upcoming opportunities and threats have to be forecast. A special aspect has to be mentioned here. Unlike the approach applied in many companies, the identification of challenges has to focus on the whole industry – and not on the company in question. If the internal and external perspectives are mixed, a synthesis of the key findings at the end is impossible. Relevant criteria to identify opportunities and threats are directly linked to the drivers of the Five Forces Concept as shown in Figure 12.6.

Threat of new entrants

The threat of new entrants (with comparable products) into the printing machine industry is quite limited, because the general outlook of the sector is challenging. The growth rates within the industry that existed before the global economic crisis will not be achieved again and are expected to remain volatile (Heidelberg, 2010, p. 31). The direct effects of the economic crises were a significant decline in sales, overcapacities and financial problems of the key players in the industry. In Germany, the printing machine industry has had to cope with a decline of 41 percent in incoming orders in 2009, because many customers postponed investments in machinery (Heidelberg, 2010, pp. 59, 62; ibid. p. 117). Furthermore, the market is highly saturated and dominated by six key players. The development costs for sheet-fed machines are very high, so that the expected ROI for new entrants is limited and entry barriers are also high (cf. Heidelberg, 2008, p. 2). These barriers of entry are not only based on capital requirements, but also on huge economies of scale and learning curve effects. In addition, customers' loyalty – mostly impacted by their switching costs – should not be neglected (Kreutzer, 2009, p. 177).

In addition, it has to be noted that the printing industry in general no longer has huge growth potential (N. A., 2011a, p. 23). In the developed markets in particular, a stagnation or even decline of print volume of magazines, newspapers and books can be expected, and this could eventually lead to a 60–70 percent reduction of the former market volume (N. A., 2011d, p. 16). This might be one reason why this industry was not defined as a core area of development in China. The producers of printing equipment will not be challenged by new entrants from China or from other emerging markets (Gorpe, 2011). As no powerful new entrants are expected, the threat of new entrants is low.

Bargaining power of suppliers

The example of Heidelberg shows a vertical range of manufacture of about 40 percent (Heidelberg, 2008, p. 6). Therefore the company is highly dependent on the reliability of its suppliers and the quality of their components. Since the suppliers of the printing machine industry were also hit by the economic crises, many of them are still facing significant financial problems. Therefore they are also heavily dependent on their key accounts (e.g. Heidelberg). A mutual dependence can be seen here, which leads to limited bargaining power for the suppliers.

The number of suppliers is still high and they are not concentrated or organized, which weakens their bargaining power and increases the competition between them. In some areas, however, the costs of switching suppliers are high as some of them are integrated into the workflow of the producers of printing machines, and this increases the suppliers' bargaining power. There is no risk of suppliers integrating downstream due to the complexity of the production of printing machines. All in all, the bargaining power of these suppliers is quite limited.

In Germany, industry as a whole was challenged by the *collective bargaining round* of 2011, during which the trade unions tried to achieve a wage increase of 5.5 percent. The employers intended to repeal the 35-hour working week, and came across significant resistance from the trade unions. Negotiating partners have to take into consideration the fact that industry, in total, lost more than 60,000 jobs within the last ten years. In addition, a price increase of raw material and energy has to be considered (N. A., 2011g, p. 14). Some pressure from these suppliers can be expected to increase prices.

Threat from substitute products

The entire printing industry is intensively challenged by new technologies. These have an influence on the printing process itself, as well as on the behavior of end users. The background of this development can be seen in Figure 12.19.

A dramatic change, from one-to-mass communication to one-to-many communication, can be identified in most industries. Some companies go further and try

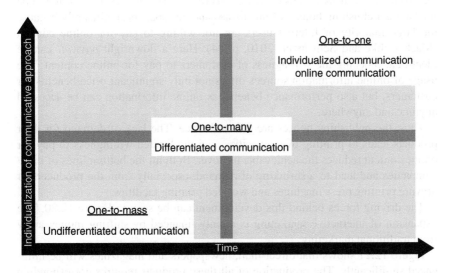

Figure 12.19 Changes in the communication approach.

We will increase budget for interactive by shifting money away from traditional marketing — 60%

We will increase budget for interactive with no budget change to traditional marketing — 15%

We will increase budget for both interactive and traditional — 14%

We have no plans to increase our interactive marketing budget — 7%

Don't know — 8%

Figure 12.20 How do you finance the expansion of interactive marketing? (Basis: 204 marketers; Forrester Research, 2009).

to achieve a one-to-one communication by using concepts of mass customization (Peppers and Rogers, 2011, pp. 189–92). By using data from CRM (customer relationship management) systems to tailor messages, companies expect higher response rates to advertising campaigns (Kreutzer, 2009, p. 8). Digital printing offers the possibility to achieve a high level of individualization because it can deliver one-to-one printing solutions. This technology challenges the traditional printing processes, but, even so, offset technologies could be used in this context as well – by delivering a much higher printing quality at reasonable prices (Gorpe, 2011; Heidelberg, 2010, p. 116).

In many areas of the world, the younger generation (and also younger adults) has a high affinity with online channels of communication. This leads to a dramatic worldwide decline of the newspaper and magazine business and a shrinking interest in printed books, to the benefit of online editions of newspapers and magazines as well as e-books (N. A., 2011c, p. 14). This shift towards online media hits publishing houses of magazines and newspapers significantly because the large majority of Internet users are not willing to pay for online content (Machatschke and Schwarzer, 2010, p. 44). Here a downright *paywall* can be identified, blocking the willingness of customers to pay for online content. The usage of online information sources offers not only significant price benefits for customers, but also performance benefits as online information can be accessed anytime and anywhere.

Thus, the publishing houses are affected twice. The lack of demand for their products leads to printing overcapacities, and the limited willingness to pay for online content reduces the achievable turnover. Both hit the bottom lines of these companies and lead to a shrinking of demand, especially from the producers of gravure printing press machines and web-fed printing facilities.

The driving forces behind this development can be seen in Figure 12.20. The expansion of interactive marketing is mainly financed by shifting money away from traditional marketing.

Figure 12.21 shows that direct mail, newspapers and magazines will be influenced significantly. The production of all these products requires corresponding printing machines.

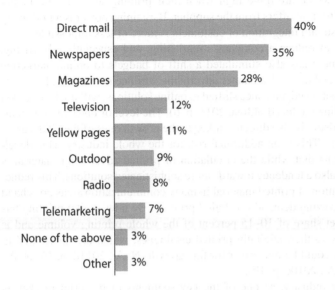

Figure 12.21 Which traditional marketing budgets will be reduced in favor of interactive marketing? (Basis: 118 marketers, Forrester Research, 2009).

Bargaining power of buyers

The printing industry is highly dependent on overall economic development, and the global economic crisis led to a significant decrease in the demand for printing machines. Additionally the increase in online usage leads to a decrease in print products in general. Advertising material generates an average of 60 percent of the production value of printing companies and fluctuates directly with the ups and downs of the world economy (Heidelberg, 2010, p. 61). Due to the above-mentioned overcapacities of printing shop suppliers, an intensive competition for market share connected with price battles is expected. There we can really talk of a "red ocean". The pressure on prices might even force competitors to exit the market (Heidelberg, 2010, p. 115).

In addition to this, customers of printed material are in a very powerful bargaining position due to the overcapacities of the 400,000 printing shops operating worldwide (Heidelberg, 2008, p. 16). Here too, price pressure and price wars concerning printed material are part of daily business. The industry has to face another challenge, which is influenced by the growing purchasing power of huge producers of packaging material like Mayr-Melnhof. A further consolidation in the market is expected (Gorpe, 2011).

On the one hand, the bargaining power of customers could be regarded as high because the depreciation of printing machines can represent a significant fraction of buyers' costs. Therefore these costs have a direct impact on the prices of final print products. On the other hand, bargaining power is limited by buyers' switching costs, which are quite high when their printing solutions are highly connected with different offers from the supplier. Bargaining power is additionally limited, as an upstream integration of customers is more or less impossible.

The necessity to reduce a company's marketing, and especially advertising, budgets during the crisis also stimulated a shift of budgets to online marketing solutions (e.g. social networks, banner advertising, affiliate marketing). Forecasts show that advertising budgets, once shifted to online solutions, will not be returned to traditional offline media (Bialdiga, 2011, p. 6). The level of investment in marketing and advertising is also directly linked to the growth rates of the GDP (gross domestic product). This is an additional risk for the whole industry. This development also means that while the circulation of printed advertising material is reduced, there is also a tendency towards more sophisticated solutions. This reduction in the circulation of printed material in many communication areas goes hand in hand with a growing demand for digital printing. By now, digital printing has achieved a market share of 10–15 percent of the whole printing volume and is expected to grow further. Digitally printed catalogues, which are distributed in smaller numbers, could be one driver for this growth (N. A., 2011d, p. 16; N. A., 2011c, p. 16; N. A., 2010c, p. 19).

The packaging industry, as one of the key segments of the print market, is not as volatile as the advertising market. A considerable increase in demand for packed goods in threshold and emerging markets leads to a constantly increasing request for respective printing machines. This development offers a significant opportunity for producers of sheet-fed machines. It is not yet clear whether a similar print product level per capita can be achieved in the threshold countries, as in the industrialized nations, or whether there will be an enforced substitution of print media by online offers. In any case, the increase in population in the threshold countries will boost the demand for packaged goods and therewith, also, the demand for printing equipment (see Heidelberg, 2011b, p. 123; see also Figure 12.22).

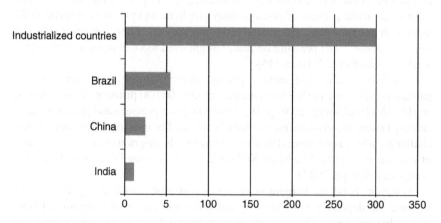

Figure 12.22 Printing volume per capita in euros, 2010 (Heidelberg, 2011b, p. 123).

In addition, *country specific criteria* have to be taken into consideration. Here, the overall investment environment in target markets, exchange rates between key countries, patent protection, new environmental protection laws, local content requirements, availability of new sales channels and the development of local input prices have to be mentioned (Kreutzer, 2010b, pp. 78–82). In particular, the development of the exchange rate between the euro and the yen could tighten competitiveness with Japanese suppliers (Heidelberg, 2010, p. 117) This in-depth analysis of the printing industry has revealed the following key findings (see Figures 12.23 and 12.24).

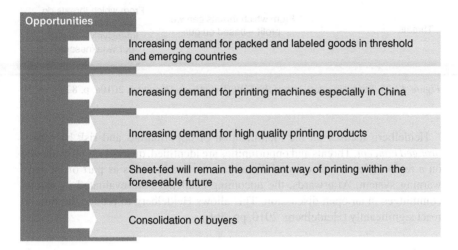

Figure 12.23 Opportunities in the printing industry.

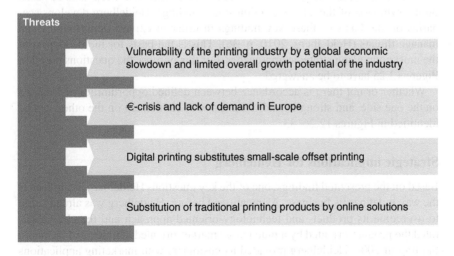

Figure 12.24 Threats in the printing industry.

Internal perspective / External perspective	Own strengths	Own weaknesses
Opportunities	Which opportunities can be used perfectly – based on our strengths?	Which opportunities cannot be used – due to our weaknesses?
Threats	From which threats can we profit – based on our strengths?	From which threats do we have to suffer intensively – due to our weaknesses?

Figure 12.25 Strategic questions of the SWOT synthesis (Kreutzer, 2010a, p. 82).

Heidelberg focuses on the identification of opportunities and risk by a *two-pronged concept*. Threats and opportunities are identified, quantified and evaluated on a regional level and reported directly to the headquarters as part of an early warning system. Afterwards, the upcoming challenges are evaluated in several committees in an open discussion. This allows Heidelberg to reduce the time to react significantly (Heidelberg, 2010, pp. 36f.).

Synthesis of the key findings as background for strategic decisions

The information platform for the development of a strategic concept is to be based on the synthesis of the above-mentioned key findings. Heidelberg develops scenarios on the basis of these key findings in order to exploit opportunities and manage threats (Heidelberg, 2010, p. 36). This is the basis for the deduction of the most convincing strategic approaches. For this purpose the questions posed in Figure 12.25 have to be answered.

Whether or not there is accordance between defined opportunities and threats on the one side, and strengths and weaknesses of Heidelberg on the other, can be identified in Figures 12.26–33.

Strategic implications for Heidelberg

Based on the presented findings, one of the key questions Heidelberg has to face is the way it defines its business. As mentioned before, Heidelberg was already able to overcome its product- and technology-oriented approach and thereby substituted the product-oriented by a much more market-oriented definition of business. Starting in 2004, Heidelberg provided its customers with marketing applications and business consulting solutions, seeing itself as the dominant player in business

Internal perspective / External perspective	Strengths of Heidelberg	Weaknesses of Heidelberg
Opportunity : Increasing demand for packed and labeled goods in emerging and threshold countries	• Heidelberg's sales force and branches cover the relevant markets • Positive reputation of Heidelberg in keymarkets • Innovative products & services for this industry	• Reduced financial strength due to significant losses in the years 2008/09, 2009/10, 2010/11 • Weakened workforce due to employee bleeding in the crisis
Opportunity : Increasing demand for printing machines in China	• Own production facility for smaller printing and folding machines in Qingpu/China • Reduced vulnerability by trade barriers	• Reduced financial strength due to significant losses in the years 2008/09, 2009/10, 2010/11 • Weakened workforce due to employee bleeding in the crisis

Figure 12.26 Key findings of the SWOT analysis of Heidelberg – opportunities I.

Internal perspective / External perspective	Strengths of Heidelberg	Weaknesses of Heidelberg
Opportunity: Increasing demand for high quality printing products	• Heidelberg delivers equipment and a wide variety of services to achieve premium quality • Coverage of the global market via 250 branches, 4 logistic centers, 3,200 specialists in equipment, services and consumables • Print Media Academy to train specialists and managers globally	• Reduced financial strength due to significant losses in the years 2008/09, 2009/10, 2010/11 • Weakened workforce due to employee bleeding in the crisis

Figure 12.27 Key findings of the SWOT analysis of Heidelberg – opportunities II.

competence. By doing this, the company is in a good position to understand its customers' needs in order to guarantee convincing solutions. Its b2b2c-approach delivers convincing solutions to support further prospective development (Nuneva, 2011c, p. 19). The implications of this concept can be seen in Figure 12.34. Heidelberg's broader horizon also tries to understand the requirements of its direct customers' own print buyers.

Further development is based on the *brand steering wheel 2012*, as developed by Heidelberg management (see Figure 12.35). Within this steering

Internal perspective / External perspective	Strengths of Heidelberg	Weaknesses of Heidelberg
Opportunity: Sheet-fed will remain the dominant way of printing	• Sheet-fed is the core competence of Heidelberg • Coverage of the global market via 250 branches, 4 logistic centers, 5,000 specialists in equipment, services and consumables	• Reduced financial strength due to significant losses in the years 2008/09, 2009/10, 2010/11 • Weakened workforce due to employee bleeding in the crisis • High reliance on suppliers for they deliver 60% of the value of the equipment

Figure 12.28 Key findings of the SWOT analysis of Heidelberg – opportunities III.

Internal perspective / External perspective	Strengths of Heidelberg	Weaknesses of Heidelberg
Opportunity: Consolidation of buyers	• Large buyers are looking for full service suppliers to reduce the number of interfaces • Heidelberg has perfect offers for these large customers • Large customers expect a high operational availability which can be guaranteed by the quality and the service of Heidelberg	• Reduced financial strength due to significant losses in the years 2008/09, 2009/10, 2010/11

Figure 12.29 Key findings of the SWOT analysis of Heidelberg – opportunities IV.

wheel positioning/USP, personality/tonality, reason why and visual signs are defined.

The overall convincing point of the strategic approach of Heidelberg 2012 and beyond, is to meet the following customer expectation (Heidelberg, 2011a):

I need a committed partner providing products, flexible solutions and services on a premium level which are not only focused on my needs but also give me the flexibility of adaption to changing market trends. A partner who not

Internal perspective / External perspective	Strengths of Heidelberg	Weaknesses of Heidelberg
Threat: Vulnerability of the printing industry by a global economic slowdown and limited overall growth potential of the industy	• Heidelberg focusses on the packaging industry which is less growth-sensitive • Significant growth rates in services and consumables • Potential area of future growth: make-to-order production under the label Heidelberg System Manufacturing • Powerful distribution network by partnering solutions	• Reduced financial strength due to significant losses in the years 2008/09, 2009/10, 2010/11 • Weakened workforce due to employee bleeding in the crisis • Task: necessity to identify new growth areas for Heidelberg (market field) • Task: define which additional services and products could be sold via the existing distribution network

Figure 12.30 Key findings of the SWOT analysis of Heidelberg – threats I.

Internal perspective / External perspective	Strengths of Heidelberg	Weaknesses of Heidelberg
Threat: €-crisis and lack of demand in Europe	• Coverage of the global market via 250 branches, 4 logistic centers, 5,000 specialists in equipment, services and consumables • High level activities in emerging and threshold countries with high growth rates • Make-to-order production under the label Heidelberg System Manufacturing	• Reduced financial strength due to significant losses in the years 2008/09, 2009/10, 2010/11 • Weakened workforce due to employee bleeding in the crisis • Still high dependency on the European market • Only limited lateral diversification to spread risks

Figure 12.31 Key findings of the SWOT analysis of Heidelberg – threats II.

only contributes new ideas and opportunities to my business success but also broadens visions and plays a forward taking role.

By fulfilling this customer expectation the following emotion has to be reached (Heidelberg, 2011a): "I have the right business partner."

This could be regarded as the next logical step in order to implement an overall business competence approach to deepen the level of customer intimacy once more (see Figure 12.36). Heidelberg is achieving this position by gaining a deep understanding of the latest commercial and social trends and transforming these into

Internal perspective / External perspective	Strengths of Heidelberg	Weaknesses of Heidelberg
Threat: Digital printing substitutes small-scale offset printing	• Strategic cooperation with Ricoh to provide market with digital printing equipment integrated in the overall workflow of Heidelberg • Piggybacking strategy to sell third party digital printing machines via Heidelberg sales channels • High flexibility and high speed of Heidelberg's offset machines partially outperforms digital print (exception small circulations)	• Dependency on strategic supplier (Ricoh)

Figure 12.32 Key findings of the SWOT analysis of Heidelberg – threats III.

Internal perspective / External perspective	Strengths of Heidelberg	Weaknesses of Heidelberg
Threat: Substitution of traditional printing products by online solutions	• Heidelberg focusses also on packaging and consumables (magazines, newspapers, books no Heidelberg core business)	• Reduced financial strength due to significant losses in the years 2008/09, 2009/10, 2010/11 • Weakened workforce due to employee bleeding in the crisis • Lack of solutions to participate from the shift to online activities of core customers

Figure 12.33 Key findings of the SWOT analysis of Heidelberg – threats IV.

adequate solutions for its customers. This could be regarded as a huge, constant and never-ending challenge for the whole company. By this business definition of Heidelberg, it is clear that the company regards itself as a global driver for adequate technological change – going hand in hand with the requirements of the different tiers of its customers.

This approach converges with a specific version of the value chain, which could be named the value-adding information chain. Figure 12.37 shows that

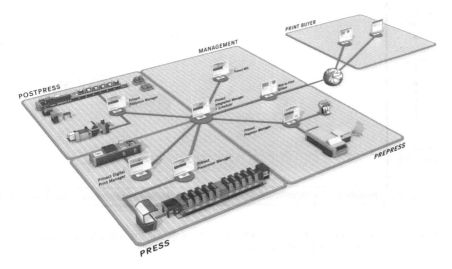

Figure 12.34 To think beyond the borders of Heidelberg's direct customers (Heidelberg, 2011a).

Customer Expectation
I need a committed partner providing products, flexible solutions and services on premium level which are not only focussed on my needs but also give me the flexibility of adaption to changing market trends. A partner who not only contributes with new ideas and opportunities to my business success but also broadens visions and plays a forward taking role.

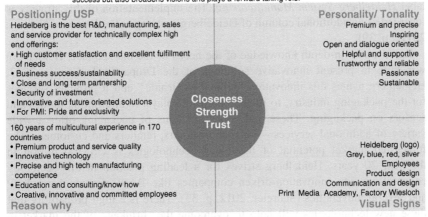

Positioning/ USP

Heidelberg is the best R&D, manufacturing, sales and service provider for technically complex high end offerings:
- High customer satisfaction and excellent fulfillment of needs
- Business success/sustainability
- Close and long term partnership
- Security of investment
- Innovative and future oriented solutions
- For PMI: Pride and exclusivity

160 years of multicultural experience in 170 countries
- Premium product and service quality
- Innovative technology
- Precise and high tech manufacturing competence
- Education and consulting/know how
- Creative, innovative and committed employees

Reason why

Closeness Strength Trust

Personality/ Tonality

Premium and precise
Inspiring
Open and dialogue oriented
Helpful and supportive
Trustworthy and reliable
Passionate
Sustainable

Heidelberg (logo)
Grey, blue, red, silver
Employees
Product design
Communication and design
Print Media Academy, Factory Wiesloch

Visual Signs

Desired Feelings
"I have the right business partner."
For Print Media Industry (PMI) only: Pride ("I am a member of the Heidelberg Family")

Figure 12.35 Brand steering wheel 2012 and beyond (Heidelberg, 2011a).

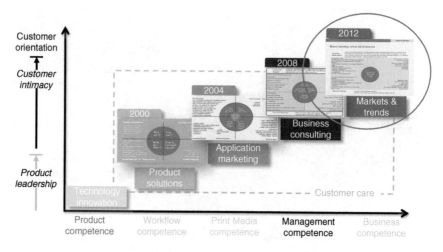

Figure 12.36 Heidelberg developed from a product competent towards a business competent brand (Heidelberg, 2011a).

the information focus of Heidelberg reaches far beyond its direct customers. To achieve the necessary business competence in the whole industry, Heidelberg implemented a complex value-adding information chain in order to understand not only its direct customers, but also its indirect ones.

In addition to this strategic perspective, Heidelberg is looking for additional growth areas. These have been defined in the area of print-to-order production, where Heidelberg can use its core competencies to attract additional customers from market segments that are not yet covered. This approach is marked under the label *Heidelberg System Manufacturing*. The implementation of this strategy is regarded as an additional column of Heidelberg's strategic development (Nuneva, 2011c, p. 39).

Based on its in-depth knowledge of the needs of the marketplace, Heidelberg was able to present innovative solutions at the Drupa Trade Fair in 2012. Heidelberg names this innovation "printed electronic," and it provides services for the packaging industry, to include chips, displays, light-emitting diodes and sensors on packaging. These additional functions of packaging offer a wide variety of additional services – for manufacturers, retailers and customers. The forecasted market potential of these new technologies is US$300 billion in the next 20 years. Heidelberg strives for a leading position in this sector by cooperating with innovation-driven companies like BASF, Freudenberg, SAP and several universities (Schreier, 2012, p. 33). There is a high probability that these new technologies will help to overcome the shrinkage of the market in other areas. Heidelberg possesses a convincing position to master the difficulties ahead and to remain a profitable and reliable partner of the printing industry in future.

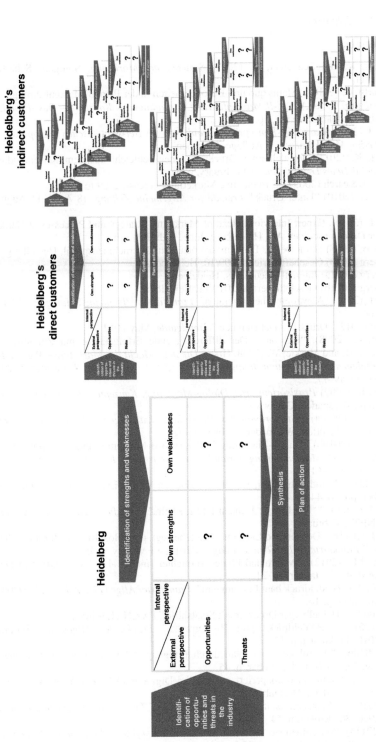

Figure 12.37 Specific value-adding information chain.

References

Backhaus, K. and Schneider, H. (2007) *Strategisches Marketing*, Stuttgart: Schäffer-Poeschel.

Baumgarth, C. (2010). "Status quo und Besonderheiten in der B-to-B-Markenführung," in: Baumgarth, C. (ed.) *B-to-B-Markenführung, Grundlagen – Konzepte – Best-Practice*, Wiesbaden: Gabler Verlag, pp. 37–62.

Becker, J. (2009) *Marketing-Konzeption, Grundlagen des ziel-strategischen und operativen Marketing-Managements*, 9. Auflage, München.

Bialdiga, K. (2011) "Heidelberger Druckmaschinen schleicht aus dem Krisenmodus," *Financial Times Deutschland*, 10 February, p. 6.

Forrester Research (2009) US Interactive Marketing Forecast, 2009 to 2014.

Freytag, B. (2010) "Unter Druck," *Frankfurter Allgemeine Zeitung*, 18 April, 11 August, p. 16.

Gorpe, T. (2011), Expert Interview, Head of Marketing Strategy and Processes at Heidelberger Druckmaschinen AG, Heidelberg, June, 16th, July 4th.

Heidelberg (2008) Heidelberger Druckmaschinen, Ein Unternehmensprofil, Heidelberg.

Heidelberg (2010) Geschäftsbericht 2009/10, Heidelberg.

Heidelberg (2011a) Internal Documents, Heidelberg.

Heidelberg (2011b) Geschäftsbericht 2010/11, Heidelberg.

Hock, M. (2011) "Abwarten scheint geraten," *Frankfurter Allgemeine Zeitung*, FAZ.NET, 16 June.

Horizont (2012) "Druck erfindet sich neu," *Trendguide*, May 2012.

Kreutzer, R. (2008), "Passion – Der differenzierende Erfolgsfaktor mit Zukunft," in: Kreutzer, R. and Merkle, W. (2008, Hrsg.) *Die neue Macht des Marketing – Wie Sie Ihr Unternehmen durch Emotion, Innovation und Präzision profilieren*, Wiesbaden: Gabler Verlag, pp. 49–77.

Kreutzer, R. (2009) *Praxisorientiertes Dialog-Marketing, Konzepte – Instrumente – Fallbeispiele*, Wiesbaden: Gabler verlag.

Kreutzer, R. (2010a) *Praxisorientiertes Marketing, Grundlagen – Instrumente – Fallbeispiele*, 3rd edition, Wiesbaden: Gabler Verlag.

Kreutzer, R. (2010b) "Dialog-Marketing in der B-to-B-Markenführung," in: Baumgarth, C. (ed.), *B-to-B-Markenführung, Grundlagen – Konzepte – Best-Practice*, Wiesbaden: Gabler, pp. 575–611.

Machatschke, M. and Schwarzer, U. (2010) "Endlich Weltmeister," *Manager Magazine*, October, pp. 36–44.

Mejias, J. (2011a) "'The Daily': Denken und Lächeln," *Frankfurter Allgemeine Zeitung*, FAZ.NET, 3 February.

Mejias, J. (2011b) "Denken und Lächeln – Bunt, bewegt, papierlos: Rupert Murdochs 'The Daily'," *Frankfurter Allgemeine Zeitung*, 29/2011, 4 February, p. 35.

Murphy, M. (2012) "Manroland-Pleite vernichtet mehr als 2000 Arbeitsplätze," *Handelsblatt*, 25 January, p. 21.

N. A. (2009a) "Heideldruck baut Führung um," *Frankfurter Allgemeine Zeitung*, 275/2009, 26 November, p. 16.

N. A. (2009b) "Heidelberger Druck erhält Staatshilfe," FAZ.NET, 9 June.

N. A. (2010a) "Heideldruck spürt Rückenwind," *Frankfurter Allgemeine Zeitung*, 184/2010, 11 August, p. 13.

N. A. (2010b) "Manroland: Sozialplan durch Einigungsstelle," *Frankfurter Allgemeine Zeitung*, 293/2010, 16 December, p. 45.

N. A. (2010c) "Manroland kooperiert mit Océ im Digitaldruck," *Frankfurter Allgemeine Zeitung*, 281/2010, 2 December, p. 19.

N. A. (2010d) "Manroland baut Verwaltungsstellen ab," *Frankfurter Allgemeine Zeitung*, 253/2010, 30 October, p. 54.

N. A. (2011a) "Maschinenbau weiterhin im Wachstumszyklus," *Frankfurter Allgemeine Zeitung*, 100/2011, 30 April, p. 23.

N. A. (2011b) "Manroland erhofft sich Gewinn," *Frankfurter Allgemeine Zeitung*, 65/2011, 18 March, p. 19.

N. A. (2011b) "Zeitungsdruck macht KBA zu schaffen," *Frankfurter Allgemeine Zeitung*, 72/2011, 26 March, p. 14.

N. A. (2011c) "KBA steigt in Digitaldruck ein," *Frankfurter Allgemeine Zeitung*, 52/2011, 3 March, p. 16.

N. A. (2011d) "Manroland will sich aus der Defensive befreien," *Frankfurter Allgemeine Zeitung*, 60/2011, 12 March, p. 16.

N. A. (2011e) "Von der Rolle," *Frankfurter Allgemeine Zeitung*, 112/2011, 14 May, p. 20.

N. A. (2011f) "Heideldruck schöpft Hoffnung," *Frankfurter Allgemeine Zeitung*, 100/2011, 30 April, p. 15.

N. A. (2011g) "Drucker vor schwieriger Tarifrunde," *Frankfurter Allgemeine Zeitung*, 99/2011, 29 April, p. 14.

N. A. (2011h) "Heideldruck fasst langsam wieder Fuß," *Frankfurter Allgemeine Zeitung*, 139/2011, 17 June, p. 17.

N. A. (2011i) "Koenig & Bauer baut weitere Stellen ab," *Frankfurter Allgemeine Zeitung*, 139/2011, 17 June, p. 17.

N. A. (2011k) "KBA sieht schwarz," *Frankfurter Allgemeine Zeitung*, 112/2011, 14 May, p. 17.

N. A. (2011l) "Heidelberger Druck kooperiert mit Ricoh," *Frankfurter Allgemeine Zeitung*, 46/2011, 24 February, p. 14.

N. A. (2011m) "Heideldruck zahlt Kredite zurück," *Frankfurter Allgemeine Zeitung*, 17/2011, 21 January, p. 18.

N. A. (2012a) "Heideldruck erwartet abermals einen Verlust," *Frankfurter Allgemeine Zeitung*, 137/2012, 15 June, p. 19.

N. A. (2012b) "KBA bleibt profitabel," *Frankfurter Allgemeine Zeitung*, 62/2012, 3 March, p. 16.

N. A. (2012c) "Manroland wird in drei Gesellschaften aufgespalten," *Frankfurter Allgemeine Zeitung*, 17/2012, 19 January, p. 14.

Nuneva, A. (2011a) "Global Marketing at Heidelberger Druckmaschinen," presentation at the Berlin School of Economics and Law, Berlin, 27th January, 2011.

Nuneva, A. (2011b) Expert Interview, Vice President Global Marketing & Communications at Heidelberger Druckmaschinen AG, Heidelberg, 6 June, 2011.

Nuneva, A. (2011c) "Reputation Management bei der Heidelberger Druckmaschinen AG," in: Wüst, C./Kreutzer, R. (Editors); *Corporate Reputation Management*, Wiesbaden.

Pepels, W. (2006) *Produktmanagement , Produktinnovation – Marketingpolitik – Programmplanung – Prozessorganisation*, 5th edition, München: Oldenbourg, Wissensch. Vlg.

Peppers, D. and Rogers, M. (2011) *Managing Customer Relationships, A Strategic Framework*, 2nd edition, Hoboken: John Wiley and Sons.

Porter, M. (1996) "What is strategy?", November–December, 1996, pp. 61–78.

Porter, M. (2008) *Wettbewerbsstrategie, Methoden zur Analyse von Branchen und Konkurrenten*, Frankfurt: Campus Verlag.

Porter, M. (2010) *Wettbewerbsvorteile, Spitzenleistungen erreichen und behaupten*, Frankfurt: Campus Verlag.

Reichwald, R. and Piller, F. (2006) *Interaktive Wertschöpfung, Open Innovation, Individualisierung und neue Formen der Arbeitsteilung*, Wiesbaden: Gabler Verlag.

Schreier, B. (2012) "Wir sind Ideengeber fürs Marketing", *Horizont*, 26 April, p. 33.

Simon, H. (2007) *Hidden Champions des 21. Jahrhunderts, Die Erfolgsstrategien unbekannter Weltmarktführer*, Frankfurt: Campus Verlag.

Smolka, K. M. (2012) "Heidelberger Druck jagt Manroland verunsicherte Kunden ab," *Financial Times Deutschland*, 9 February, p. 4.

13 Competitive strategy of small firms

The two mechanisms of competitive advantage

Kenichi Tamai

Introduction

Following recent changes in global business environments, the competitiveness of manufacturing firms in Japan is beginning to be recognized (Fujimoto, 2004). However, this argument focuses on large manufacturing firms. By contrast, the attention paid to small manufacturing firms (SMFs) is insufficient and thus we need to articulate the competitiveness of these firms, which underpin the strength of manufacturing capabilities in Japan. The examination of the competitiveness of Japanese SMFs may help researchers understand their distinct characteristics for the first time. Therefore, this study captures the fundamental factors that bring about their competitiveness.

The theoretical framework of generic strategies proposed by Porter (1980, 1985) can be applied to explore these factors. Since Porter proposed three generic competitive strategies in the 1980s, a paradigm of strategic management theory has been established (Mintzberg *et al.*, 1998; Campbell-Hunt, 2000). In this paradigm, the theoretical approach of using the concept of generic strategies became possible and the constructs of strategy were operationalized. As a result, many empirical studies based on this framework have been conducted in various industries in order to develop the theory.

The unit of analysis of this framework is the business unit. Therefore, the development of this theory would increase the applicability to SMFs, which usually have only one or a few related business units. More importantly, however, is that competitive scope as a fundamental dimension of generic strategies is included in this theory. If we assume that the competitive advantage of SMFs cannot be discussed in the same dimension as that of large manufacturing firms because of their differences in size or market power, the aspect of competitive scope would seem to be important to the explanation of the strategies of those firms. Through the analysis of strategy in terms of competitive scope (Porter, 1985), it would be possible to ascertain the distinctive strategies for acquiring competitive advantage in SMFs, because the analysis of competitive scope can capture a unique position according to market choice. However, the concept of competitive scope is not yet developed fully. Further, the relationship of this concept with competitive advantage is unclear. Therefore, it is necessary to clarify its conceptual meaning and to determine its position in competitive strategy in order to clarify competitive advantage in SMFs.

Previous research

The theoretical development of competitive strategy

The theory of competitive strategy has been developed as an accompanying critical argument since Porter (1980) suggested cost leadership, differentiation, and focus as generic strategies based on the aspects of competitive advantage and competitive scope. In particular, the view that a firm that is stuck in the middle, namely "failing to develop its strategy in at least one of the three directions (three generic strategies)" (Porter, 1980: 41), has inferior competitive advantage and has been the focus of criticism by many scholars of strategic management.

Murray (1988) pointed out that it is possible to pursue different generic strategies concurrently because a differentiation strategy depends on customers' preferences, while cost leadership is based on industry structure. Thus, pursuing generic strategies simultaneously is possible, owing to differences in the source of competitive advantage.

In addition, Hill (1988) stated that a differentiation strategy results in competitive advantage because it is based on firm-specific skills, while a cost leadership strategy based on economies of scale, the experience curve, and economies of scope, does not because there is no such unique low-cost position in many industries. He regarded a differentiation strategy as the only source of competitive advantage and stated the logic of the concurrent pursuit of generic strategies: "Only when the increase in cost due to differentiation is outweighed by cost reductions associated with expanding volume can differentiation be seen as a way of achieving a low-cost position" (Hill, 1988: 406).

These arguments suggest that market factors such as customers' preferences and demand are significant for the explanation of competitive advantage through the concurrent pursuit of generic strategies. Therefore, it is necessary to understand the logic of competitive advantage including the view of competitive scope.

In spite of criticism about being stuck in the middle, generic strategies were established as a building block of empirical studies. Some studies even elaborated on their constructs. In such studies, the underlying dimensions that classify generic strategies were distinguished more strictly to enable the accurate assessment of strategies (Hambrick, 1983). In addition, the demonstration of generic strategies based on Porter's model provides empirical evidence of construct validity (Dess and Davis, 1984).

In such attempts, Miller (1986) formulated the constructs of generic strategies following previous studies. First, the strategy for low-cost position was distinguished between cost leadership and asset parsimony. Second, innovative differentiation and marketing differentiation as a differentiation strategy were also clarified, with a focus on strategy in terms of competitive scope only.

In this manner, generic strategies were divided into fundamental dimensions and each dimension was combined to develop types of strategies. Each type consisted of a combination of the strategy for competitive advantage and that for competitive scope. This analysis of how both strategies are related is indispensable for seizing competitive advantage. However, despite such progress in the development of the dimensions of strategies, there is insufficient empirical evidence about how the strategy for competitive scope is related to that for competitive advantage (Kim and Lim, 1988; Miller, 1988; Davis *et al.*, 1991). Therefore, we need to articulate the theoretical meaning of this strategy and, based on this, capture the relation with strategies for competitive advantage.

Furthermore, we must also reconsider the dimensions of strategies for competitive scope. As mentioned above, the dimension of focus⇔non-focus (variety of product market) is assumed to be unitary. In other words, if a firm pursues a focus strategy, it would not heighten its non-focus (variety) strategy and vice versa. However, we can assume that this dimension is not at opposite ends of a single continuum. Therefore, conceptual consideration is needed to assess whether this dimension is indeed unitary.

Such consideration would express the nature of the relationship between the strategy for competitive advantage and the strategy for competitive scope. Further, this clarification would meet the request of the analysis of the interaction among the constructs of competitive strategies, which has not been fully examined in previous studies (Galbraith and Schendel, 1983; Miller, 1992).

Competitive scope and market segmentation

Studies of market segmentation hint at the development of the dimensions of the strategy for competitive scope. Dickson and Ginter (1987) explained the difference between a market segmentation strategy and a differentiation strategy against the insistence that both strategies were alternatives (Smith, 1956). They found that a differentiation strategy had, in previous discussions, been classified between a change in the perceived attributes of the product (variables that compose the demand function) and a change in the functional relationship of the demand function[1] (parameters that compose the demand function). Further, they called the former a differentiation strategy and the latter a demand function modification strategy.

Market segmentation strategy was developed using the above two strategies for market segments that have distinct demand functions. The first is a segment-based product differentiation strategy, which adapts a differentiation strategy to existing segments with the distinct demand function. The second is a segment development strategy, which creates unique market segments through a demand function modification strategy.

Thus, both market segmentation strategies are related to the heterogeneity of the demand function as a variant of a differentiation strategy or a demand function modification strategy. In addition, they are both dependent on a differentiation strategy. Therefore, they can converge to become a dimension of strategy that positions heterogeneous segments relative to competitors in the pursuit of a differentiation strategy. Further, this dimension can be regarded as the strategy for competitive scope. We call this a specification strategy. In addition, the competitive advantage of a specification strategy would be caused by improving customer value through the adaptation of a differentiation strategy to specific segments and lowering costs by relaxing competition.

In addition to a specification strategy, one study of strategic management that included a view on market segmentation indicated another dimension of strategy for competitive scope. Mintzberg (1988) articulated that this strategy is thought of as one that transfers a differentiation strategy to the market. Further, he proposed that the strategy is related to "how narrowly or comprehensively it [the firm] competes, and to what extent it relies on segmentation" (Mintzberg, 1988: 27). This refers to expanding the number of responding market segments, which we call a variety strategy.

The competitive advantage of a variety strategy is caused by extending the coverage of a differentiation strategy, namely increasing the domain that acquires customer value. Further, this strategy brings about a cost advantage through economies of scope. As mentioned above, studies of market segmentation have articulated two types of strategies for competitive scope and anticipated that they are related to competitive advantage by cost advantage and differentiation.

Standardization and customization in competitive scope

In strategic management theory, the central analysis concerns the strategies of differentiation or cost advantage rather than a variety strategy or a specification strategy as stated above. However, some scholars have sought a theoretical foundation in the theory of population ecology, in which generalists and specialists are demonstrated as organizations that adapt to specific environments. While a generalist is an organization that adapts to a broad domain, a specialist is one that adapts to a narrow domain (Hannan and Freeman, 1977).

This theory led to a search for strategies in strategic management theory that can adapt to the different competitive scopes of each organization (Zammuto, 1988; Ketchen *et al.*, 1993). In such a movement, the consideration of the difference in strategies for both types of organizations clarified significant elements of the variety strategy for competitive scope.

Miller (1991) insisted that generalist strategies and specialist strategies can be regarded as exclusive means of securing competitive advantage and adapting to the external market. Further, a central distinction of both means "is whether firms customize their products to meet the needs of individual clients" (Miller, 1991: 6). Thus, the strategies of generalists founded on customization and the strategies of specialists based on standardization were classified as mutually exclusive. However, successive considerations about standardization and customization showed that these two elements are in fact complementary. Such features have been clarified by scholars examining not only the external product market but also the internal organizational process of creating value. Indeed, the fact that standardization and customization are used in some value chain activities has been articulated and thus two elements have been recognized as significant factors in a variety strategy. These are closely related to value creation activities in an organization.

On this point, Pine (1993) described these states by proposing the concept of mass customization. This concept did not capture firms that make products for small specific markets, but rather those that make products for the mass market. The remarkable feature of firms that adopt mass customization is that they skillfully combine standardization with customization. Based on this feature, the author showed types of strategies for competitive scope.

Lampel and Mintzberg (1996) put standardization and customization into two opposites and pointed out that standardization begins upstream and customization begins downstream in a value chain. Based on this perspective, they proposed pure standardization, segmented standardization, customized standardization, tailored customization, and pure customization on a continuum of five strategies between the aggregation of customers and the individualization of them. We can anticipate the various means by pursuing a variety strategy in this study.

Subsequent studies of customization and standardization have aimed to classify how to combine both elements and assess the effectiveness of these systems (Pine *et al.*, 1993; Gilmore and Pine, 1997; Zipkin, 2001). These studies agree that standardization and customization are used concurrently to implement a variety strategy effectively. Further, there is also recognition that a variety strategy is related not only to firms' market choice but also to those value chain activities that generate competitive advantage.

In brief, the advantage of competitive scope relies on how firms use customization and standardization in a value chain, and both are essential elements in a variety strategy. Furthermore, pursuing them lowers costs or improves quality. This means that competitive advantage is acquired through close interactions between standardization and customization.

Competitive strategy in manufacturing firms

Alongside the development of a general theory for competitive strategy, studies of strategies for manufacturing firms have also progressed. These studies focus on the product development and/or production process, and they have derived primary manufacturing strategies from the dimensions of generic strategies, especially those of a differentiation strategy. Although these strategies are similar to those already proposed by general theory, distinctive strategies for manufacturing firms have also been found and operationalized.

First, relating to product development, a strategy for innovative differentiation through a change in product technologies, as proposed by innovation theory, has been pointed out (Abernathy, 1978; Henderson and Clark, 1990). Second, relating to production, strategies about quality and flexibility have been clarified. Originally, the role of manufacturing was to improve efficiencies to achieve lower costs and reliable production in the progress of manufacturing automation (Parthasarthy and Sethi, 1992). However, the strategic importance of the differentiation strategy in manufacturing was emphasized later.

A quality strategy aims to improve product quality in terms of reliability, adaptability, and durability using a production process that is different from quality advancement through product development or marketing[2] (Garvin, 1987). By contrast, a flexibility strategy is concerned with the agility, adaptability, and responsiveness of a production process by the introduction of computers in the automation process (Parthasarthy and Sethi, 1992). This strategy has been recognized as a strategic factor for acquiring competitive advantage through flexible production, especially in changing environments (Kotha, 1991).

A flexibility strategy can be classified into delivery flexibility, namely "to scale production up and down quickly" (Yondt *et al.*, 1996: 843), and scope flexibility "to quickly expand the scope of a firm's product offerings" (ibid.: 843). This distinction highlights two aspects of production flexibility. Delivery flexibility is regarded as a differentiation strategy that aims to improve the convenience of product supply, while scope flexibility is regarded as a strategy for competitive scope that deals with diversifying customers' requests (Upton, 1994).

Moreover, these two flexibilities are described as the relation between the differentiation strategy for competitive advantage and the strategy for competitive scope that includes a specification strategy and a variety strategy. First, a variety strategy is needed to respond swiftly to customers' requests. Therefore, delivery flexibility promotes scope flexibility (a variety strategy). Next, a specification strategy is required to construct close customer relationships. Thus, delivery flexibility promotes a specification strategy (Schlie and Goldhar, 1995). As such, studies of the competitive strategies of manufacturing firms have clarified specific strategies in the context of the product development and production process. We expect these strategies to be explained in the relationships between the fundamental dimensions that comprise competitive strategy.

Hypotheses development

Competitive advantage in SMFs is assumed to exist in the relationship between the strategy for competitive advantage and that for competitive scope. As a fundamental assumption, we postulate that this advantage arises from the effect of a differentiation strategy to a specialization or a variety strategy and the effect of these strategies to a low-cost strategy.

This assumption is espoused for two reasons. The first reason is that competitive advantage is assured through the adaptation of a differentiation strategy to specific market segments and/or the reduction of competitive costs when a differentiation strategy facilitates a specialization strategy. The second reason is that competitive advantage is assured by increasing the domain that acquires customer value and/or through cost reductions owing to economies of scope.

However, the pursuit of a specialization strategy can lead to a decrease in competitiveness because the bargaining power of buyers is strengthened by the limited number of customers. This suggests that a variety strategy with a specialization strategy that develops multiple specialized market segments is needed to acquire competitive advantage.

From these points, we anticipate that two mechanisms generate competitive advantage. These mechanisms can be described as a variety strategy that is

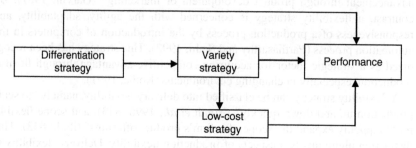

Figure 13.1 Research framework.

facilitated by a differentiation strategy corresponding to the degree of market specialization (i.e. either high or low). Thus, the following two hypotheses are formulated:

- H1: There is a mechanism of competitive advantage in the general markets.
- H2: There is a mechanism of competitive advantage in the specialized markets.

Figure 13.1 shows the research framework that is used in order to examine the validity of these hypotheses. In this framework, we will also examine mediation effects as well as direct effects. The mediation effects are about the effect of a differentiation strategy that influences performance through a variety strategy, and the effect of a variety strategy that influences performance through a low-cost strategy.

Methods

Data and procedures

This research deals with the competitive strategies of SMFs that engage in single businesses autonomously. Firms were selected from the membership directory of *Hokkaido kigyoka doyukai*. Following the definition of small firms in "Minor Enterprise Basic Law," we chose firms that had fewer than 300 employees or capital of ¥300 million or less. However, firms that met these criteria until five years ago were also included.

Questionnaires were then sent to the presidents of 416 SMFs in Hokkaido prefecture, while the final sample consisted of 110 firms (response rate: 26.4 percent). Capital ranged from ¥4 million to ¥335.92 million with a mean of ¥42.97 million. The number of employees ranged from 7 to 350, with a mean of 61. Turnover ranged from ¥113 million to ¥3.037 billion with a mean of ¥1.722 billion. Those industries defined by the first two digits of the SIC (standard industrial classification) code were extended to 17 industries in the sample. Thus, sample bias was prevented.

Measures

Questionnaire items in this study concern the strategy for competitive scope, the strategy for competitive advantage, financial performance, the environment, and control variables (described below). The exact wording of items that originated in or were adapted for this study appears in Appendix 13.1.

Strategy for competitive scope

Two components of the strategy for competitive scope pursued for the past five years, relative to competitors, were measured as follows. A specialization strategy was assessed using a three-item scale that measured the extent to which a firm has specialized its products and/or customers. These items were based on the description of a focus strategy (Porter, 1980). A variety strategy was assessed using a six-item scale that measured the extent to which a firm responds to the breadth of its products and/or customers (Miller and Dess, 1993). In addition, standardization and customization items were also included in a variety strategy based on the earlier description of generalists and specialists (Miller, 1991). Each scale was a five-point Likert-type scale and measurement items were averaged to form a composite score.

Strategy for competitive advantage

The strategy for competitive advantage was distinguished by four differentiation strategies as well as a low-cost strategy The four differentiation strategies measured the degree of improvement in customer value through (1) change in basic product design, (2) modification of product design, (3) improvement in product quality, and (4) manufacturing flexibility. The former two measures were based on the product innovation model (Henderson and Clark, 1990), while the latter two measures were modified items from the manufacturing strategy proposed by Dean and Snell (1996). These measures consisted of 16 items. A low-cost strategy was measured using a four-item scale that operationalized the means of generating cost advantage. This scale was a five-point Likert-type scale and the average of the items of each strategy was used as a composite score.

Financial performance

Financial performance was composed of the growth rates of turnover and operating profit for the past three years. We did not use real numbers, but, rather, subjective measures of performance relative to competitors, because firms were spread over multiple industries. Each measure was composed of only one item. The scale was a five-point Likert-type scale.

Control variables

Both organizational size and environmental uncertainty affect financial performance. In order to investigate potential confounding due to the possible influence of firm size and the environment, these variables were used as controls in the analysis. Number of employees was a proxy for organizational size. Environmental uncertainty was composed of nine items that modified Miller's (1983) measures of dynamism, unpredictably, and heterogeneity. The scale was a five-point Likert-type scale and an average of nine items was used as a composite score. Table 13.1 shows the means, standard deviations, coefficient alphas, and Pearson correlations. All coefficient alphas exceeded 0.70. Thus, the scales demonstrated internal consistency.

Results

Path analysis was used to examine the two hypotheses of this chapter. For analysis, the sample was divided into two subgroups: the high specification group ($N = 53$) and the low specification group ($N = 57$). Table 13.2 and Figure 13.2 present the results relevant to H1. The direct effect and mediating effect were examined.

The direct effects on performance could not be confirmed for all differentiation strategies or for the low-cost strategy. On the contrary, the variety strategy was shown to strongly influence the growth rates of turnover and operating profit. Further, a change in basic product design had a positive impact on the variety strategy.

In terms of mediating effects, the effects of the differentiation strategy on the low-cost strategy through the variety strategy (Table 13.3) and the effects of the variety strategy on the growth rates of turnover and operating profit through the low-cost strategy (Table 13.4) could not be confirmed. However, we confirmed that a change in basic product design in the differentiation strategy influences indirectly the growth rates of turnover and operating profit through the variety strategy (Table 13.5).

Thus, we showed that competitive advantage is based on the relationship between the variety strategy and technological differentiation in the low specification group. The fit of this model was good, and thus H1 was supported (chi-square $= 11.090$, DF $= 16$, $p = 0.804$, GFI $= 0.966$, AGFI $= 0.858$).

Table 13.6 and Figure 13.3 present the results of the analysis relevant to H2. In terms of the direct effects, the growth rates of turnover and operating profit were not influenced by the differentiation strategies. However, the low-cost strategy and the variety strategy both influenced financial performance. In addition, the effect of a manufacturing flexibility on the variety strategy was confirmed.

In terms of mediating effects, the effects of the differentiation strategy on the low-cost strategy through the variety strategy (Table 13.7) and the effects of the variety strategy on the growth rates of turnover and operating profit through the low-cost strategy (Table 13.8) could not be confirmed. However, we confirmed that a manufacturing flexibility influences financial performance through the variety strategy (Table 13.9).

As a result, we showed that competitive advantage is based on the variety strategy facilitated by flexible manufacturing as a differentiation strategy in the high specification group. The fit of this model was adequate (chi-square $= 13.826$, DF $= 16$, $p = 0.612$, GFI $= 0.960$, AGFI $= 0.837$). H2 was thus supported.

Table 13.1 Descriptive statistics

Variable	Means	s.d.	1	2	3	4	5	6	7	8	9	10
1 Environmental uncertainty	3.51	0.718	(0.832)									
2 Number of employees	63.3	67.8	−0.68	(−)								
3 Change in basic product design	3.40	0.704	0.123	0.058	(0.834)							
4 Quality	3.65	0.541	0.168	−0.077	0.473***	(0.783)						
5 Low cost	3.25	0.634	0.048	0.146	0.289**	0.246*	(0.762)					
6 Manufacturing flexibility	3.72	0.606	0.176	−0.067	0.401***	0.406***	0.322**	(0.773)				
7 Modification of product design	3.20	0.530	0.075	0.020	0.564***	0.443***	0.303*	0.405***	(0.823)			
8 Specification	3.24	0.750	0.153	0.019	0.455***	0.450***	0.344***	0.481***	0.492***	(0.859)		
9 Variety	3.46	0.584	−0.038	0.065	0.576***	0.407***	0.314**	0.520***	0.462***	0.389***	(0.745)	
10 Growth rate of turnover	3.12	0.968	−0.222*	0.124	0.284**	0.237	0.268**	0.278**	0.222*	0.234*	0.495***	(−)
11 Growth rate of operating profit	3.17	0.966	−0.251**	0.167	0.230*	0.198*	0.347***	0.210*	0.169	0.269**	0.472***	0.643***

Notes: $N = 110$, $^+ P < 0.1$, $^* P < 0.05$, $^{**} P < 0.01$, $^{***} P < 0.001$; Cronbach alphas are on the diagonal.

Table 13.2 Path coefficients of low specification group

Path	Estimate	SE	CR
Change in basic product design → growth rate of turnover	−0.109	0.228	−0.475
Change in basic product design → growth rate of operating profit	−0.262	0.212	−1.238
Quality → growth rate of turnover	0.256	0.289	0.888
Quality → growth rate of operating profit	0.414	0.268	1.545
Manufacturing flexibility → growth rate of turnover	0.223	0.290	0.768
Manufacturing flexibility → growth rate of operating profit	0.079	0.269	0.293
Modification of product design → growth rate of turnover	−0.054	0.293	−0.184
Modification of product design → growth rate of operating profit	−0.090	0.271	−0.333
Low cost → growth rate of turnover	−0.062	0.181	−0.344
Low cost → growth rate of operating profit	0.267	0.168	1.594
Variety → growth rate of turnover	0.817	0.268	3.044**
Variety → growth rate of operating profit	0.921	0.249	3.703**
Variety → low cost	0.174	0.300	0.579
Change in basic product design → variety	0.404	0.104	3.890**
Quality → variety	0.019	0.149	0.130
Manufacturing flexibility → variety	0.166	0.148	1.121
Modification of product design → variety	−0.035	0.151	−0.233
Environmental uncertainty → growth rate of turnover	−0.360	0.143	−2.527
Environmental uncertainty → growth rate of operating profit	−0.416	0.132	−3.145**
Number of employees → growth rate of turnover	0.003	0.002	1.611
Number of employees → growth rate of operating profit	0.004	0.002	2.226*

Note: $N = 53$, $^*P < 0.05$, $^{**}P < 0.01$.

Discussion

Overview and implications of the findings

The presented results determined that two types of strategic mechanisms generate competitive advantage in SMFs. We term the first mechanism in the general market "top-down segmentation." Firms that adopt this mechanism aim to penetrate submarket segments by generating a technologically superior core product based on changing the basic product design as a core strategy.

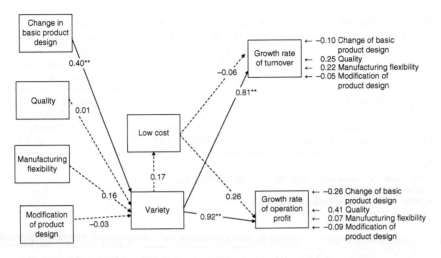

Figure 13.2 Path diagram of low specification group.

Notes: $^*P < 0.05$, $^{**}P < 0.01$.

Table 13.3 Mediating effect of differentiation to low cost through variety

	Low cost β (t-value)
Change in basic product design	0.046 (0.424)
Quality	0.002 (0.144)
Manufacturing flexibility	0.018 (0.393)
Modification of product design	−0.003 (−0.178)

Notes:
β represents the standardized coefficients of the mediating effects.
t-values are in parentheses.
Significance is examined using the sobel test.
$^+P < 0.1$, $^*P < 0.05$, $^{**}P < 0.01$.

Table 13.4 Mediating effect of variety to performance through low cost

	Growth rate of Turnover	Growth rate of Operating profit
	β (t-value)	β (t-value)
Variety	−0.007 (−0.278)	0.030 (0.612)

Notes:
β represents the standardized coefficients of the mediating effects.
t-values are in parentheses.
Significance is examined using the sobel test.
$^+P < 0.1$, $^*P < 0.05$, $^{**}P < 0.01$.

Table 13.5 Mediating effect of differentiation to performance through variety

	Growth rate of turnover β (t-value)	Growth rate of operating profit β (t-value)
Change in basic product design	0.330* (2.216)	0.372* (2.490)
Quality	0.019 (0.153)	0.022 (0.153)
Manufacturing flexibility	0.128 (0.956)	0.144 (0.969)
Modification of product design	−0.025 (−0.195)	−0.028 (−0.195)

Notes:
β represents the standardized coefficients of the mediating effects.
t-values are in parentheses.
Significance is examined using the sobel test.
$^+P < 0.1$, $^*P < 0.05$, $^{**}P < 0.01$.

By developing multiple market segments in a general purpose product market, such firms sell standard goods that use freely available components. As a result, scale advantages rather than differentiation advantages generate competitive advantage. Thus, SMFs find it difficult to exert competitiveness compared with large manufacturing firms.

In such a situation, they tend to adopt state-of-the-art technology or new product concepts to overcome their lack of differentiation. In brief, they create innovative products through integral product development. For this reason, technological differentiation brings about the development of an unspecified number of customers in submarket segments by promoting the diffusion of products.

This is similar to comprehensive market segmentation (Mintzberg, 1988) or mass customization (Pine, 1993), which multiplies products and markets through coordinating with specific customer requests by offering catalogs, derivative products, and segment products. In other words, product technologies and core products meet customers' basic needs, and such a differential advantage can adapt to market segments or customized markets. Thus, competitive advantage based on the mechanism of top-down segmentation is secured.

The second mechanism in specific markets is termed herein a "bottom-up multi-niche." Firms that adopt this mechanism aim to multiply in specific product markets. In general, firms that deal with specific products suffer increases in coordination costs with specific customers and among internal functions. In addition, they find it difficult to generate competitive advantage because of their inferior bargaining power and because they rely on a limited number of customers.

To avoid such cost disadvantages, a variety strategy is applied from the outset by using freely available components rather than customized ones. However, differentiated products cannot be generated by using such components. For this reason, customer value is increased by responding swiftly and appropriately to individual customer requests and through flexible production processes rather than through the products themselves. In addition, flexible production processes can develop modular products by combining various technologies available from

Table 13.6 Path coefficients of high specification group

Path	Estimate	SE	CR
Change in basic product design → growth rate of turnover	0.067	0.191	0.349
Change in basic product design → growth rate of operating profit	0.072	0.186	0.390
Quality → growth rate of turnover	−0.121	0.225	−0.537
Quality → growth rate of operating profit	−0.306	0.218	−1.404
Manufacturing flexibility → growth rate of turnover	−0.028	0.196	−0.144
Manufacturing flexibility → growth rate of operating profit	−0.249	0.190	−0.131
Modification of product design → growth rate of turnover	−0.190	0.235	−0.808
Modification of product design → growth rate of operating profit	−0.213	0.228	−0.933
Low cost → growth rate of turnover	0.457	0.190	2.402*
Low cost → growth rate of operating profit	0.435	0.185	2.356*
Variety → growth rate of turnover	0.528	0.228	2.319*
Variety → growth rate of operating profit	0.593	0.221	2.685**
Variety → low cost	0.573	0.200	2.869**
Change in basic product design → variety	0.169	0.102	1.648
Quality → variety	0.186	0.121	1.540
Manufacturing flexibility → variety	0.352**	0.098	3.588**
Modification of product design → variety	0.234	0.125	1.873
Environmental uncertainty → growth rate of turnover	−0.365	0.153	−2.386*
Environmental uncertainty → growth rate of operating profit	−0.319	0.148	−2.151*
Number of employees → growth rate of turnover	−0.001	0.001	−0.402
Number of employees → growth rate of operating profit	−0.001	0.001	−0.514

Notes: $N = 53$, $^* P < 0.05$, $^{**} P < 0.01$.

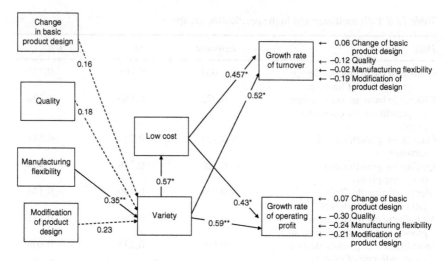

Figure 13.3 Path diagram of the high specification group.

Notes: *$P < 0.05$, **$P < 0.01$.

Table 13.7 Mediating effect of differentiation to low cost through variety

	Low cost β (t-value)
Change in basic product design	0.016 (0.560)
Quality	0.019 (0.557)
Manufacturing flexibility	0.038 (0.597)
Modification of product design	0.018 (0.551)

Notes:
β represents the standardized coefficients of the mediating effects.
t-values are in parentheses.
Significance is examined using the sobel test.
+$P < 0.1$, *$P < 0.05$, **$P < 0.01$.

Table 13.8 Mediating effect of differentiation on performance through low cost

	Growth rate of turnover β (t-value)	Growth rate of operating profit β (t-value)
Variety	0.134 (1.581)	0.128 (1.568)

Notes:
β represents the standardized coefficients of the mediating effects.
t-values are in parentheses.
Significance is examined using the sobel test.
+$P < 0.1$, *$P < 0.05$, **$P < 0.01$.

Table 13.9 Mediating effect of differentiation on performance through variety

	Growth rate of turnover β (t-value)	*Growth rate of operating profit β (t-value)*
Change in basic product design	0.089 (1.202)	0.100 (1.258)
Quality	0.100 (1.171)	0.113 (1.223)
Manufacturing flexibility	0.203* (1.785)	0.228* (1.987)
Modification of product design	0.097 (1.112)	0.109 (1.157)

Notes:
β represents the standardized coefficients of the mediating effects.
t-values are in parentheses.
Significance is examined using the sobel test.
$^+P < 0.1$, $^*P < 0.05$, $^{**}P < 0.01$.

external markets. Thus, competitive advantage based on the mechanism of the bottom-up multi-niche is secured.

Limitations and directions for future research

Although we find that two types of mechanisms generate competitive advantage in SMFs, it remains unknown whether the two relational patterns of each mechanism between the strategy for competitive scope and that for competitive advantage are distinctive to SMFs only. These relational patterns may be found in large manufacturing firms as well. Thus, the distinctive competitive advantage in SMFs may be constructed in a different domain apart from large manufacturing firms rather than in different relational patterns with them.

Therefore, future research should first articulate a specific technological domain in which SMFs can differentiate in their general purpose markets. Second, it is necessary to clarify the attributes of the domain in which these firms can construct exclusive and close customer relationships in specific markets. Third, an examination of the processes and paths that create strategic patterns is needed to understand why they generate competitive advantage in each market.

Appendix 13.1

Questionnaire items

Change in basic product design

Developing and selling products based on new concepts
Adding unique product functions
Developing and selling state-of-the-art products
Developing and selling products of different designs
Changing the design process or development procedure

Quality

Improving quality of products

Improving performance of products
Improving durability of products
Improving reliability of products

Low cost

Pursuing low unit cost
Pursuing low labor cost
Pursuing low material cost

Manufacturing flexibility

Meeting release dates for new products
On-time delivery
Short lead time from order to delivery
Change in basic design

Modification of product design

Solving problems on product functions
Changing the architecture of products
Adding product functions to respond to customers' needs

Specification

Focusing on customers
Focusing on product type
Focusing on customers' needs

Variety

Diversifying product type
Extending the number of customers
Extending the products made to order

Environmental uncertainty

Our firm must change its practices extremely frequently
The rate of obsolescence of products is very high
The actions of competitors are unpredictable
Demand and tastes are almost unpredictable
The modes of production and product design change often and in a major way
Customers' buying habits are heterogeneous
The methods of production or turnovers of competitors are heterogeneous
The nature of competition is heterogeneous

Notes

1 The equation of the demand function is $Q = F(p, x_1, \ldots, x_n)$. "It postulates that the demand, Q, for a particular product offered by an individual supplier is a function of the price, p, and the product characteristics of that offering, $x_1, \ldots, x_n$" (Dickson and Ginter, 1987: 4). In brief, the demand function is delineated as the "functional relationship between perceived product characteristics and market segment and demand" (Dickson and Ginter, 1987: 5).
2 Garvin (1987) proposed performance, features, reliability, conformance, durability, serviceability, aesthetics, and perceived qualities as the dimensions of quality.

References

Abernathy, W.J. (1978) *The Productivity Dilemma*, Baltimore: Johns Hopkins University Press.

Campbell-Hunt, C. (2000) "What have we learned about generic strategy? A meta-analysis," *Strategic Management Journal*, 21, pp. 127–54.

Davis, P.S., R.B. Robinson, and J.A. Pearce (1991) "The contingent effects of competitive market scope on strategy-share-performance relationships," *Academy of Management Proceedings*, 2, pp. 16–20.

Dean, J.W. and S.A. Snell (1996) "The strategic use of integrated manufacturing: an empirical examination," *Strategic Management Journal*, 17, pp. 459–80.

Dess, G.G. and P.S. Davis (1984) "Porter's (1980) Generic strategies as determinants of strategic group membership and organizational performance," *Academy of Management Journal*, 27, pp. 46–88.

Dickson, P.R. and J.L. Ginter (1987) "Market segmentation, product differentiation, and marketing strategy," *Journal of Marketing*, 51, pp. 1–10.

Fujimoto, T. (2004) *Nihonnomonozukuritetsugaku*, Tokyo: Nihonkeizaisinbunsya.

Galbraith, C.G. and D. Schendel (1983) "An empirical analysis of strategic types," *Strategic Management Journal*, 4, pp. 153–73.

Garvin, D.A. (1987) "Competing on the eight dimensions of quality," *Harvard Business Review*, 65, pp. 101–09.

Gilmore J.H. and B.J. Pine (1997) "The four faces of mass customization," *Harvard Business Review*, 75, pp. 91–101.

Hambrick, D.C. (1983) "High profit strategies in mature capital goods industries," *Academy of Management Journal*, 26, pp. 687–707.

Hannan, M. and J. Freeman (1977) "The population ecology of organizations," *American Journal of Sociology*, 82, pp. 929–64.

Henderson, R.M. and K.B. Clark (1990) "Architectural innovation: the reconfiguration of existing product technologies and the failure of established firms," *Administrative Science Quarterly*, 35, pp. 9–30.

Hill, C.W.L. (1988) "Differentiation versus low cost or differentiation and low cost: a contingency framework," *Academy of Management Review*, 13, pp. 401–12.

Ketchen, D.J., J.B Thomas, and C.C. Snow (1993) "Organizational configurations and performance: a comparison of theoretical approaches," *Academy of Management Journal*, 36, 6, pp. 1278–313.

Kim, L. and Y. Lim (1988) "Environment, generic strategies, and performance in a rapidly developing country," *Academy of Management Journal*, 31, 4, pp. 802–27.

Kotha, S. (1991) "Strategy, manufacturing structure, and advanced manufacturing technologies – a proposed framework," *Academy of Management Proceedings*, 1, pp. 293–97.

Lampel, J. and H. Mintzberg (1996) "Customizing customization," *Sloan Management Review*, 38, pp. 21–30.

Miller, A. and G.G. Dess (1993) "Assessing Porter's model in terms of its generalizability, accuracy and simplicity," *Journal of Management Studies*, 30, pp. 553–85.

264   *K. Tamai*

Miller, D. (1983) "The correlates of entrepreneurship in three types of firms," *Management Science*, 29, pp. 770–91.

Miller, D. (1986) "Configurations of strategy and structure," *Strategic Management Journal*, 7, pp. 233–49.

Miller, D. (1988) "Relating Porter's business strategies to environment and structure: analysis and performance implications," *Academy of Management Journal*, 31, pp. 280–308.

Miller, D. (1991) "Generalists and specialists: two business strategies and their contexts," *Advances in Strategic Management*, 7, pp. 3–41.

Miller, D. (1992) "The Generic Strategy Trap," *The Journal of Business Strategy*, 13, pp. 37–41.

Mintzberg, H. (1988) "Generic strategies: toward a comprehensive framework," *Advances in Strategic Management*, 5, pp. 1–67.

Mintzberg, H., B. Ahlstrand, and J. Lampel (1998) *Strategy Safari*, New York: Free Press.

Murray, A.I. (1988) "A contingency view of Porter's generic strategies," *Academy of Management Review*, 13, pp. 390–400.

Parthasarthy, R. and S.P. Sethi (1992) "The impact of flexible automation on business strategy and organizational structure," *Academy of Management Review*, 17, pp. 86–111.

Pine, B.J. (1993) *Mass Customization*, Cambridge MA: Harvard Business School Press.

Pine, B.J., B. Victor, and A.C. Boynton (1993) "Making mass customization work," *Harvard Business Review*, 71, pp. 108–19.

Porter, M.E. (1980) *Competitive Strategy*, New York: Free Press.

Porter, M.E. (1985) *Competitive Advantage*, New York: Free Press.

Schlie, T.W. and J.D. Goldhar (1995) "Advanced manufacturing and new directions for competitive strategy," *Journal of Business Research*, 33, pp. 103–14.

Smith, W. (1956) "Product differentiation and market segmentation as alternative marketing strategies," *Journal of Marketing*, 21, pp. 3–8.

Upton, D.M. (1994) "The management of manufacturing flexibility," *California Management Review*, 36, pp. 72–89.

Yondt, M.A., S.A. Snell, J.W. Dean, and D.P. Lepak (1996) "Human resource management, manufacturing strategy, and firm performance," *Academy of Management Journal*, 39, pp. 836–66.

Zammuto, R.Z. (1988) "Organizational adaptation: some implications of organizational ecology for strategic choice," *Journal of Management Studies*, 25, pp. 105–20.

Zipkin, P. (2001) "The limits of mass customization," *Sloan Management Review*, 42, pp. 81–87.

Index

Note: The abbreviation Heidelberg is used throughout to denote the company Heidelberger Druckmaschinen AG.

For Product Safety Concerns and Information please contact our
EU representative GPSR@taylorandfrancis.com Taylor & Francis
Verlag GmbH, Kaufingerstraße 24, 80331 München, Germany